Her Gates Will N

Her Gates Will Never Be Shut

Hell, Hope, and the New Jerusalem

BRADLEY JERSAK

WIPF & STOCK · Eugene, Oregon

HER GATES WILL NEVER BE SHUT
Hell, Hope, and the New Jerusalem

Copyright © 2009 Bradley Jersak. All rights reserved. Except for brief quotations
in critical publications or reviews, no part of this book may be reproduced in any
manner without prior written permission from the publisher. Write: Permissions,
Wipf and Stock Publishers, 199 W. 8th Ave., Suite 3, Eugene, OR 97401.

Wipf & Stock
An imprint of Wipf and Stock Publishers
199 W. 8th Ave., Suite 3
Eugene, OR 97401

ISBN 13: 978-1-60608-882-1

Manufactured in the U.S.A.

For Little Granny

Elsie (Fisher) Ditchfield (1905–2009)

IF GRANNY WERE STILL alive to read this book, she probably wouldn't. I doubt that she would understand what I'm talking about. But since she is with the Lord now, I believe she would say that it's me who doesn't understand what I'm talking about. I get that.

On the day I was born, Granny walked a long distance to the bus stop and then rode all the way across the city to the hospital where my mother was facing a long, difficult labor and assisted delivery. She sat in the waiting room all day, praying for my safe arrival.

From there, I believe she interceded for me every day of my life up until she died at the age of 103. Her prayer list also included at least 200 other descendants. Even into her nineties, she still prayed every night on her knees by her bed.

On the day she died, she hopped another bus, C. S. Lewis's heavenly transit, and traveled across the divide to another City. I believe she continues to pray me through another long, difficult labor and assisted delivery. I imagine she occupies some sort of heavenly waiting room, interceding for my safe arrival.

Thank you, Little Granny. Is it everything we dreamed it would be?

Contents

Contents

Illustrations and Tables

Acknowledgments

For walking, praying, and coaxing me through hell—some at great cost, others without knowing it, and a few by sharing their own—thank you.

Eden, Stephen, Justice, and Dominic, Brita Miko, Robin Emberly, Steve Imbach, Ron and Karin Dart, Archbishop Lazar, Brian Klassen, Philip Cilliers, S. J. Hill, Peter and Anne-Marie Helms, Kim and Darlene, Eric Janzen, Eric McCooeye, Andre Harden, Michael Hardin, Eugene Peterson, Bob and Gracie Ekblad, James Alison, Andrew Klager, Walter Unger, Ted Grimsrud, Hermit Gregory, John Caputo, Rene Girard, Abraham J. Heschel, Jason Upton, Al Sergel, Walter Brueggemann, Anne Rice, N. T. Wright, Nik Ansell, Jonathan Stanley, Dan Johnston, John and Diane, Dwight and Lorie, Bill and Jamie, Harmen, Gary, Lauren and Jelly-Bean, Keagen, Brian West, Steve Schroeder, Charles Littledale, Adit, Fi, Anne, Barb, Heidi, Jorden and Norah Dekkers, mom and dad, Heinz and Doreen, Dar and Ted, Pam and Chad, Candice, Julia, Andy, Jacquie, Steph, Duane, Bob, Brian Schmidt, Jacki, Eve, Sava, Jana, the Karen people, Christian, Patrick, and Raydeen, at Wipf and Stock, and as always, Kevin Miller.

Special thanks to Michael and Lorri Hardin, whose work with me on *Stricken by God?* led me to revisit the question of hell. Their welcome to the *Compassionate Eschatology* conference, introductions to Rene Girard and John Caputo, and the invitation to write a chapter for the follow-up text unlocked the first pages of what would become this book. I originally set out to simply write a short piece on eschatological hope in Rev 21–22 for Michael, but it just kept snow-balling. Thanks for your generosity.

Many thanks also to Nik Ansell, whose article, "Hell: The Nemisis of Hope?" I came across after the first draft of *Her Gates* was already on my editor's desk. The find was providential in that we had come to several identical conclusions independently and Ansell had already confirmed what I thought were my own discoveries. The overlap, even of our quotations from Dante, led me to contact him and he subsequently agreed to refresh his essay and contribute it as the Afterword for this book. Beyond that, we exchanged a flurry of e-mails in which Ansell offered many helpful challenges and suggestions, opening a dialogue that I've imported into the footnotes along the way.

Abbreviations

PRIMARY SOURCES AND COLLECTIONS

1 Esd	1 Esdras (Apocrypha)
2 Esd	2(4) Esdras (Pseudepigrapha)
ANF	Ante-Nicene Fathers
APOT	The Apocrypha and Pseudepigrapha of the Old Testament
Contra Cels.	Origen, *Contra Celsus*
De Civ. Dei	Augustine, *The City of God*
De Genesi	Augustine, *De Genesi ad litteram*
De Princ.	Origen, *De Principiis*
De Res. Carn.	Tertullian, *De resurrectione carnis*
EPE	*Ellines Pateres tis Ekklisias (Greek Fathers of the Church)*
Frag. Hom.	Hyppolytus. *Fragments of Discourses or Homilies: Homily on the Paschal Supper*
HL	*Hebraic Literature*
Matt Hom.	Chrysostom, *Homilies on the Gospel of Saint Matthew*
NHC	Nag Hammadi Codex
NPNF	Nicene and Post-Nicene Fathers
NT	New Testament
OT	Old Testament
Paed.	Clement, *Paedagogus*
PG	*Patrologia graeca,* edited by J.-P. Migne
Rhet	Aristotle, *Rhetoric*

Sib.	The Sibylline Oracles (Pseudepigrapha)
Sim.	Similitudes of Enoch (1 Enoch 37–71)
Strom	Clement, *Stromata*
Syr Bar	Syriac Apocalypse of Baruch, or 2 Baruch (Pseudepigrapha)
TM	*Talmudic Miscellany*
Wis Sol	Wisdom of Solomon
Odes Sol	Odes of Solomon

MODERN JOURNALS AND REFERENCES

ATR	*Anglican Theological Review*
BDB	*A Hebrew and English Lexicon of the Old Testament,* edited by Brown, Driver, and Briggs
BSac	*Bibliotheca Sacra*
CSR	*Christian Scholars Review*
CRIJ	*Christian Research Institute Journal*
DJG	*Dictionary of Jesus and the Gospels*
EDB	*Eerdmans Dictionary of the Bible*
HDB	*Dictionary of the Bible,* edited by James Hasting
ISBE	*International Standard Bible Encyclopedia*
JE	*Jewish Encyclopedia*
JBL	*Journal of Biblical Literature*
NIDNTT	*New International Dictionary of New Testament Theology*
TDNT	*Theological Dictionary of the New Testament* [*Abridged,* 1985], edited by Kittel, Friedrich, and Bromiley
TLOT	*Theological Lexicon of the Old Testament,* edited by Ernst Jenni and Claus Westerman
TMSJ	*The Masters Seminary Journal*

1

Presumptions and Possibilities

Through me the way into the suffering city,
Through me the way to the eternal pain,
Through me the way that runs among the lost.
Justice urged on my high artificer;
My maker was divine authority,
The highest wisdom, and the primal love.
Before me nothing but eternal things were made,
And I endure eternally.
Abandon every hope, ye who enter here.[1]

THE INFERNO

IF DANTE WERE TO revisit the *Inferno* today, he would find his visions of hell deeply embedded in our Western psyche, culture, and religion. Images of fire and brimstone, dungeons and torture, demons and judgment continue to ignite imaginations and controversy. In our era of CGI, everything Dante described in poetry can be recreated on the big screen for those who want to face their deepest fears in a climate-controlled environment where the smell of buttered popcorn masks the stench of sulfur. Modernized upgrades of medieval artwork imbue movies like *Jacob's Ladder* (1990) and *What Dreams May Come* (1998); comic books like *Hellblazer* and *Hellboy*; and video games like *Inferno*. One can even take the *Dante's Inferno Test* online,[2] where visitors are exhorted, "Test your impurity, find out which level of *Dante's* hell you will be spending eternity in." And for a personal taste of hell, why not marinate some chicken wings

---

1. Dante Alighieri, *Inferno,* Canto 3.
2. http://www.4degreez.com/misc/dante-inferno-test.mv.

in *Dan-T's White Hot Inferno* sauce? I'm sure even Dante would be confused: Is hell a place, a state, or a brand?

Western civilization does not hold a monopoly on the dreams and nightmares of the afterlife. Taoist and Buddhist mythology contain their own layered maze of terrifying torture chambers (*Diyu*),[3] and the Hindu *Naraka*[4] features the usual fire, boiling oil, and other instruments of abuse for karmic atonement between incarnations. And Dante's hell barely holds a torch to the hellish punishments described in the Koran:[5]

> Garments of fire have been prepared for the unbelievers. Scalding water shall be poured upon their heads, melting their skins and that which is in their bellies. They shall be lashed with rods of iron. Whenever, in their anguish, they try to escape from Hell, back they shall be dragged, and will be told: "Taste the torment of the Conflagration!" (22:19–23)

Global belief in some form of divine judgment remains as unquenchable as its flames, the New Atheists[6] notwithstanding. For their part, writers like Christopher Hitchens and Richard Dawkins give voice to those whose atheism is rooted less in unbelief than in hatred of a religion-projected god whose mind reflects humanity's need to best one eternal excruciation with another. They and Bill Maher mock such notions as patently *religulous* and write off faith as laughable were it not for its dangerous capacity to incite fear and violence.[7]

Do they have a point? I can only offer my own experience in response. As a sensitive little boy raised in the evangelical church, I was a horrified but Bible-convinced infernalist.[8] I accepted in good faith the word of camp counselors who described the fate of the lost as we stoked orange coals during late night marshmallow roasts. Seeing as I had prayed the "sinner's prayer," they assured me I had no need to worry. But worry I did. What about the unchurched cousins I loved so dearly? God loved them, but if they didn't love him back, he would skewer them on an

3. "Diyu," http://www.viswiki.com/en/Diyu.

4. Subhangi Devi Dasi, "Vedic Knowledge Online," para. 3.

5. Koran 18:23–30; 40:67–73; 44:40–49; 73:12, etc. See also "Descriptions of Hell in Islam," *Shariah Program Articles Library.*

6. In particular, see Hitchens' *God is Not Good* and Dawkins' *The God Delusion.*

7. See Bill Maher's recent documentary *Religulous* (2008).

8. "Infernalism" is belief in hell as eternal, conscious torment of the unbeliever.

everlasting rotisserie—just like the stick I used for roasting my marsh-mallows. My great commission was to "snatch others from the fire and save them" (Jude 24). And if I failed, I feared their blood would be on my hands (Ezek 33:6).

Just as awful as being that traumatized eight-year-old camper was the fact that I was being groomed to become the next zealous counselor. My first convert responded quickly to the choice between eternal life and everlasting flames. I remember being troubled by his expression—not the wide-eyed fear I expected, just incredulity and a rushed prayer before the dinner bell rang. I sensed that he was unconvinced of the gravity of the decision, especially when I discovered that he had "fallen away" within days of returning home.

Highly visual, I became overwhelmed by mental images of bubbling skin and the attendant shrieks of the masses with whom I went to school, stood in line with at McDonalds, and prayed for every night before bed. Unlike Hitchens and Dawkins, I knew and loved (and feared) a living God too much to junk my entire worldview just because the idea of eternal, conscious torment in hell clashed with what I conceived to be his loving character. I tried to swallow the discrepancies in denial or wallpaper over the holes like a writer trying to hide glitches in a bad plot. But eventually, the necessary rational and emotional disconnect got caught in my throat. There it would remain until I could discover an alternative view that was just as faithful to the Bible—not that I even dared to hope one existed. If only I had realized that the Christian theologians were already on the case—had been for centuries.

RENOVATING HELL: THEOLOGICAL OPTIONS
FOR DIVINE JUDGMENT

Sheltered in my tiny corner of Christendom, like many evangelicals I was unaware of the heated discussion around damming up the river of fire through various alternative perspectives on hell that did not trans-form God into a wrathful tyrant-judge who consigns the unrepentant to Dante-esque tortures for eternity. As it turns out, the view of hell with which I grew up—infernalism—is only one of several options handed down to us through our forefathers in the faith. We will survey each of them briefly here.

Infernalism

Many or even most Christians across the church spectrum are still convinced that to be a good, Bible-believing Christian, they must accept a hell of eternal, conscious torment. They may secretly repress doubts or privately concede to skepticism, but they still believe that the Bible teaches infernalism only. Infernalists range in opinion from belief in hell as a literal place with actual flames to a spiritual state of anguish of the soul. They are taught to presume that hell must be populated by the damned: those who refused salvation during their lifespan. After all, they reason, how else can one interpret key texts like Matt 25:31–46 (the goats who go into eternal punishment), Luke 16:19–31 (the rich man who is in inescapable "agony in this fire"), and the "lake of burning sulfur where the smoke of torment rises forever and ever" (Rev 14, 20, 21)? This view of hell leads to evangelical fervor, a desire to see as few people as possible condemned to such a terrible place.

Annihilationism

Others teach that "perishing" (John 3:16) is synonymous with death or eradication, rendering a full stop to the existence of the unredeemed. Some annihilationists believe that death itself is the end and that only those prepared for everlasting life will experience the resurrection ("conditional immortality"). Others believe that the wicked will be raised to life again, judged for their deeds, and then damned to the lake of fire, where they are completely consumed. Rather than being supernaturally sustained to endure endless torture, "both body and soul are destroyed" (Matt 10:28) in a "second death" (Rev 21:8), which vaporizes the whole person (Ps 37) to ashes (Mal 4). The annihilationist sees justice done justly, with spiritual capital punishment performed quickly and compassionately. Any weeping, wailing, or gnashing of teeth refers to the grief over receiving one's sentence, not some ongoing, agonized state of consciousness.[9]

Universalism

A breadth of other views find shelter under the umbrella term "universalism." Many modern universalists believe that hell doesn't exist and that

---

9. See also Matt 7:13; John 10:28; 17:12; Rom 2:12; 9:22; 1 Cor 1:18; 15:18; 2 Cor 2:15; 4:3; Phil 1:28; 3:19; 1 Thess 5:3; 2 Thess 1:9; 2:10; Heb 10:39; Jas 4:12; 2 Pet 3:9; Rev 17:8, 11.

everyone goes to heaven—whatever that happens to be. No particular faith is necessary, and not even the most heinous crimes can disqualify anyone from Paradise. After all, in God's indiscriminate grace, "He causes his sun to rise on the evil and the good, and sends rain on the righteous and the unrighteous" (Matt 5:45). At the opposite end of the universalist continuum is the doctrine of "ultimate redemption." Ancients like Origen of Alexandria and Gregory of Nyssa are often labeled "universalists," but they certainly believed in the existence of a lake or river of fire and insisted that many must pass through it. But for them, the cleansing fire would be curative chastisement that prepares one for God's presence. In fact, the fire might even be God's presence. Therefore, hell would eventually be empty or its refining purpose would come to an end.[10]

All of these points of view reflect theological concerns for representing God's character aright, pastoral concerns for guarding and guiding God's flock in the truth, evangelistic concerns for presenting the Gospel with integrity, and biblical concerns for faithfulness to Christian Scripture.[11] So how is it that we've come to such differing positions?

INFORMING THEOLOGY

How do we arrive at our cosmology of hell? What informs our biases, preferences, or sense of obligation to adopt a particular teaching? In

10. To some readers, this type of universalism will sound much like purgatory. Some Roman Catholics would agree, because purgatory functions redemptively. The Eastern Orthodox would not, since Catholic purgatory was historically punitive rather than pedagogical or medicinal. Besides, Augustine, the infernalist, believed in purgatory, too, but only for the elect. The damned were not given any postmortem opportunity of redemption. God's refinery (Mal 3) cleanses and perfects us but is not necessarily equated directly to purgatory or even the afterlife.

11. Jonanthan Stanley comments: "I think it is helpful to include 'ethical concerns' to communicate that all views are concerned with not undermining justice (though they employ very different notions of justice in the process). You flag and deal with the question of justice in terms of God's character (just? merciful? wrathful?), but I think flagging the way our views of final judgment frame and guide our attempts to do and establish justice in the real interpersonal, social, and political conflicts of history draws things together and foreshadow your very helpful suggestion in the end of the book that the final judgment will be something like a grand 'truth and reconciliation commission.' Our view of final judgment must not undermine our commitment to justice, or as Moltmann says, leaning on Horkheimer, our view of final judgment must not allow 'the perpetrator to triumph over his innocent victim'—according to Moltmann, infernalism, annihilationism, and presumptive universalism allow this to happen (in their own ways)." (Jonathan Stanley, email to me, June, 2009).

addition to the Scriptures we choose for our focus, how we view hell also depends on:

1. **Our View of God**: Is God primarily a God of love, justice, and mercy or righteous anger? Is his primary posture toward humanity enmity or compassion? Does God's holiness allow or prevent fellowship with sinful people? Is God free to forgive or bound by righteousness to punish? Is he absolutely approachable (Heb 4:16) or infinitely unapproachable (1 Tim 6:16)?

2. **Our View of the Atonement**: Was the Cross about God pouring out his wrath upon Christ or us pouring our wrath out upon God? Was God punishing Jesus in our place (ultimate justice) or were we murdering God's perfect love (ultimate injustice)? Was it about final payment for sin-debts or final forgiveness of sin-debts? Does the Cross save us from God, the devil, sin, death, or ourselves?[12]

3. **Our Approach to Scripture**: When we read the Bible, do we tend to interpret the images literally or metaphorically? Do we feel we are more faithful to the text when we take it as literally as the language allows or when we are most sensitive to the authors' use of symbols? Are we more prone to ignore verses that don't fit our doctrinal presuppositions or are we more apt to bend them into our framework?

4. **Our Personal Need**: Do we feel the need to ignore, minimize, or do away with hell because we cannot allow that a loving God could conceive, create, or implement such a monstrosity? Or do we desperately need hell, because in this world of atrocities, God could not be considered holy, righteous, and just without it? Do we require such a place with which to threaten unbelievers into salvation and believers into faithfulness? Or, like the annihilationists, do we look for a proportionate combination of compassion and punishment in our desire to prevent God from vanquishing evil with a far greater evil?

HEREIN LIES THE PROBLEM

The stubborn fact is that Scripture is richly polyphonic on the topic of hell and judgment—*as if by design*. Thus, if we become dogmatic about any

---

12. See also Jersak and Hardin, *Stricken by God?*

one position, we reduce ourselves to reading selectively or doing interpretive violence to those verses that don't fit our chosen view. Our theological prejudgments blind us to passages we may have read many times but never really seen. Even a tentative removal of traditionalist lenses leads to the question, "Why didn't I ever see that verse before?" The complexity of the text is not a deficiency! If we can momentarily suspend our penchant for forcing the text to harmonize with our systems or even with itself, we'll see some magnificent tensions between those old Moroccan leather covers.

For example, the Bible repeatedly affirms that God has given humanity the real capacity for authentic choice. To choose between life and death, heaven and hell, and mercy and wrath implies the real possibility that some could choose the way that leads to destruction. The Bible testifies that some may opt for choices that result in permanent posthumous exclusion (the lake of fire, outer darkness, etc.).

On the other hand, the Bible just as plainly teaches that God is also free: free to relent, free to forgive, free to restore even when judgment is promised (Hos 11; Jonah 1:1; 3:4, 10; 4:2, 11), free to pursue lost sheep "until he finds them," free to play out a cosmic history where, in the end, "every knee will bow," "all things will be restored," "everything will be reconciled," and "all will be made alive," a time when absolutely everything will be "summed up in Christ," and when Christ will, in turn, hand a saved cosmos over to his Father so "that God may be all in all." The Alpha purposes of God for the universe will come to their Omega point in Jesus Christ. Thus, before we plant our flag on any one version of hell, we must take all of the biblical texts on hell and judgment, mercy and restoration into account.

These three types of passages, which I will call infernalist, annihilationist, and universalist texts, cannot be integrated easily into a cogent dogmatic system. In fact, my argument for hope over presumption is just this: the Bible doesn't allow us to settle easily on any of these as "isms." Perhaps that's because humankind needs all of these voices. Maybe God would have the wicked tremble before the infernalist passages and renounce their evil works. He would comfort the afflicted with the promise of justice and a day of accounting, and he would have "the elect" embrace the broader hope of the universalist verses. We joyfully hope for the best but bow heart and knee to the justice and mercy of God. Thus, one voice cannot be absolutized without negating the others. Our obsessive attempts to harmonize the Scriptures into artificially coherent, stackable propositions—as if they required us to contend for their reliability or authority—actually do violence to their richness.

PRESUMPTIONS AND POSSIBILITIES

So where does that leave us? Setting aside preconceptions as best we can, what does the Bible actually teach us about judgment and hell when we read it carefully and take it seriously? Not "what do I imagine about hell?" or "what do I wish about hell if it were up to me?" Furthermore, what do judgment and hell say about God's character? For that is the real issue at stake here. Is there a way to approach the subject of hell that doesn't presume or negate any of these positions, one that accepts the reality of judgment but hopes that somehow everyone might one day be reconciled to God?

Rather than painting themselves into universalist or infernalist corners, a great many of the Church Fathers and early Christians found refuge in the humility of hope. They maintained the *possibility* (not the presumption) of some version of judgment and hell and the twin *possibility* (not presumption) that at the end of the day, no one need suffer it forever. For several centuries, scholars and mystics engaged in experimental theology, warning that none should presume upon universal redemption because of the possibility of damnation *and* that none should presume upon hell for anyone else other than perhaps oneself. For them, peace came not from certainty of knowing how it would all pan out but from a solid hope in God's great love and mercy—that Jesus' plan to save the whole world might actually work.[13]

13. Jonathan Stanley, editor of *The Other Journal*, comments: "I appreciate the distinction between 'presumption' and 'hope' which allows you to distinguish between presumptive and hopeful universalisms, and opens the door to an evangelical universalism of the hopeful sort. Following Moltmann, I think it might be helpful to expand your taxonomy of universalisms to 'presumptive' (or dogmatic), 'wishful,' and 'hopeful'—that would further distinguish between 'wishful thinking' and 'hopeful thinking' and the types of universalism that follow. For Jurgen Moltmann, there is a 'knowing (in hope)' that while not presumptive (it must happen) surpasses wishful thinking (it might happen) and provides the ground to confess 'I know (i.e., in the knowledge of hope) it will happen.' I think your 'hopeful universalism' is more hopeful than wishful (and thus very close to Moltmann), but I think it would help to critique the 'presumptive' (liberal) and the 'wishful' (agnostic) equally to really create the space for the distinctiveness of your proposal of a 'hopeful' (evangelical) universalism." (Jonathan Stanley, email to me, June 2009). I hear Stanley—though I cannot quite say, "I know," I experience peaceful confidence when I pray for mercy from the One who is Love.

This eschatological hope has little in common with the fashionable pop-universalism that scorns judgment and hell as medieval myths and that assumes everybody is "in" regardless of their beliefs and behaviors in this life. Quite the opposite: the hope of ultimate redemption is as inclusive in its judgment as it is in its salvation. All are held to account, all pass through the fire so that all may be purified and glorified. Mercy triumphs over judgment; it does not skirt it.

BIASED TOWARD HOPE

We all have a bias. The important thing is to recognize your bias and be able to defend or explain it. As a "critical realist,"[14] I spend a good deal of time and energy studying my biases—how they emerged, and how they influence my thinking. Rather than pretending to be perfectly objective, I confess that since my early days as a terrified infernalist, I have developed a strong preference for hope. I hope in the Good News that God's love rectifies every injustice through forgiveness and reconciliation. The Gospel of hope that I can preach boldly is this:

God is not angry with you and never has been. He loves you with an everlasting love. Salvation is not a question of "turn or burn." We're burning already, but we don't have to be! Redemption! The life and death of Christ showed us how far God would go to extend forgiveness and invitation. His resurrection marked the death of death and the evacuation of Hades. My hope is in Christ, who rightfully earned his judgment seat and whose verdict is restorative justice, that is to say, mercy.

Hope. That is my bias, and I believe that Scripture, tradition, and experience confirm it. I want to explain and validate my hope in those contexts. This book will address the central problem of this "heated" debate: *not* infernalism versus annihilationism versus universalism, but rather, authentic, biblical Christian hope vis-à-vis the error of dogmatic presumption (of any view).[15] Hope presumes nothing but is rooted in a

---

14. Critical realism acknowledges objectively knowable, mind-independent reality whilst admitting the limitations of perception and cognition. E.g., God is real. I can know God, but I know God through subjective filters that may distort God's image significantly. "For now we see through glass, darkly" (1 Cor 13:11 KJV).

15. This statement by Wright, reminiscent of von Balthasar and Karl Rahner, lays out my thesis exactly. "All this should warn us against the cheerful double dogmatism that has bedeviled discussion on these topics—the dogmatism, that is, of the person who knows exactly who is and who isn't 'going to hell' and of the universalist who is absolutely cer-

deeper confidence: the love and mercy of an openhearted and relentlessly kind God.

In short, I do not intend to convince readers of a particular theology of divine judgment. I hope, rather, to recall those relevant bits of Scripture, history, and tradition that ought to inform whatever view we take on this important topic. That said, the data summarized herein did lead me to four conclusions, which you may or may not share after all is said and done:

1. We cannot presume to know that all will be saved or that any will not be saved.

2. The revelation of God in Christ includes real warnings about the possibility of damnation for some *and also* the real possibility that redemption may extend to all.

3. We not only dare hope and pray that God's mercy would finally triumph over judgment; the love of God *obligates* us to such hope.

4. Revelation 21–22 provides a test case for a biblical theology of eschatological hope.

To summarize our direction, I quote Hermann-Josef Lauter.

> Will it really be all men who allow themselves to be reconciled? No theology or prophecy can answer this question, but love hopes all things (1 Cor 13:7). It cannot do otherwise than to hope for the reconciliation of all men in Christ. Such unlimited hope is, from a Christian standpoint, not just permitted but commanded.[16]

---

tain that there is no such place or that if there is, it will, at the last, be empty." (N. T. Wright, *Surprised by Hope*, 177).

16. Hermann-Josef Lauter, *Pastoralblatt*, 123.

PART ONE

"Who Then Can Be Saved?"

Possibilities in Biblical Tradition

2

The Biblical Possibility of Ultimate Judgment

It is generally known that, in the New Testament, two series of statements run along side by side in such a way that synthesis of both is neither permissible nor achievable: the first series speaks of being lost for all eternity; the second, of God's will, and ability, to save all men.[1]

THE MYSTERY OF AFTERLIFE

THE MYSTERIOUS POSSIBILITIES OF the afterlife have been sought out from time immemorial and across every culture. Religions, mythologies, and philosophies have always featured freely evolving visions of existence beyond the grave and have frequently borrowed terms (including "hell") and images (especially flames) from those traditions otherwise regarded as pagan. Even in the Bible we see an evolution of understanding concerning judgment, an unfolding of revelation toward resurrection, and the free use of metaphors without endorsing the cosmology behind them. A careful examination of the text grants so many possibilities that categorical statements seem altogether ignorant. But examine it we shall, for the possibilities may perchance lead us to hope.

THE POSSIBILITY OF DIVINE JUDGMENT IN SCRIPTURE

No matter our view on hell, if we stand back and look at Jesus' character, preaching, and ministry as a whole, we can probably all agree that the defining characteristic of the God whom he revealed is love (John 3:16; 1 John 3–4). He is not willing that any should perish but that all should come to repentance (2 Pet 3:9). Further, he sent his Son into the world as

---

1. von Balthasar, *Dare We Hope?*, 29.

Biblical Terms Associated with Hell and Judgment	
Words traditionally translated "hell" in English	Occurrences of Hebrew and Greek words relating to divine judgment
Sheol Deut 32:22; 2 Sam 22:6; Job 11:8; 26:6; Ps 9:17; 16:10; 18:5; 55:15; 86:13; 116:3; 139:8; Prov 5:5; 7:27; 9:18; 15:11; 15:24; 23:14; 27:20; Isa 5:14; 14:9; 14:15; Isa 28:15; 28:18; 57:9; Ezek 31:16, 17, 31:17; 32:21; 32:27; Amos 9:2; Jonah 2:2; Hab 2:5.	**Sheol (grave, pit, unseen)** Gen 37:35; 42:38; 44:29, 31; Num 16:30, 33; Deut 32:22; 1 Sam 2:6; 2 Sam 22:6; 1 Kng 2:6, 9; Job 7:9; 11:8; 14:13; 17:13, 16; 21:13; 24:19; 26:6; Ps 6:5; 9:17; 16:10; 18:5; 30:3; 31:17; 49:14, 14, 15; 55:15; 86:13; 88:3; 89:48; 116:3; 139:8; 141:7; Prov 1:12; 5:5; 7:27; 9:18; 15:11, 24; 23:14; 27:20; 30:16; Eccl 9:10; Song Sol 8:6; Isa 5:14; 14:9, 11, 15; 28:15, 18; 38:10, 18; Isa 57:9; Ezek 31:15, 16, 17; 32:21, 27; Hos 13:14, 14; Amos 9:2; Jonah 2:2; Hab 2:5.
Hades Matt 11:23; 16:18; Luke 10:15; 16:23; Acts 2:27, 31; Rev 1:18; 6:8; 20:13, 14.	**Hades (grave, pit, unseen)** Matt 11:23; 16:18; Luke 10:15; 16:23; Acts 2:27, 31; 1 Cor 15:55; Rev 1:18; Rev 6:8; 20:13, 14.
	Tehom (deep, depths) Gen 1:2; 7:11; 8:2; 49:25; Exod 15:5, 8; Deut 8:7; 33:13; Job 28:14; 38:16, 30; 41:32; Ps 33:7; 36:6; 42:7; 71:20; 77:16; 78:15; 104:6; 106:9; 107:26; 135:6; 148:7; Prov 3:20; 8:24, 27; Isa 51:10; 63:13; Ezek 26:19; 31:4; 31:15; Amos 7:4; Jonah 2:5; Hab 3:10. **Abussos (Abyss, bottomless pit)** Luke 8:31; Rom 10:7; Rev 9:1, 2, 11; 11:7; 17:8; 20:1, 3.
Gehenna Matt 5:22, 29, 30; 10:28; 18:9; 23:15, 33; Mark 9:43, 45, 47; Luke 12:5; Jas 3:6.	**Ge Hinnom (Valley of Hinnom)** Josh 15:8; 18:16; 2 Kgs 23:10; 2 Chr 28:3; 33:6; Neh 11:30; Jer 7:31, 32; 19:2, 19:6; 32:35. **Topheth (a place in the Valley of Hinnom)** Job 17:6; 2 Kgs 23:10; Jer 7:31, 32; 19:6, 11, 12, 13, 14; Isa 30:33. **Gehenna (the Valley of Hinnom)** Matt 5:22, 29, 30; 10:28; 18:9; 23:15, 33; Mark 9:43, 45, 47; Luke 12:5; Jas 3:6.
	Lake of fire / fire / brimstone (sulfur) Gen 19:24; Deut 29:23; Job 18:15; Ps 11:6; Isa 30:33; 34:9; Ezek 38:22; Luke 17:29; Rev 19:17, 18; 19:20; 20:10; 21:8.
Tartarus 2 Pet 2:4.	**Tartarus** 2 Pet 2:4.

Savior to forgive us and reconcile us to himself (2 Cor 5:19). He welcomes all, the righteous and the wicked, to the heavenly banquet (Matt 22:10). Jesus says his Father has rendered all judgment into his hands (John 5:22–27), and yet Jesus said he did not come to judge or condemn (John 8:15; 12:47) but to extend unilateral mercy, which trumps all judgment (Jas 2:13).

With this revelation of God as our foundation, a punitive judgment of eternal torture in burning flames that can never satiate God's wrath is not merely a paradox—it is a flat out contradiction. Can we not, therefore, dismiss the texts that bear such threats? How could we, especially when some of the Bible's direst warnings about hell come from the mouth of Jesus, himself? Instead, if we truly are people of the book and followers of Jesus of Nazareth, we must heed such warnings with the utmost respect.

So is that it, then? Are we stuck with the apparent paradox of a loving God who will at the same time abandon us to eternal agony in hell if we fail to respond properly to his Son? Will we have to wait until the next life to see how this contradiction is resolved? Before rushing to answer this question, let's revisit the Scriptures, noting carefully what they actually do and do not say about hell and judgment and the various images they associate with these concepts.

THE BIBLICAL SPECTRUM OF TERMS FOR "HELL" (AND THEIR TERMINI)

In modern street-English, we use "hell" as a catchall term to describe the bad place (usually red hot) where sinful people are condemned to punishment and torment after they die. This simplistic, selective, and horrifying perception of hell is due in large part to nearly 400 years of the King James Version's monopoly in English-speaking congregations (not to mention centuries of imaginative religious art). Rather than acknowledge the variety of terms, images, and concepts that the Bible uses for divine judgment, the KJV translators opted to combine them all under the single term "hell." In truth, the array of biblical pictures and meanings that this one word is expected to convey is so vast that they appear contradictory. For example, is hell a lake of fire or a place of utter darkness? Is it a purifying forge or a torture chamber? Is it exclusion from God's presence or the consuming fire of God's glory?

While modern scholarship acknowledges the mis- or over-translation of Sheol, Hades, and Gehenna as "hell"—especially if by "hell" we refer automatically to the eternal punishment of the wicked in conscious torment in a lake of fire[2]—the thoroughly discussed limitations of hell language and imagery have been slow to permeate the theology of pulpits and pews in much of the church. Why the reluctance? Do we resist out of ignorance? Or are we afraid that abandoning infernalism implies abandoning faithfulness to Scripture and sound doctrine? After all, for so long we were taught that to be a Christian—especially an evangelical—is to be an infernalist. And yet, not a few of my friends have confessed that they have given up on being "good Christians" because they can no longer assent to the kind of God that creates and sends people to hell as they imagine it.

Perhaps we subconsciously believe we need visions of a literal, flaming hell ever before us to keep ourselves (and others) in moral check. If so, it is only natural to be intuitively suspicious of any exegetical move that might, on the surface, diminish the gravity of these texts and jeopardize souls. Good intentions, but I can't think of a better place to point out that the road to hell is paved with such! I think we need to ask ourselves which is more important, protecting our received dogma or truly listening to what the Bible has to say, how it says it, and what it intends? We may find that in our supposed doctrinal faithfulness we actually "nullify the word of God for the sake of our tradition" (Matt 15:3, 6). It is possible that even though we sincerely think we are being biblical that we are really only reading a narrow swath of pet texts in a wooden, literalist way that misses the authors' point? Reading biblical hell language in the way Jesus, Paul, or John intended it, even if this includes metaphorical or rhetorical uses, will not castrate the images of their power or negate their reality.

2. "English Etymology: The modern English word 'hell' is derived from the Old English *hel/helle* (originated about AD 725 to refer to a netherworld of the dead) reaching into the Anglo-Saxon pagan period, and ultimately from Proto-Germanic *halja*, meaning 'one who covers up or hides something.' The word has cognates in related Germanic languages such as Old Frisian *helle, hille;* Old Saxon *hellja;* Middle Dutch *helle* (modern Dutch *hel*); Old High German *helle* (Modern German *Hölle*); and Gothic *halja.* Subsequently, the word was used to transfer a pagan concept to Christian theology and its vocabulary. The English word 'hell' has been theorized as being derived from Old Norse *Hel.* Among other sources, the *Poetic Edda,* . . . and the *Prose Edda,* written in the thirteenth century by Snorri Sturluson, provide information regarding the beliefs of the Norse pagans, including a being named *Hel,* who is described as ruling over an underworld location of the same name." (R. Barnhart, *Concise Dictionary of Etymology,* 348).

Let us observe what is actually in the text and note again the spectrum of possibilities that defy neat harmonization. By the time we're finished, you'll see that far from presenting a unified voice on the topic, the Bible documents a progressive revelation and interpretation concerning the afterlife, an evolution that both borrows from and defines itself against other ancient traditions.[3] Moreover, between the covers of our Bible, the authors plainly teach infernalism, annihilationism, and universalism—and none of these briefly! Scripture includes a breathtaking breadth of possibilities suffused with incompatible details, making presumption and easy harmonization virtually impossible.

Nevertheless, what is generally overlooked is that each of the terms most commonly translated as "hell" in our English translations—Sheol, Hades, Gehenna, and Tartarus—all share one thing in common: a potential terminus. That is, the biblical writers declare a definite end to each. Imagine that: We've barely begun our study, and we're already facing a substantial challenge to the traditional definition of divine punishment! I will note each of these termini along the way.

SHEOL/HADES

We begin with Sheol (Hebrew) and Hades (Greek), in part because they occur more frequently than the other terms traditionally translated as "hell" and partly because they are among the first terms that modern translations have moved to either transliterate as place names (NASB, NRSV) or retranslate as "grave" (NIV, NKJV). I have combined these words, because they roughly correspond in biblical usage, and the Septuagint (LXX) translates Sheol as Hades some sixty-five times.[4]

While the King James Version was too quick to render Sheol and Hades as equivalents to hell, we are probably saying too little if we consistently reduce these words to "the grave" in the narrowest modern sense of simply being dead in a grave. Whether we read Sheol, Hades, or the grave, we need to keep in mind that the terms came into the Bible loaded with interfaith mythology.[5] Biblical writers borrowed these words to cover a

---

3. Cf. Brian McLaren, *The Last Word*, ch. 8–9; N. T. Wright, *The Resurrection of the Son of God*, Part I.

4. For a comparative chart, see http://www.what-the-hell-is-hell.com/HellStudy/HellCharts.htm.

5. Sheol from Assyrian-Babylonian mythology; Hades from the Greeks.

diversity of intermediate states between death and the final Judgment Day (when both Sheol and Hades will be eradicated). In the OT, Sheol (Hades in the LXX) can refer to death or the grave where everyone goes—righteous or wicked (Ps 16:10), but the faithful hope to be rescued from it (Ps 16:10). Sometimes it is under the earth (Isa 7:11; 57:9; Ezek 31:14; Ps 86:13), under the mountains (Job 26:5), under water (Jonah 2:7), or far from heaven (Job 11:8; Amos 9:2; Ps 139:8). It is monotonous and gloomy (Job 3:17–19), a place of sorrows (Ps 18:5), a place for the wicked (Ps 9:17; Isa 14:9–19), parallel to destruction (Prov 15:11), or a place of torment (Luke 16:23). It can be a pit, an abyss, or a prison (Ezek 31:16–17).

Theologian Emil Hirsch offers an even more nuanced understanding of these terms:

> The dead continue after a fashion their earthly life. Jacob would mourn there (Gen. xxxvii. 35; xlii. 38); David abides there in peace (I Kings ii. 6); the warriors have their weapons with them (Ezek. xxxii. 27), yet they are mere shadows ("rephaim"; Isa. xiv. 9; xxvi. 14; Ps. lxxxviii. 5, A. V. "a man that hath no strength"). The dead merely exist without knowledge or feeling (Job xiv. 13; Eccl. ix. 5). Silence reigns supreme; and oblivion is the lot of them that enter therein (Ps. lxxxviii. 13; xciv. 17; Eccl. ix. 10). Hence it is known also as "Dumah," the abode of silence (Ps. vi. 6; xxx. 10; xciv. 17; cxv. 17); and there God is not praised (*ib.* cxv. 17; Isa. xxxviii. 15). Still, on certain extraordinary occasions the dwellers in Sheol are credited with the gift of making known their feelings of rejoicing at the downfall of the enemy (Isa. xiv. 9, 10). Sleep is their usual lot (Jer. li. 39; Isa. xxvi. 14; Job xiv. 12). Sheol is a horrible, dreary, dark, disorderly land (Job x. 21, 22); yet it is the appointed house for all the living (*ib.* xxx. 23). Return from Sheol is not expected (II Sam. xii. 23; Job vii. 9, 10; x. 21; xiv. 7 *et seq.*; xvi. 22; Ecclus. [Sirach] xxxviii. 21); it is described as man's eternal house (Eccl. xii. 5). It is "dust" (Ps. xxx. 10; hence in the Shemoneh 'Esreh, in benediction No. ii., the dead are described as "sleepers in the dust").[6]

In the NT, Hades may still refer to either death or the place where the dead are confined until Judgment Day (Rev 20:13). It can be a place of conscious torment opposite to paradise or the "bosom of Abraham" (Luke 16), a fate reserved for the unregenerate (Matt 11:23; Luke 10:15). Hades also represents the forces of darkness that oppose the Church (Matt 16:18). Hades is finally exterminated in the lake of fire (Rev 6:8; 20:14).

---

6. Emil Hirsch, "Sheol," *JE* (1906), para. 2.

NT preaching put David's prayer of faith on Jesus' lips, expecting that God would not abandon his soul to Hades (Acts 2:25–28).

With such a stunning array of ideas about the state of the dead within the Jewish worldview, it is no wonder that Jesus' disciples might believe they had seen a ghost (Matt 14:26) or that Rhoda mistook Peter for his angel[7] (Acts 12:15).

Descent into Hades

In the early church, Christ's *descensus* (descent into Hades) on Holy Saturday (Eph 4:8–9; 1 Pet 3:18–21; 4:6) was preached widely, even entering our creeds. There was a diversity of interpretations as to what this actually meant (e.g., Cyril, John Damascene, Gregory of Nyssa, Augustine, and Aquinas), but the common hope was that Jesus invaded Hades not to suffer further but to conquer its gates and rescue the dead.

On what basis did the church hope for posthumous rescue of the dead from Sheol/Hades? This was not just the wishful thinking or sentimentalism characteristic of so many contemporary funerals. The ancient Christian tradition in which Christ descended into Hades to destroy its gates and plunder its goods (Matt 12:29) was rooted in the apostolic message. Christ's descent into Hades and offer of salvation are explicit in the epistles of Peter:

> 1 Pet 3:18–20 (NASB)—For Christ also died for sins once for all, the just for the unjust, so that He might bring us to God, having been put to death in the flesh (*thanatōtheis men sarki*), but made alive in the spirit (*zōopoiētheis de pneumati*); in which also He went and made proclamation (i.e., preached: *ekēruxen*) to the spirits now in prison, who once were disobedient, when the patience of God kept waiting in the days of Noah, during the construction of the ark, in which a few, that is, eight persons, were brought safely through the water.

> 1 Pet 4:6 (NASB)—For the gospel has for this purpose been preached even to those who are dead (*nekrois euēngelisthē*), that though they are judged in the flesh as men (*krithōsi men kata anthrōpous sarki*), they may live in the spirit according to the will of God (*zōsin de kata theon pneumati*).

---

7. They didn't think Peter had a doppelgänger for a guardian angel but that the spirits of the departed might on occasion reappear as angels.

Two items come to my attention when I read these texts. First, the Greek could not be much clearer. The dead are being evangelized. Jesus' proclamation is more than gloating. The effects of his preaching show us that. Namely, the rebellious people who had formerly been judged in the body and whose spirits were kept in prison are now made alive in/by the s/Spirit,[8] exactly as Jesus was put to death in the body but made alive in/by the s/Spirit (note the parallels in the Greek—Jesus shares their death in the flesh that they might share in his life in the spirit). Peter was teaching that what happened to Jesus, the Firstborn from the dead, also happened to those from Noah's day who had died in rebellion once they heard the Gospel preached.[9]

Could this conquest tradition also be at the heart of Heb 2:14–15? "[Jesus] himself likewise shared [flesh and blood], so that through death he might destroy the one who has the power of death, that is, the devil, and free those who all their lives were held in slavery by the fear of death."

Finally, there is also an odd Easter story, mentioned only in Matthew's Gospel, which may be a relevant confirmation of the descent tradition. Are these representatives or firstfruits of those that Jesus set free from the place of the dead?

> Matt 27:52–53—The tombs broke open and the bodies of many holy people who had died were raised to life. They came out of the tombs, and after Jesus' resurrection they went into the holy city and appeared to many people.

Prison break language, metaphors, and passages made for dynamic Gospel preaching throughout the first few centuries of Christianity. In his essay, "Descent to the Underworld," Richard Baukham says this drama was common in early Christian proclamation. "Jesus breaks down the gates of the underworld (*Odes Sol* 17:9–11; *Teachings of Silvanus, NHC* 7.110.19–34; Tertullian, *De Res. Carn.* 44), releases the captive dead (*Odes Sol* 17:12;

---

8. Whether they are made "in their human spirits" or "by the Holy Spirit" is ambiguous in the Greek.

9. Ansell: "The flood is a huge transition, in a way parallel to the Cross. I think of Moberly's "the old testament of the Old Testament" idea (Moberly, *The Old Testament of the Old Testament*), intensified so that Gen 6–8 is the old testament of the old testament of the Old Testament! [there is something to having a dispensational sensitivity in a way contrary to the 'zamboni' (leveling) hermeneutic of covenant theology] After the flood, God's attitude to judgment changes. So in that light, those who were judged before/in this, need special attention in the dynamics of grace. So Jesus goes to the lowest of the low first of all." (Nik Ansell, email to me, May 29, 2009).

22:4; *Acts Thom* 10), or destroys death or Hades (Melito, *Peri Pascha* 102)."[10] Second century Christians also loved to pray, preach, and sing on the theme of Christ's invasion of the grave.[11] Clement of Alexandria asserts that:

> The Lord descended to Hades for no other end but to preach the Gospel . . . since God's punishments are saving and disciplinary, leading to conversion, and choosing rather the repentance than the death of a sinner; and especially since souls, although darkened by passions, when released from their bodies, are able to perceive more clearly, because of their being no longer obstructed by the paltry flesh.[12]

Hippolytus of Rome (ca. AD 170–236) preached that Jesus was "He who rescued from the lowest hell the first-formed man of earth when he was lost and bound with the chains of death; He who came down from above, and raised the earthly on high; He who became the evangelist of the dead, and the redeemer of the souls, and the resurrection of the buried."[13] However, for Hippolytus this salvation was specific to the saints, and he believed God's judgments were both eternal and infernal.[14] The early Christians also used Christian translations of Sirach that say, "I shall go through all the regions deep beneath the earth, and I shall visit all those who sleep, and I shall enlighten all those who hope on the Lord; I shall let my teaching shine forth as a guiding light and cause it to shine afar off."[15] Justin and Irenaeus repeatedly quoted a Jewish text attributed to Jeremiah (meanwhile accusing the Jews of deleting it): "The Lord God hath remembered his dead among those of Israel who have been laid in the place of burial, and has gone down to announce to them the tidings of his salvation."[16]

---

10. Bauckham, "Descent to the Underworld," 157.

11. For a collection of numerous early texts on Christ's descent, see Hugh W. Nibley, "Baptism for the Dead in Ancient Times."

12. *Strom* 6.6 (ANF 2).

13. *Frag. Hom.* 7.2 (ANF 5).

14. *Against Plato on the Cause of the Universe*, 1 (ANF 5). *Scholia on Daniel, 7.14* (ANF 5).

15. "Sirach 24:32," in Schmidt, *Gespräche Jesu*, 473.

16. Justin, *Dialogue with Trypho* 72 (ANC 1); Irenaeus, *Against Heresies* 3:20.4; 4:22.1; 5:31.1 (ANF 1); Jerome, *Commentary on Matthew* 4.27 (NPNF-2 6).

Some streams of Christ's descent limit the salvation offered to the righteous dead while others treat it as a general offer of salvation to all prisoners. Church historian Jeffrey Trumbower, in his study on posthumous salvation in early Christianity, posits numerous examples of biblical and extra-biblical texts that support the descent theory, zeroing in on the apocryphal Gospel of Nicodemus as a favorite.[17] The book is composed of the Acts of Pilate (a trial and crucifixion account) and Christ's descent into Hades. Justin Martyr referred to it by the middle of the second century (*Apology* 1, 35, 48) as did Tertullian (*Apologeticum* 5, 21, 24), although it apparently underwent later editing and additions in Latin. Though late, the Gospel of Nicodemus was influential and well received as orthodox (i.e., esp. not Gnostic). The final act of this colorful narrative recounts Jesus' successful search and rescue of Adam and the parade of captives that follow them out of their prison into freedom.[18] It includes a beautiful glimpse of St. John the Forerunner preparing the way for Christ even in Hades:

> For this reason he sent me to you, to preach that the only begotten son of God comes here, in order that whoever believes in him should be saved, and whoever does not believe in him should be condemned. Therefore I say to you all: When you see him, all of you worship him. For now only have you opportunity for repentance because you worshiped idols in the vain world above and sinned. (Gosp. Nicod. 18)

Later theologians expounded on this tradition, from the poetic language of Gregory the Great to the scholastic dissections of Aquinas. So Gregory: "Christ descended into the profoundest depths of the earth when he went into the lowest hell in order to bring out the souls of the chosen. Thus God made of this Abyss a path."[19] But we give last word to von Balthasar: "From now on, even hell belongs to Christ."[20]

---

17. Trumbower, *Rescue for the Dead,* ch. 5.

18. "The Gospel of Nicodemus, or Acts of Pilate," *The Apocryphal New Testament.*

19. Gregory the Great, cited in von Balthasar, *Dare We Hope?,* 112. See also Thomas Aquinas, *Summa Theologica,* 3.Q52, Christ's Descent into Hell.

20. von Balthasar, *Dare We Hope?,* 112.

Sheol/Hades' Terminus

Until Easter weekend, Sheol/Hades held the dead, imprisoned behind its gates (Job 17:16; 38:17; Ps 9:14; Isa 38:10). By conquering death, Christ now holds the keys to those gates (Rev 1:18). In this present age, the NT pits the gates of Hades in a losing battle against the Church (Matt 16:18). Though death and Hades are given temporary power to wage war on the earth (Rev 6:8), Christ ultimately triumphs. Death and Hades must give up their dead (Rev 20:13) and then come to their own decisive terminus.

> Isa 25:7–8—On this mountain he will destroy the shroud that enfolds all peoples, the sheet that covers all nations; he will swallow up death forever. (cf. 1 Cor 15:54–55)

> 1 Cor 15:25–26—For he must reign until he has put all his enemies under his feet. The last enemy to be destroyed is death.

> Rev 20:13–14—The Sea gave up the dead that were in it, and death and Hades gave up the dead that were in them, and each person was judged according to what he had done. Then death and Hades were thrown into the lake of fire.

The Good News about Sheol/Hades

We must all face death, because it continues to hold sway in this world. But by virtue of his resurrection, Jesus Christ has beaten its power to tyrannize. Death's reign will finally come to an end, its shroud (Isa 25:7) and its stinger removed (1 Cor 15:55), and we hold fast to the promise of resurrection beyond the grave.

THE DEEP/THE ABYSS/TARTARUS

I have linked these three terms—*Tehom* (the deep), Abyss (pit), and Tartarus (place name for the prison of the Greek Titans or NT demons)—because in spite of some distinctions, they also overlap in meaning or are even treated as synonymous. For example, while *Tehom* usually refers to the watery depths, the Abyss and Tartarus connote a fiery pit. Yet all three share two things in common: they have sometimes been associated with hell but not normally as the place of punishment for the unredeemed. They are regularly connected with fallen angels or demonic spirits as their source, abode, or prison.

The Deep (Tehom)

In contrast to Sheol/Hades,[21] *Tehom* is used in the creation and flood narratives (Gen 1:2; 7:11; 8:2) and elsewhere to describe the primordial deep or Abyss that is always threatening to overtake creation with chaos.[22] "*Tehom*," the Semitic word for "sea," comes to acquire literal or poetic meanings for "the deep" or "deep waters." Genesis 1:2 describes darkness on the surface of the Abyss and the Spirit of God on the surface of the water trembling it or shaking it.[23] Eugene Peterson's *The Message* paints a poignant picture of this moment:

> Earth was a soup of nothingness, a bottomless emptiness, an inky blackness.
> God's spirit brooded like a bird above the watery abyss.

So literally from the beginning, we have a metaphorical connection between the waters of the sea and the depths of the Abyss. Later on, the chaotic and destructive potential of the deep sea comes to be associated with the demonic depths of the underworld. One can imagine how this might have come about as Mediterranean sailors identified flash storms and treacherous tidal straits with mythological beasts seeking to devour their little ships. By the time the Septuagint was written, Hebrew scholars were already regularly translating *Tehom* with the Greek "*abussos*." Early Judaism and the NT shift the meaning of *Tehom* and *abussos* to the depths of the earth as the prison of spirits.[24] Perhaps an earth-bound prison for supernatural beasts provided ancient imaginations with more solace than a deep-sea lair.

The Abyss (abussos)

Thus, in the NT, the Abyss combines two diverse OT pictures—chaotic sea/fiery pit—both ideas of what lay deep beneath the earth's crust. On the one hand, the Abyss is equivalent to the OT *Tehom* as a source of primal chaos. In Revelation, the Beast actually comes up out of the Abyss (9:1-2; 11:7; 17:8), parallel to the emergence of the dragon and beast from out of

21. The *deep* in contrast to *Sheol* or *Hades*: Cf. Samuel Terrien, "The Metaphor of the Rock," 166–69.

22. Cf. Walter Brueggemann, *Genesis: Interpretation*, 124–26; Ibid., *Theology of the Old Testament*, 155–59.

23. Brita Miko, email to me, Feb 2009.

24. Jenni and Westerman, *TLOT*, 3:1410.

the sea (*thalasses*—12:18; 13:1). Conversely, Legion begged Jesus not to be sent there (Luke 8:31), and Satan is bound in the Abyss for 1,000 years (Rev 20:3). Later, we discover that the Abyss precedes and is separate from the eternal lake of fire. Satan is released from the Abyss to briefly deceive the nations, and thereafter thrown into the "lake of burning sulfur" to be "tormented day and night forever and ever" (Rev 20:10).

The Abyss also hearkens back to the furnace imagery of Sodom and Gomorrah, where God rained down fire and brimstone and turned the cities to ash. Abraham witnessed smoke rising from the land "like smoke from a furnace" (Gen 19:28). We hear echoes of this in Revelation 9:2: "When he opened the Abyss, smoke rose from it like the smoke from a gigantic furnace. The sun and sky were darkened by the smoke from the Abyss."

This is not to say that Sodom and Gomorrah were the Abyss or became the Abyss. Nor are their citizens pictured as going there. Rather, the memory of their fiery destruction provides a visual of what the Abyss might be like and what it can release in our world. Notice that whenever the Abyss is opened in Revelation and "all hell breaks loose," the results recorded or foreseen are destructive "woes" on the earth: war, famine, disease, and death are *on earth, as it is in hell,* so to speak. The wrath of the Lamb is that he honors our demands to release humanity's chaotic will to self-destruct.

Tartarus

Like Abyss and *Tehom, Tartarus* means "deep place" but came to be a proper place name for the underworld prison. Tartarus has a rich backstory in ancient Greek mythology,[25] but it occurs just once in the Bible (where it has often been translated "hell"). There, it is a dense, dark pit that serves as a pre-trial holding tank for fallen angels.

> 2 Pet 2:4—God did not hold back from punishing the angels that
> sinned, but, by throwing them into *tartarus*, delivered them into

---

25. In Greek myth, Tartarus was both a deity and a place in the underworld far beneath Hades. Hesiod's *Theogony* (116–38), Homer's *Odyssey* (11.576–600), and most Greek mythology reserves *Tartarus* as a prison used by the Titans (Cronus) and gods of Olympus (e.g., for defeated Titans, Cyclopes, Sisyphus, Tantalus, et al). Others, like Plato (*Gorgias*) and Virgil (*Aeneid* 6, 539–627) also consign sinners there. In Plato's *Gorgias,* he has Socrates say, "he who has lived unjustly and impiously shall go to the house of vengeance and punishment, which is called Tartarus."

pits of dense darkness to be reserved for judgment (see also Jude 6; 1 Enoch 20:2; Gen 6:1–4).

Distinct from Sheol, Hades, and Gehenna, *Tartarus* is roughly synonymous with the Abyss, a place where unclean spirits are driven and bound (1 Enoch 10:4–6; 22:11–12). Thus, if our concern for redemption is exclusive to people, both the Abyss and the *Tartarus* of 2 Peter become irrelevant, seeing as their inhabitants are strictly fallen angels or unclean spirits.

For those, however, who were concerned with the ultimate redemption of all things, speculation arose (and was later condemned) that in the end, even devils (and Satan himself!) might one day bow the humbled knee and find mercy. Would this not exemplify the supreme extension of God's call to love and bless our enemies? Does the injunction to forgive not rise from the depths of God's own nature? What a glorious victory for Christ if even the prodigal archangel[26] finally found grace in the Father's arms! Nor was this mere conjecture or ignorance of the directness of Rev 20:10. Those who wondered aloud had a measure of biblical warrant:

> 1 Cor 15:28; Acts 3:21—When all things are subjected to Christ's authority [including the fallen angels], then Christ will subject himself to God, who gave him all authority, so that God [in whom no evil dwells] may be all in all. [Including the fallen angels?]

> Phil 2:10; Rev 5:13—Every creature will bow and worship Jesus, including those on the earth [all living things], in the heavens [angelic beings] and under the earth. [Including fallen angels/ demonic spirits?]

> Col 1:16–20—For by him all things were created: things in heaven and on earth, visible and invisible, whether thrones or powers or rulers or authorities; all things were created by him and for him . . . [including people and angels, holy or fallen] For God was pleased to have all his fullness dwell in him, and through him to reconcile to himself all things, whether things on earth or things in heaven, [what invisible things in heaven need reconciling?] by making peace through his blood, shed on the Cross. [Beyond humankind and earthly creation?]

I hope you can see that if we take these verses and the implied questions seriously, the salvation of demons and Satan can come up for discussion

---

26. For more food for thought, see Nik Ansell, "The Call of Wisdom/the Voice of the Serpent," 31–57.

not as mere philosophical speculation but as a matter of serious biblical exegesis and theological inquiry. And so it did, with the Synod of Constantinople (543 AD) rendering the verdict of "anathema" against Origen's speculations (while, for political reasons, allowing others like Gregory of Nyssa to track similar lines of thought).

> If anyone says or thinks that the punishment of demons and of impious men is only temporary, and will one day have an end, and that a restoration (*apokatastasis*) will take place of demons and of impious men, let him be anathema.[27]

The Deep/Abyss/Tartarus' Terminus

The question remains: Is there any biblical hope for a final end to this Abyss as a holding tank for chaos and evil? Beyond the aforementioned texts, I believe we can cling to such an eschatological hope, because in the new heaven and new earth, the watery Abyss of Gen 1:2 is completely gone:

> Rev 21:1—Then I saw a new heaven and a new earth, for the first heaven and the first earth had passed away, and there was no longer any sea (*ē thalassa ouk estin eti*).

For those prone to strictly literalist interpretations of such passages, don't panic! We need not fear the loss of our saltwater oceans and their wondrous creatures (Rev 5:13). The sea that disappears forever is the old order destruction, chaos, or any abode (whether prison or fortress) for the dragon, his beasts, and the demonic hordes of hell. In the new cosmology, that entire realm no longer exists.

The Good News about the Deep/Abyss/Tartarus

Evil, chaos, and destruction do exist in this era, but they have been bound and limited somehow until their final destruction. Many beastly horrors continue to emerge in our world from the depths, but the kingdom of God will have the last word, eradicating even the Abyss from the universe.

---

27. "The Anathematisms of the Emperor Justinian Against Origen," *The Seven Ecumenical Councils* 5.9 (NPNF-2 14).

ETERNAL PUNISHMENT (*KOLASIN AIŌNION*)
AND TORMENT (*BASANOS*)

Even if we are satisfied that the Bible directly identifies a terminus for all the specific terms [mis]translated as "hell," Jesus' most haunting messages of judgment may—and should—continue to niggle at our self-assurance. The words that we've translated as "eternal punishment" and "torment" require close attention, because they are words used unblushingly by the Jesus of the Gospels.

In his story of the sheep and the goats, we read the fateful verdict for those who have failed to love Christ in the least of his brothers and sisters:

> Matt 25:41,46—Then [the King] will say to those on his left, "Depart from me, you who are cursed, into the eternal fire prepared for the devil and his angels." Then they will go away to *eternal punishment* (*kolasin aiōnion*), but the righteous to eternal life (*zōēn*).

aiōnios, aiōnion

The debate around the term "eternal punishment" goes back at least as far as Gregory and Augustine. Infernalists argue that "eternal" must mean everlasting in duration. Therefore, the punishment must be the forever and ever punitive torment of the wicked (as it is for the dragon and the beast in Rev 20).[28] Universalists argue that "eternal" (*aiōnios*) can also literally mean an "age" (period of time) or an "unquantifiable duration of time."[29] If so, then one can make a case for a punishment of limited duration (as parts of 1 Enoch and the Talmud supposed). If the punishment is corrective and redemptive, *aiōnion* could mean that the chastisement continues for as long as is necessary to save the "goats." The fact is: each side makes the case they prefer. Either is possible; neither is presumable. Wright offers a simple solution without tipping the scales:

> *Aiōnian* relates to the Greek *aiōn*, which often roughly translates the Hebrew *olam*. Some Jews thought of there being two "ages"— *ha῾olam ha-zeh*, the present age, and *ha῾olam ha-ba*, the age to

---

28. Cf. Alan W. Gomes, "Evangelicals and the Annihilation of Hell," *Christian Research Journal* (Summer 1991) 8.

29. Cf. Canon F. W. Farrar, *Mercy and Judgment*, 378–99.

come. *Aiōnian* punishment and the like would be punishment in the age to come.[30]

Thus, for Wright, *aiōnion* addresses the question of "when" rather than "how long." Whatever the judgment or punishment is, it belongs to *aiōnion, in the age to come.* This resonates with me and does justice to the passage, reinforcing Jesus' central point: how you live in this age impacts your life in the next age. In other words, Jesus will actually enforce the "golden rule." This might sound a little like the Hindu concept of karma, but I prefer to think of it in terms of "sowing and reaping."

Nik Ansell goes an important step further than Wright. For him, the judgment is not merely scheduled for the age to come; the birth pangs of judgment actually usher in the new age foretold by the prophets. God's judgment is not meant to clear the wicked out of the path of the righteous, but to bring about the new era of hope for the salvation for all.[31]

For those who insist on nailing down the duration question, why not partner Matt 25 with Ps 136, where we read (twenty-six times) that God's love "endures forever" (NIV); "His mercy endureth forever" (KJV); "His faithful love endures forever" (NLT); "His lovingkindness is everlasting" (NASB). Apparently God's mercy can endure and exceed any length of time required by his corrections.

Moreover, while the parallel statements of Matt 25 compare eternal life and eternal judgment as if the eternity of one state is equivalent to the eternity of the other, why not hold this passage in tandem with the counterpoints of Ps 103:9–10: "He will not . . . harbor his anger forever; he does not treat us as our sins deserve or repay us according to our iniquities"? Or how about, "'In a surge of anger I hid my face from you for a moment, but with everlasting kindness I will have compassion on you,' says the LORD your Redeemer" (Isa 54:8).

Moving past "when" or "how long," we come to the question of "what?" What is this punishment to which Jesus refers?

---

30. N. T. Wright, "Your Questions to N. T. Wright," para. 3. Wright treats hell as a real possibility. Without presuming its nature, he speculates: "If it is possible . . . for human beings to choose to live more and more out of tune with their divine intention, to reflect the image of God less and less, there is nothing to stop them finally ceasing to bear that image, and so to be, as it were, beings who were once human but are not now." (N. T. Wright, *Following Jesus*, ch. 10).

31. Nik Ansell, "Hell: The Nemesis of Hope?" (Taken from para. 31 of Ansell's online version. A revised and expanded version appears in the Afterword below).

kolasis

Had penal retribution been intended, Matthew could have used the applicable Greek word, *timōreō/timōria* (Acts 22:5; 26:11; Heb 10:29). Instead, he chose the restorative term *kolasis*, usually [over]translated as *punishment*, but which actually carries a connotation of corrective discipline or chastisement.

> The Greek word for punish and punishment appears just three times in the NT . . . Our common version translates two Greek words, *timōreō*, "punish," and *kalazō*, "chastise," with the same English word, "punish." Chastising carries the idea of correcting with a view to amendment of one's mistakes, while punishment is penal action. These two words were defined by Aristotle in his *Rhet. 1, 10, 17*, as, "*kolasis* is corrective, *timōria* alone is the satisfaction of the inflictor." Archbishop Trench states in his synonyms of the N.T. (p. 23–24): "*timōria* indicates the vindictive character of punishment; *kolasis* indicates punishment as it has reference to correcting and bettering the offender."[32]

If so, then the goats of Matthew 25 are not dismissed to eternal, retributive torment. Rather, we have something more like Malachi's refiner's fire, which by implication, finds its terminus when the subject's "pruning"— the root meaning of *kolasis*—is complete.

In John's gospel, both perspectives on pruning (cut back versus cut off) play off against each other in chapter 15 (without using *kolasis*). On the one hand, God prunes disciples who abide in his love and bear fruit, just like branches on a vine (vs 2, 8). In this case, what is the nature of the pruning? How are the limbs cut back in practical life? What is it about this pruning that makes for greater fruit bearing? In the latter case, Jesus warns that "every branch of mine" (v 2) that does not abide in the vine or bear fruit is cut off, withers, is gathered, thrown into the fire, and burned (v 6). To whom is Jesus referring here? They are his, but they do not abide. Is the fire temporal destruction? Spiritual destruction? Eternal destruction? Jesus doesn't specify, but his point is made. The faithful are cut back and the unfaithful are cut off. Therefore, abide in him!

---

32. Louis Abbott, *An Analytical Study of Words*, ch. 9, para. 7.

Torment (*basanos, basanizō, basanismos, basanistēs*)

According to J. Schneider's article on the *basanos* word group,[33] the word for "torment" was used in the ancient world of economics, first by coin inspectors, then by those checking calculations. Thus, it became a figurative term for testing, and ultimately the supreme test of trial by torture[34] (specific to judicial punishment, whether justly or not).

Unfortunately, we do not have ancient dictionaries. We infer meanings by usage in context over time. Through the Septuagint,[35] the emphasis of this word group shifts somewhat from purpose to description ("tortures"[36]) to the agony itself. *Basanos* is also used with regard to the judgment of sin, whether inflicted by God[37] or self-inflicted as the consequences of sin or fear.[38] This judgment can vary from the "stumbling blocks"[39] of sin to physical agony in death[40] to bearing the "disgrace" of judgment[41] or the "eternal" or "unceasing torment" of fire prepared for the wicked.[42]

In the NT, we read about the torments experienced in Hades (Matt 4:24; Luke 16:23). However, our theology predetermines to what degree we see the suffering as testing or merely retributive punishment. For example, *basanazein* refers only to the suffering of the Centurion's paralytic servant (Matt 8:6), and the demons feared that Jesus would torment them before their time of judgment (Matt 8:29). Yet the sense is not quite so narrow as all that. Elsewhere, the boat was "battered" by waves (Matt 14:24), Lot was "afflicted" by the wickedness in Sodom/Gomorrah (2 Pet 2:8), and the woman clothed with the sun cried out in "birth pains" (Rev 12:2). *Basinismos* appears only in Rev 9:5 (where demonic locusts torment un-

33. J. Schneider, "Basanos," *TDNT*, 96–97.

34. Wis Sol 2:19.

35. Or LXX, the Greek translation of the Hebrew Scriptures, extant during the life of Christ.

36. "Tortures" of the Maccabeans (2 Macc 7:8; 4 Macc 8:19; 9:5, 6; 14:4, 8, 11; 15:11, 18, 19, 20, 21, 22, 32; 16:1, 2, 17; 17:3, 7, 10, 23; 18:20, 21) and decree of Ptolemy (3 Macc 3:27).

37. On Pharaoh's armies (Wis Sol 17:13; 19:4) and on Antiochus (2 Macc 9:5).

38. Wis Sol 17:13.

39. Ezek 3:20; 7:19; 12:18.

40. 1 Macc 9:56.

41. Ezek 16:52, 54; 32:30.

42. 4 Macc 9:9; 12:13; 13:15.

sealed humanity for five months) and 18:7 (a double-measure of suffering is paid out on Babylon for its deeds). Finally, *basanistēs* (Matt 18:34) is an anomaly. First, the master or king seems to represent God, who is initially benevolent with his servant's great debt, but whose subsequent judgment is more about angry retribution than it is about divine justice. Second, the settling of accounts occurs at some point in the present, rather than at a final judgment, because the servant is released to go hound his own debtor. Third, the master delivers the man to the jailer to be tormented. Is this about a living experience of sowing and reaping, or does it involve an afterlife punishment? In either case, who is the jailer? The devil? Angels? The conscience? And finally, the torture is a judicial verdict that continues only until the debt is paid in full (although repayment seems impossible). The parable does not exactly suit the traditional doctrine of hell, nor does it need to. Whether the torment is in this lifetime or in some sort of Hades, the message is the same: forgive and you will be forgiven. If you want to receive mercy, then show mercy.

In summary, without denying that the central focus of *basanos* can describe torment and that sometimes the reference is to Hades, we ought to remember that the word does not automatically include or preclude implications of testing or terminus. I.e., torment is not necessarily endless or pointless. But whether in the best or worst case, Jesus is about the Father's business of salvation from judgment, torment, and Hades.

3

The Gehenna Tradition(s)

A LTHOUGH THE MAJOR TRANSLATIONS no longer use the word "hell" in the OT, some continue to introduce the term through Jesus in the synoptic Gospels whenever he refers to Gehenna[1] (although some footnote this distinction). I have devoted an entire chapter to the Gehenna tradition, because it is not just another term for hell: it represents a pivotal point in our understanding of divine judgment. Our understanding—or misunderstanding—of the Gehenna tradition(s) shapes our view of hell and judgment. More than that, it profoundly influences our understanding of Jesus' ministry and message. I don't presume to have it all figured out, but so much essential data has been overlooked (esp. Jesus' use of the Jeremiah tradition[2]) that it behooves me to share some of the results of

1. The Scriptural references for Hinnom/Gehenna are: Josh 15:8; 18:16; 2 Kgs 9:7; 15:3, 4; 23:10, 36, 39; Ezra 23:37, 39; 2 Chr 28:3; Lev 18:21; 20:2; Jer 7:30–32; 19:2–6; 32:35. This place is *never* referred to as "hell" in the OT. References to Gehenna in the NT are: Matt 5:22, 29, 30; 10:28; 18:9; 23:15; 23:33; Mark 9:43, 45, 47; Luke 12:5; Jas 3:6. Most of these come from Jesus, and every reference to this word was addressed to God's covenant people (the Jewish nation, her religious leaders, or Jesus' listeners). "The 11 references may be seen in three groups: (a) warnings addressed to the disciples concerning stumbling blocks (Matt 5:29–30; 18:8–9; Mark 9:43–48); (b) warnings addressed to the disciples in relation to their personal destiny (Matt 5:22; 10:28; Luke 12:4–5); and (c) condemnation of the scribes and Pharisees (Matt 23:15, 33)." (Hans Scharen, "Gehenna in the Synoptics," 330).

2. When I refer to Jeremiah or the Jeremiah tradition in this chapter, I am generally recalling the Jeremiah (the prophet) of Jeremiah (the book). I am following Brevard S. Childs' "canonical contextual approach" (*Introduction to the Old Testament as Scripture*) in which the primary context of Jeremiah is the canon of Scripture itself rather than speculative reconstructions of his life setting. Thus, the quest for the historical Jeremiah, questions of redaction, or whether the book is prophetic or retrospective are of little importance here. What matters is that the community of faith received the book of Jeremiah as authoritative and that Jesus locates his mission and ministry within the stream of that tradition. See also Brueggemann, *Jeremiah*, 266.

my spadework. I've included a chart that may help readers follow my train of thought (see chart 1).

GEHENNA'S BACKSTORY—THE VALLEY OF THE SONS OF HINNOM[3]

Gehenna is a gorge that bends around the west and south sides of the Old or First Wall of Jerusalem like an L, right beneath the hill we know as Mount Zion.[4] From Jerusalem's Zion and Dung Gates, one could peer down into the valley, known in OT times as the "Valley of the Sons of Hinnom"[5] (Josh 15:8). The valley descends from the west side of Jerusalem (Wadi el-Mes), then bends eastward across the south side (Wadi Er Rababi), where it meets the Kidron ravine[6] near the lower pool of Siloam at the southeastern corner of the city. There they join to become the modern day Wadi en-Nar (the "Ravine of Fire"), descending southeast to the Dead Sea.[7]

By the time the gorge became a byword, a layered backstory had developed through many generations of fiery conflict. The images it evoked have given it symbolic importance among the Jews and Christians of every stripe. Ultimately, it became our inspiration (via the apocalyptic writers and Talmudic rabbis) for post-resurrection hell. However, I would propose at the outset that (i) Jeremiah plainly tells us what the valley symbolizes: he calls it "the Valley of Slaughter" (Jer 7:28–34); and (ii) that

---

3. Cf. Also "Tophet," a piece of the Valley of Hinnom referred to by Isaiah when he predicted the destruction of the Assyrian armies by fire there, where Yahweh would consume her princes and kings as in a fiery furnace (Isa 30:31–33; 31:9).

4. Whether this hill is the original City of David is contested, but the name has stuck. The hill to the northeast, where the Dome of the Rock is situated, is traditional Mount Moriah (where Abraham took Isaac to be sacrificed). A third valley, Tyropoean, divides the two hills.

5. Also used synonymously with Tophet (and often in tandem with Kidron to its east; e.g., 2 Kgs 23:6, 12), or in its infamy, it is simply "the Valley" (Jer 2:23). It is probably also the Valley of Baca of Ps 84 (approaching Gehenna from the south). And if we stretch our geographical imaginations a little, might we also see Ezekiel's valley of dry bones?

6. Or *Valley of Jehoshaphat* (lit. "The Lord Judges"—Joel 3:2, 12), *Valley of Decision* (Joel 3:14). Kidron cuts down the east side of Old Jerusalem between Mount Moriah and the Mount of Olives. It becomes the sight for Joel's judgment of the nations (Joel 3)

7. Re: issues of location, see E. G. W. Masterson, "Hinnom, Valley of," *ISBE*, para. 3. Note too that the topography has changed somewhat from ancient times, but the location is fairly well established now. See also *Case's Bible Atlas*, 14.

The Gehenna Tradition(s)

Gehenna's Backstory—The Valley of the Sons of Hinnom

1. The Unholy Fire of Child Sacrifice

Ahaz (2 Chr 28) and Manasseh (2 Chr 33) sacrifice children to the flames of Molech in the Valley of Hinnom outside Jerusalem. God says that burning people is "something I did not command, nor did it enter my mind." (Jer 7:31)

2. The Cleansing Fire of Josiah's Reforms

Josiah (literally "fire of God") destroys the altars, idols, and false priests in flames in Hinnom. It is a "cleansing defilement" of smouldering rubble. (2 Kgs 23)

3. The Destructive Fire of Foreign Conquest

Jeremiah prophesies the destruction of Jerusalem and the temple, with corpses, rubble, and flames in Hinnom. (Jer 7, 19, 32)

4. The Memorial Fire of Gehenna's Dump

Even after Jerusalem is rebuilt, the fires continue to burn outside the city, the defiled valley used as a dump for rubble, refuse, and wormy carcasses. (Isa 66:24; Mk 9:48)

Jeremiah's Hinnom Prophecies			
Warning: Jer 7	**Judgment: Jer 19**	**Promise: Jer 31–32**	**Fulfillment: Jer 52**
Destruction of the temple and the city in death, rubble, and flames	Prophetic act in temple (broken pottery) confirms destruction	New Covenant destruction and restoration of the city and Hinnom (Jer 31:38–40)	Siege and destruction fulfilled (587 BC) Jerusalem falls to Babylon

Two Gehenna Traditions Develop

1. The Historic-Prophetic Tradition: Jeremiah—Jesus

a. Jesus' use of Gehenna intentionally references Jeremiah's prophetic use of Hinnom to represent literal destruction. He recalls the fall of Jerusalem in 587 BC as a warning of the impending fall of Jerusalem to Rome in AD 70.

Warning: Jer 7:11	**Judgment: Jer 19**	**Promise: Jer 31:31**	**Fulfillment:**
The temple is a "den of thieves" to be overthrown (Mt 21:12–13)	Prophetic act in the temple confirms destruction (Mt 21, Mk 11, Lk 19)	New Covenant (Lk 22:20) / Destruction and restoration of his temple (Jn 2:12–22)	Siege and destruction fulfilled (AD 70) Jerusalem falls to Rome

b. Jesus also uses the term Gehenna at times as a spiritual metaphor for self-destructive trajectories, the torment of alienation from God, and the spiritual refiner's fire that purges sin and prepares us for the presence of God—whether in this life or in the life to come. (Mk 9:47–49; Jn 3:16–18)

2. The Apocalyptic-Infernalist Tradition: Enoch—Talmud—Church

This tradition uses historic Hinnom as a metaphor for a literal place of punishment in the afterlife. It can be punitive or purgative, permanent or temporary, annihilation or torment.

a. Jewish Apocalyptic (Enoch et al)	b. The Talmudic Rabbis	c. The Christian Infernalists
	A place of literal afterlife suffering but:	Conflated Gehenna with:
• Eternal conscious torment (Jth 16:17) • Permanent annihilation (En 48:8–10) • Purifies or punishes (En 67:4, 90:20) • Spectacle for the righteous (En 90:24–27) • Pit of fire/torment 2(4) Esd 7:33–44) • Punishment by angels (Sim of Enoch 62:11–13) • Spirits in a fiery furnace (En 98–99)	• can be for purification (Zech 13:9) • often has a time limit (e.g., 12 months) • may exit by good deeds, esp. to the poor • can be rescued by God (1 Sam 2:6) • hell, itself, is consumed or transformed • by the righteous (Ps 49:14, 84:5–7)	• Hebrew Sheol • Greek Hades • lake of fire • literal afterlife hell • eternal, conscious torment (Rev 20)

PLAN DE LA VILLE DE JERUSALEM ANCIENNE ET MODERNE

PAR LE Sr. D'ANVILLE

BEZETHA

TEMPLI

ACRA

SION

VALLIS BEN-HINNOM

Jesus employs Jeremiah's historic sense of destruction in his use Gehenna. Historically, four fires burned there:

1. The Unholy Fire of Child Sacrifice

Under Ahaz and Manasseh, Gehenna became a site for sacrifices to Molech[8] (2 Chr 28; 33), where the people of Judah burned their children in an effort to satiate this ravenous fire-deity. They did this even though child sacrifice was explicitly forbidden in the Law:

> Do not give any of your children to be sacrificed [or *to be passed through the fire*–NIV note] to Molech, for you must not profane the name of your God. I am the LORD. (Lev 18:21)

> The LORD said to Moses, "Say to the Israelites: 'Any Israelite or any alien living in Israel who gives [or *sacrifices*–NIV note] any of his children to Molech must be put to death. The people of the community are to stone him. I will set my face against that man and I will cut him off from his people; for by giving his children to Molech, he has defiled my sanctuary and profaned my holy name. If the people of the community close their eyes when that man gives one of his children to Molech and they fail to put him to death, I will set my face against that man and his family and will cut off from their people both him and all who follow him in prostituting themselves to Molech.'" (Lev 20:2–5)

If Israel as a nation should ever mimic the other nations in this kind of sin, the sentence was expulsion from the land. Defiling the land with the blood of child-sacrifice has dire national results: "[The land] will vomit you out like it vomited out the nations that were before you" (Lev 18:24–28).

And yet they had committed that very abomination, not once, but twice over the course of a century and a half. The scene is too disturbing to imagine as reality. Judah had stooped to the "low place" of Gehenna's ravines and crags (Isa 57:5) to sacrifice children to underworld deities like Molech. Did they believe they left their offspring at the doorway to his domain?[9] To faithful Jews, "the valley" (Jer 2:23) had become the most defiled real estate in the immediate vicinity of Jerusalem—or anywhere.

8. Or Moloch (LXX), Baal (in Palestine). Cf. Lev 18:21; 20:2–5; 1 Kgs 11:7 (Solomon's high place for Molech, mentioned as an Ammonite god).

9. See also Bailey, "Gehenna: The Topography of Hell," 189.

2. The Cleansing Fire of Josiah's Reforms

Under the reign of Josiah, whose name literally means "fire of God,"[10] the valley underwent a "cleansing defilement" so that "no man might make his son or his daughter pass through the fire to Molech" (2 Kgs 23:10). Josiah left it a cursed place as a reminder of the people's shameful acts (Jer 2:23). The desecration was dramatic and thorough.

> 2 Kgs 23:6, 12, 14, 16—[Josiah] took the Asherah pole from the temple of the LORD to the Kidron Valley outside Jerusalem and burned it there. He ground it to powder and scattered the dust over the graves of the common people. . . . He pulled down . . . the altars Manasseh had built in the two courts of the temple of the LORD. He removed them from there, smashed them to pieces and threw the rubble into the Kidron Valley, . . . Josiah smashed the sacred stones and cut down the Asherah poles and covered the sites with human bones. . . . when he saw the tombs that were there on the hillside, he had the bones removed from them and burned on the altar to defile it.

So Josiah's act of repentance took the form of fire and destruction: defilement of the temple, the high places, and the valleys of Kidron and Hinnom were no doubt remembered for their fire, rubble, ashes, and human bones.[11] The fire of God had come to judge and to cleanse.

3. The Destructive Fire of Foreign Conquest

Josiah's cleansing defilement of the valley was merely a foreshadowing of the more devastating fire of God yet to be released through foreign conquest. Note the fire imagery in the text:

> 2 Kgs 23:26–27—Nevertheless, the LORD did not turn away from the heat of his fierce anger, which burned against Judah because of all that Manasseh had done to provoke him to anger. So the LORD said, "I will remove Judah also from my presence as I removed Israel, and I will reject Jerusalem, the city I chose, and this temple, about which I said, 'There shall my Name be.'"

10. "Josiah is an Anglicized version of the Hebrew *Yoshihahu,* meaning *fire of God.*" (A. Kolatch, *Complete Dictionary of Names,* 126). Thanks to Josiah Albers for pointing this out.

11. See Manasseh's initial repentance in 2 Chr 33:11–13.

As we will see later, both Jeremiah and Jesus prophesy very tangible flames in Gehenna associated with the fiery obliteration of Jerusalem, her temple, and her people.[12] For now, suffice it to say that a relationship between God's judgment, the destruction wrought by foreign armies, and the imagery of consuming fire already existed in the Israelite mind, recalling Isaiah's words:

> Who handed Jacob over to become loot, and Israel to the plunderers? Was it not the LORD, against whom we have sinned? For they would not follow his ways; they did not obey his law. So he poured out on them his *burning* anger, [=] the violence of war. It enveloped them in *flames*, yet they did not understand; it *consumed* them, but they did not take it to heart.
>
> But now, this is what the LORD says—he who created you, O Jacob, he who formed you, O Israel: "Fear not, for I have redeemed you; I have summoned you by name; you are mine. When you pass through the waters, I will be with you; and when you pass through the rivers, they will not sweep over you. When you walk through the *fire*, you will not be *burned*; the *flames* will not set you *ablaze*." (Isa 42:24—43:2)

4. The Memorial Fire of Gehenna's Dump

In the aftermath of destruction, Gehenna is said to have become a permanent, smoldering garbage dump where unburied bodies were burned. Lightfoot imagined it this way:

> It was the common sink of the whole city; whither all filth, and all kind of nastiness, met. It was, probably, the common burying-place of the city (if so be, they did now bury within so small a distance from the city). "They shall bury in Tophet, until there be no more any place," Jeremiah 7:32. And there was there also a continual fire, whereby bones, and other filthy things, were consumed, lest they might offend or infect the city.[13]

---

12. Earlier, Isaiah had prophesied the furnace of destruction for Assyria in Tophet (part of Gehenna). "Topheth has long been prepared; it has been made ready for the king. Its fire pit has been made deep and wide, with an abundance of fire and wood; the breath of the LORD, like a stream of burning sulfur, sets it ablaze" (Isa 30:33). In the siege of Jerusalem in 701 BC, 185,000 Assyrian soldiers died. See also 31:8–9.

13. John Lightfoot, "The Valley of Hinnom," ch. 39.

Imagery like "their worm does not die and the fire is not quenched" (Isa 66:24; Mark 9:48) was likely inspired more by the mundane unpleasantness of civic waste-management than by apocalyptic visions of the afterlife. Rabbi David Kimhi (ca. 1160–1235) seems to be the oldest extant source for this tradition:

> He described that Valley of Hinnom as one of Jerusalem's garbage dumps where "unclean corpses" were discarded and where fires burned continually . . . conform[ing] to first century allusions to *Hinnom* as a perpetually-burning, maggot-infested pit of putrefaction [sic]."[14]

The Hinnom dump is a well-circulated bit of folklore, considering its relatively thin and late basis. It is upheld as plausible by some scholars (e.g., Jeremias[15]), but it is contested by others[16] on the grounds that (i) its first direct mention is so late, (ii) no literary or archaeological evidence from the intertestamental or rabbinic periods support it, and (iii) Rabbi Kimhi was a medieval French Jew who never had the benefit of visiting Jerusalem.[17]

My own research has led me to a couple of observations about the garbage dump tradition. First, why not? Urban legends can still fund our symbolic repertoire. But why the near legendary status afforded to it? Why did the idea become so popular and even desperately important? Since at least as early as the 1850s, universalist and annihilationist literature relied heavily on Gehenna being an actual garbage pit as an alternative to the infernalist picture of hell. Today, we can see this precious bit of pseudo-data gaining momentum through the blogosphere as a respectable "out" for ex-infernalists and embarrassed apologists. Meanwhile, the reaction against the dump-scenario also seems excessively vehement. Why? Mainly be-

---

14. Ed Rowell, "Hinnom," *Mercer Dictionary of the Bible,* 381. Cf. Kimhi's comment on Ps 27:13.

15. "According to R. Shemaiah b. Zeira, the streets of Jerusalem were swept every day, evidently to secure the Levitical purity of the city. The fact that the Valley of Hinnom was a dump for filth and rubbish agrees with this statement. The upper end of the valley, between the tower of Hippicus and the Gate of the Essenes in the south, was called *bethso* or *bethsou* . . . 'place of filth.' The gate called the Dung Gate . . . gave immediately onto the Valley of Hinnom at its debouchment into the Kidron Valley . . . It was still in modern times the place for rubbish, carrion and all kinds of refuse." (Joachim Jeremias, *Jerusalem in the Time of Jesus,* 17).

16. L. R. Bailey, "Gehenna," 189.

17. Dennis M. Swanson, "Expansion of Jerusalem," 25.

cause some infernalists become defensive—worried at how this historic tidbit is used to undermine belief in eternal punishment. Rabbi Kimhi wouldn't have seen the problem. After describing the dump he concludes, "therefore the judgment of the wicked is parabolically called Gehenna."[18]

In my opinion, it really doesn't matter. This debate is merely a distraction from the core meaning Jeremiah gave to this place. How the valley was used after it's defilement, cleansing, and destruction is minor compared to the significance given to the atrocities that Jeremiah both remembers and prophesies. Child sacrifice, Josiah's purge, and the razing of Jerusalem make for the real ethos and pathos of Gehenna's story, whether or not memorial fires continued to burn in the aftermath.

TWO GEHENNA TRADITIONS DEVELOP

From their vivid and traumatic national memories of child sacrifice, Josiah's desecration, the city's destruction by Babylon in 587 BC, followed by smoldering carcasses (Jer 52; Lam 4:11), two distinct Gehenna traditions developed within Judaism. I will refer to them as the Apocalyptic-Talmudic-Infernalist thread (or the 1 Enoch tradition) and the Prophetic-Historic thread (or the Jeremiah tradition).

1. The Apocalyptic-Infernalist Tradition (1 Enoch—Talmud—Church)

From the Hebrew prophets to intertestamental Jewish apocalyptic writings to the Talmudic tradition of the Rabbis, Gehenna began to replace Sheol as the place of the dead, dropping from a place of physical destruction on earth into the underworld of postmortem torment. Opinions concerning Gehenna's nature, duration, and inhabitants widen and deepen greatly as we proceed through time. Without mentioning Gehenna, this sampling of Scriptures mainly retains the old destruction theme but uses language later associated with final judgment, the afterlife, and hell.

> Isa 66:24—And they will go out and look upon the dead bodies of those who rebelled against me; their worm will not die, nor will their fire be quenched, and they will be loathsome to all mankind.

> Dan 12:2—Multitudes who sleep in the dust of the earth will awake: some to everlasting life, others to shame and everlasting contempt.

---

18. Cited in James A. Montgomery, "The Holy City and Gehenna," 34.

Jdt 16:17—Woe to the nations that rise up against my kindred! The Lord Almighty will take vengeance on them in the Day of Judgment, in putting fire and worms in their flesh; and they shall feel them, and weep for ever.[19]

Jewish Apocalyptic: From Historic Destruction to Eschatological Annihilation

Defining apocalyptic literature is important and a little tricky at this point. Tom Wright's approach to apocalyptic writing is that literal earthly tragedies involving political, economic and social upheaval are described in vivid cosmic imagery because that is the only adequate language for heaven's view of those events.[20] Gehenna language is adopted to describe the desolation of Israel and the nations who reject God's Messiah and his followers. Wright sees Jesus' apocalyptic prophecies as fulfilled in first century Jerusalem. Nik Ansell kicks things up a notch. For him "apocalypse," itself, marks the transition between two ages—not the end of the space-time universe, but the cataclysmic de-creation of the old world order through the destruction of Jerusalem and its temple (Jer 4:23–28, see Mark 11:12–25; 13:28–31).[21]

Rebellion led to destruction, the end of the world as they knew it, and the rebirth of something new. In transposing Jeremiah, Jesus, and the apocalyptic writers' message to our generation, I'm echoing their thought with regard to the global fires of insanity that we witness daily in the "situation room" of our televisions, bonfires fueled as much by oil and cash as by sulfur and brimstone. This is Gehenna. But the fires of Gehenna may just consume the stage curtain behind which God's next new act is about to play. For Jesus and John, the transition was to occur in the first century.

Therefore, if we restrict our studies of apocalyptic to the canon of Scripture (Daniel, Zechariah, the Gospels,[22] and Revelation), we can make a case for drawing a sharp distinction between apocalyptic (sym-

---

19. KJV–*Apocrypha*.

20. Cf. N. T. Wright, *Jesus and the Victory of God,* 322–68. As the reader shall see, I will need to survey Gehenna as historic-prophetic from Wright's shoulders. Credit to whom credit is due.

21. Nik Ansell, "Hell: The Nemesis of Hope?" para. 29 (online version).

22. The Olivet discourse (Matt 24; Mark 13; Luke 21).

bolic imagery for this-worldly events[23]) and eschatology (theology of last things, the *parousia*, and heaven and hell[24]). We run into difficulty when we conflate and literalize the two, which is precisely what happened as the apocalyptic-Talmudic-infernalist stream developed. Their authors progressively converted imagery of God's furnace from a metaphor for historic destruction, which acts to judge and refine his people, into actual ovens of material flames into which damned souls are tossed in the afterlife or on Judgment Day.

Following the dramatic carnage depicted in Jewish apocalyptic (like 1 Enoch),[25] many mainstream Jews, and then Christians, came to transpose Gehenna (Jerusalem's legendary garbage dump) into a metaphor for the place of fiery judgment after death. The Gehenna of Jewish apocalyptic eventually became synonymous with eschatological hell (of physical and/or spiritual punishments), to which the wicked are sentenced on the Day of Judgment.[26]

> It was first conceived as a place of final punishment, later as an intermediate place, and finally as a purgatory, the latest stage of development being confined to rabbinic literature. In its earliest mention it is reserved for apostate Jews only but is gradually expanded to include all the wicked, Jews and Gentiles alike. The existence in Gehenna is depicted predominantly as for one's whole being (body and soul) rather than merely the soul. All these ideas about Gehenna exist side by side in [intertestamental] literature.[27]

---

23. Apocalyptic language is "an elaborate metaphor-system for investing historical events with theological significance" (Wright, *Jesus and the Victory of God*, 96). The Jews knew "a good metaphor when they saw one, and used cosmic imagery to bring out the full theological significance of cataclysmic socio-political events" (Wright, *New Testament and the People of God*, 333).

24. The work of Jurgen Moltmann is profoundly shifting the focus of eschatology to human destiny. E.g., J. Moltmann, *Theology of Hope*.

25. E.g., 2 Esd 7:36; Syr Bar 59:10; 85:13; Sib 1:103.

26. Cf. Hans Bietenhard, "Gehenna" *NIDNTT*, 208; N. T. Wright, *Jesus and the Victory of God*, 183 n. 142.

27. Scharen, "Gehenna in the Synoptics," 329. Scharen includes Wisdom of Solomon, 2 Maccabees, the Psalms of Solomon, and 1 Enoch as most important in the transition he's describing.

First Enoch,[28] our predominant source on Gehenna between Jeremiah and Jesus, particularly targets the kings and the mighty for a pit of consuming flames that annihilate them completely:[29]

> Enoch 48:8–10—In these days downcast in countenance shall the kings of the earth have become, And the strong who possess the land because of the works of their hands, For on the day of their anguish and affliction they shall not (be able to) save themselves. And I will give them over into the hands of Mine elect: As straw in the fire so shall they burn before the face of the holy: As lead in the water shall they sink before the face of the righteous, and no trace of them shall any more be found.
>
> And on the day of their affliction there shall be rest on the earth, And before them they shall fall and not rise again: And there shall be no one to take them with his hands and raise them: For they have denied the Lord of Spirits and His Anointed. The name of the Lord of Spirits be blessed.[30]

At this point in 1 Enoch, one can still argue that the language, while apocalyptic, points to historical referents in the prophetic tradition of Isaiah and Jeremiah: the destruction of foreign armies outside Jerusalem's walls. Gehenna ("the cursed valley") is still somewhat distinguishable from the underworld, Sheol, and Abyss references. But once Gehenna gets identified with Hades/Sheol and the Abyss by later infernalists (e.g., in the

28. Enoch is a collection of pseudonymous texts written in the last few centuries before Christ.

29. Nik Ansell traces this theme in and beyond 1 Enoch: "This prophetic interpretation of Gehenna also makes good sense of the reference to the 'cursed valley' in 1 Enoch 27:1–2 . . . It is important to note that this valley is distinct from the underworld of 1 Enoch 22 . . . This material, from what is usually considered the earliest (third century BCE) part of 1 Enoch, is in line with the geographically located portrayal of Gehenna in the Old Testament prophetic tradition. . . . The reference to Gehenna in 4 Ezra 7:36 (= 2 Esdras 7:36) seems to belong in a somewhat different—and in many ways unique—category. While in this Jewish apocalypse, Gehenna (in distinction from the rabbinic tradition) is still distinguished from Hades (see 4:7–8 and 8:53) and while there are echoes of the prophetic tradition's judgment of the nations here . . . this judgment is seen as taking place after a resurrection in the transition between the present age and the age to come. This is a significant departure from the Old Testament, where the idea of postmortem, post-resurrection judgment, found only in Dan. 12:2, is not explicitly associated with Gehenna . . . it is still important to maintain on historical grounds that the post-resurrection Gehenna of 4 Ezra 7:36 should not be read into the gospels [or] the book of Revelation" (Nik Ansell, "Hell: The Nemesis of Hope?" n. 32).

30. Enoch 48:8–10 (APOT 2).

Mishnah and early Church), they were prone to read back into 1 Enoch as identifying them all with the underworld.[31]

As we progress through Enoch and into 4 Ezra/2 Esdras, "valley of burning fire" becomes increasingly otherworldly, detached from the historical Valley of Hinnom altogether.

> Enoch 54:1–2—And I looked and turned to another part of the earth, and saw there a deep valley with burning fire. And they brought the kings and the mighty, and began to cast them into this deep valley.[32]

Early on in this tradition, the damned included angels (stars), leaders (shepherds), and the laity (sheep) cremated in a fire that consumes even their bones:

> Enoch 90:24–27—And the judgment was held first over the stars, and they were judged and found guilty, and went to the place of condemnation, and they were cast into an Abyss, full of fire and flaming, and full of pillars of fire. And those seventy shepherds were judged and found guilty, and they were cast into that fiery Abyss. And I saw at that time how a like Abyss was opened in the midst of the earth, full of fire, and they brought those blinded sheep, and they were all judged and found guilty and cast into this fiery Abyss, and they burned; now this Abyss was to the right of that house [i.e., beside the Temple? indicating Hinnom or Kidron?]. And I saw those sheep burning and their bones burning.[33]

In 2(4) Esdras, the apocalyptic tradition specifies a general resurrection when "The Most High shall be revealed upon the seat of judgment" (Esd 7:33–44). This leads to a dualist judgment in which displaying the contrast of fates is important, providing a constant spectacle for the righteous (Enoch 27:1–3; 90:24–27): "The pit of torment shall appear and over against it shall be the place of rest: and *the furnace of Gehenna* shall be showed, and over against it, the paradise of delight" (7:36). The nations

---

31. Ansell is more reluctant to surrender 1 Enoch to the infernalists than I would be: "Re: 1 Enoch, I personally don't think the infernalist tradition has a foothold here re: Gehenna. . . . From the vantage point of the Church that got into infernalism, Yes—there is indeed an Enoch-Talmud-Church tradition. But historically it doesn't begin with 1 Enoch in my view." (Nik Ansell, Email to me, May 29, 2009). Cf. n. 32 in Ansell's Afterword below.

32. Enoch 2.54:1–2 (APOT 2).

33. Enoch 4.90:24–27 (APOT 2).

that are raised to life are called to behold the contrast between the place of rest and "the place of fire and torments" (7:37f).

Later, the damned are still to be witnessed, but only temporarily (Sim of Enoch 62:12) so that Gehenna has no place in the new heavens and new earth and disappears completely from the sight of the righteous (62:13).

> Sim of Enoch 62:11-13—To execute vengeance on them because they have oppressed His children and His elect. And they shall be a spectacle for the righteous and for His elect: They shall rejoice over them, Because the wrath of the Lord of Spirits resteth upon them,
>
> And His sword is drunk with their blood. And the righteous and elect shall be saved on that day,
>
> And they shall never thenceforward see the face of the sinners and unrighteous.[34]

Another modification is introduced in Enoch 91–104. Up until this point, the punishment of the wicked was both physical and spiritual. Now incorporeal spirits, the wicked are cast into a fiery furnace (98:3), which is equated with Sheol (99:11).

The Talmudic Rabbis

The annihilationist imagery of Jewish apocalyptic was radicalized into full-blown infernalism (with a purgatorial element) among the rabbis of the Talmud-Mishna traditions.[35] The Talmud is a collection of rabbinic sayings and discussions relating to Jewish law, customs, and history. Its first component, the Mishnah (ca. AD 200), records Jewish oral law dating back to the time just prior to Christ, from the schools of Shammai and

---

34. Enoch, *Book of Noah*, 62.11-13 (APOT 2).

35. This is not the only Jewish afterlife tradition from that time. (1) The Sadducees, seeing neither a resurrection nor an infernalist judgment in the Torah, contested the theology of the Pharisaic rabbis. (2) The Essenes, according to Josephus (*Jewish Wars* 1.155), believed Gehenna to be a "murky and tempestuous dungeon, big with never-ending punishments." If the Dead Sea Scrolls were theirs, they loved apocalyptic literature, including the books of Enoch. (3) Philo of Alexandria, 30 BC—AD 40: "He was an Egyptian Jew, of the sect of the Pharisees, and a believer in punishment after death. He frequently introduces the subject, and describes the place of torment as 'a dark region, covered with profound night, and perpetual blackness;' but he never calls it Gehenna." (Thayer, *Theology of Universalism*, 389).

Hillel.[36] The Shammai school, following Zech 13:9, divided all people into three groups:

> Three classes appear on the day of judgment: The perfectly righteous, who are at once written and sealed for eternal life; the thoroughly bad, who are at once written and sealed for hell, as it is written (Dan 12:2), "And many of them that sleep in the dust of the earth shall awake, some to everlasting life and some to shame and everlasting contempt," and those in the intermediate state, who go down into hell, where they cry and howl for a time, whence they ascend again, as it is written (Zech 13:9), "And I will bring the third part through the fire, and will refine them as silver is refined, and will try them as gold is tried, they shall call on my name and I will hear them." It is of them Hannah said, (1 Sam 2:6) "The Lord killeth and maketh alive. He bringeth down to hell and bringeth up."[37]

Hillel's school emphasized God's mercy in limiting the number who suffer eternal punishment, but like Shammai, they also taught that various groups receive different treatments. The righteous go to paradise; some sinners of Israel and the Gentiles are punished in Gehenna for twelve months then reduced to ashes (Mal 4:3); while the very wicked are punished in Gehenna for "ages to ages."[38]

That said, the rabbis of the Mishnah hashed through a great range of opinions and theories about Gehenna (too many to ignore). Among them, the great Rabbi Akiva (AD 50–135)[39] is noteworthy for his insights and testimonies about the details of afterlife Gehenna. The Rabbis did not all agree on the nature or duration of Gehenna, their thoughts developing and regressing over centuries. But from what they taught, we can distill four general themes.[40]

36. Alfred Edersheim, *The Life and Times of Jesus the Messiah*, 789.

37. *Rosh Hashanah* fol. 16 col. 2, *TM* 50.

38. Alfred Edersheim, *The Life and Times of Jesus the Messiah*, 789.

39. "Rabbi Akiva developed the exegetical method of the Mishnah, linking each traditional practice to a basis in the biblical text, and systematized the material that later became the Mishnah" (Tracy R. Rich, "Sages and Scholars," para. 7).

40. Quotations from the Talmud-Mishna taken from *A Talmudic Miscellany*, 1880. Cf. *Hebraic Literature*, 1901.

1. **Gehenna is a metaphor for hell,** a real location of suffering in actual flames in the afterlife.[41] That said: Gehenna's creation,[42] size,[43] location,[44] gates[45] and vivid descriptions were much debated. Regarding location, here are two examples:

> There were two date trees in the Valley of Hinnom from between which smoke ascended and this is the gate of hell.[46]

> An Arab once said to Rabbah bar bar Channah, "Come and I will show thee the place where Korah and his accomplices were swallowed up."[47] "There," says the Rabbi, "I observed smoke coming out from two cracks in the ground. Into one of these he inserted some wool tied on to the end of his spear, and when he drew it out again it was scorched. Then he bade me listen. I did so, and as I listened, heard them groan out, 'Moses and his law are true but we are liars.' The Arab then told me that they come round to this place once in every thirty days, being stirred about in the hell-surge like meat in a boiling cauldron."[48]

41. "Rabbi Zira so inured his body (to endurance) that the fire of Gehenna had no power over it. Every thirty days he experimented on himself, ascending a fiery furnace, and finally sitting down in the midst of it without being affected by the fire. One day, however, as the Rabbis fixed their eyes upon him, his hips became singed, and from that day onward he was noted in Jewry as the little man with the singed hips." (*Bava Metzia*, fol. 85, col. i. *HL* 149).

42. "Seven things were formed before the creation of the world: The Law, Repentance, Paradise, Gehenna, the Throne of Glory, the Temple, and the name of the Messiah." (*P'sachim*, fol. 54, col. I, *HL* 84).

43. *P'sachim*, fol. 94, col. 1, *HL* 156.

44. *Tanu dby Eliyahu. HL* 260.

45. "According to Jewish tradition, there are three gates to Gehinnom: one in the desert, one in the sea, and one in Jerusalem. In the desert, as it is written, 'They went down and all that belonged to them alive into hell' (Num 16:33), In the sea, as it is written, 'Out of the belly of hell have I called,' (Jon 2:2), In Jerusalem, as it is written, 'Thus saith the Lord, whose fire is in Zion and His furnace in Jerusalem' (Isa 31:9). The gates to Gehinnom [*ptkhym lgyhnm*] must not be confounded with the [*s'ry s'vl* / gates of Sheol] of the Sacred Scriptures or the *pulai adou* of the Greek. The 'Gates of Hades' are simply the gates of death." (*TM* 28–29).

46. *Succah* fol. 32 col. 2, *TM* 28.

47. "And the earth opened its mouth and swallowed them up, with their households and all the people that belonged to Korah and all their goods. So they and all that belonged to them went down alive into Sheol, and the earth closed over them, and they perished from the midst of the assembly . . . And fire came out from the LORD and consumed the 250 men offering the incense." (Num 16:32–33, 35).

48. *Bava Bathra*, fol. 74 col. 1, *TM* 184.

2. Gehenna can have a time limit, most often seen as one year, corresponding to the Jewish bereavement time (praying the Kaddish), after which the suffering would end in either restoration or annihilation.[49] Others foresaw the truly wicked suffering for generations, or in some cases "ages of ages."[50]

> Even the wicked in Gehenna lasted no longer than twelve months.[51]

> Hezekiah saith the judgment in Gehenna is six months heat and six months cold.[52]

> Rabbi Akiva used to say, "Of five judgments, some have lasted twelve months, others will do so;—those of the deluge, of Job, of the Egyptians, of Gog and Magog, and of the wicked in Gehenna."[53]

3. Gehenna can have an exit, at least for some. For example, you can be granted a release for good deeds done, whether acts of justice on behalf of the poor performed by the one who has died or by a loved one who offers service in the synagogue on behalf of the bereaved.

> Turnus Rufus once said to Rabbi Akiva, "If your God is a friend to the poor, why doesn't He feed them?" To which he promptly replied, "That we by maintaining them may escape the condemnation of Gehenna."[54]

> He who sets aside a portion of his wealth for the relief of the poor will be delivered from the judgment of hell. Of this the parable of the two sheep that attempted to ford a river is an illustration: one was shorn of its wool and the other not, the former therefore managed to get over but the latter being heavy laden sank.[55]

49. *"Those Israelites and Gentiles who have transgressed with their bodies (the former by neglecting to wear phylacteries, and the latter by indulging in sensuous pleasures) shall go down into Gehenna and be punished there for twelve months, after which period their bodies will be destroyed and their soul consumed, and a wind shall scatter their ashes under the soles of the feet of the righteous; as it is said (Mal iv. 3)."* (*Rosh Hashanah*, fol. 17, col. 1, *TM* 155).

50. Whether this means "eternally" or not is debated. Cf. Alfred Eidersheim, *Life and Times of Jesus*, 2:791.

51. *Shabbath*, fol. 33, col. 32, *TM* 151.

52. *Midrash Reheh*, *TM* 311.

53. *Edioth*, ch. 2, mish. 10, *TM* 158–59.

54. *Bava Bathra*, fol. 10, col. 1, *TM* 152.

55. *Gittin* fol. 7 col. 1, *TM* 30–31.

Rabbi Akiva once saw in a vision the shadowy figure of a man carrying a load of wood on his shoulders. "What ails you?" asked the Rabbi. "I am one of those forlorn souls condemned for his sins to the agony of hell-fire," replied the shadow. "And there is no hope for you?" inquired the Rabbi further in great compassion. "If my little son, who was a mere infant when I died, could be taught to recite the Kaddish, then and only then would I be absolved." The Rabbi took the boy under his care and taught him to lisp the Kaddish. He was then assured that the father had been released from Gehenna.[56]

All who go down to hell shall come up again except these three: He who commits adultery, he who shames another in public, and he who gives another a bad name.[57]

4. Gehenna can be purgative, that is, it was designed not just for punishment but also for purification in preparation for Paradise.

> "God hath also set the one over against the other" (Eccl 7:14), i.e. The righteous and the wicked, in order that the one should atone for each other. God created the poor and the rich, in order that the one should be maintained by the other. He created Paradise and Gehenna, in order that those in the one should deliver those in the other. And what is the distance between them? Rabbi Chanina saith the width of the wall (between Paradise and Gehenna) is a handbreadth.[58]

These rabbis did not claim their teachings as divine revelation. Rather, the Talmud consists of discussions on Jewish law, theology, customs, and traditions. Their speculations aside, rabbis like Akiva sometimes help us to see the OT passages with first century Jewish eyes. For example, they saw Psalm 84 (a psalm of ascent sung by pilgrims on the way to Jerusalem's festivals) as pointing eschatologically to our journey from Gehenna to Zion:

> 5 Blessed are those whose strength is in you, who have set their hearts on pilgrimage.
> As they pass through the Valley of Baca, [Baca is Gehenna]

---

56. *Midrash Assereth Hadibroht.* Longer version in *TM* 305. This translation cited in Raphael, *Jewish Views of the Afterlife,* 1994.

57. *Bava Metzia,* fol. 58, col. 2, *TM* 60.

58. *Yalkut Koheleth, TM* 312.

6 they make it a place of springs; [so even Gehenna is
transformed]
the autumn rains also cover it with pools.
7 They go from strength to strength,
till each appears before God in Zion [Paradise].

Their unique translation of Psalm 49 suggests the eventual dissolution of
Gehenna.

> Gehenna itself shall be consumed, but they shall not be burned
> up in the destruction; as it is said, (Ps 49:14; *Heb* 15) . . . "and their
> figures shall consume hell from [being] a dwelling."[59]

Jesus: Rabbi and Prophet

Though still an oral tradition in the time of Jesus of Nazareth, the rabbinical discussion on Gehenna was clearly in active development. How much
of the rabbis' understanding did Jesus assume when he used the term? Did
he concede to the common usage of Gehenna or did he subvert it? Did his
understanding further clarify and supplement the apocalyptic tradition
or did he take things in an entirely new direction? We cannot presume to
know. However, I'd like to pause briefly to offer a few observations.

First, *if*[60] what we read in the Mishnah is indicative of oral tradition and rabbinical thought in the first century, then we can assert that
there was no uniform vision of Gehenna in Jesus' day. The elders did relate
Gehenna to afterlife judgment, but any penalty was justly limited in duration and scale according to one's crime and often with a view to rehabilita-
tion. They assumed the perfect justice of God's judgments—even if they
sound severe to our ears—and would have likely recoiled at the excessive
and lopsided sentence of eternal, conscious torment for something like
failing to pray the sinner's prayer before death.

59. *Rosh Hashanah*, fol. 17, col. 1, *TM* 155. I.e., Gehenna would finally cease to be a
place where anyone (the damned) would exist.

60. This "if" is a point of contention. Ansell, following the more general caveats of
Segal and Mendels (see Ansell's Afterword below, n. 32) not only resists reading the
Mishnah's portrayals of Gehenna back into the NT (agreed!), but also rejects its portrayals of Jesus' contemporaries on this subject (I'm not there yet). He sees the infernalist
view of Gehenna arising only after Jesus' lifetime and after AD 70 (which makes sense
once earthly Jerusalem is out of the eschatological picture). While I am reading the transition toward Jewish and Christian infernalism earlier on the timeline than Ansell, we are
in strong agreement on this point: Jesus' Gehenna was rooted in Jeremiah's prophetic-
historic tradition rather than the infernalist underworld.

Second, Jesus of Nazareth was an authoritative rabbi in his own right (John 3:1), hushing crowds and silencing opponents with his radical interpretation of the Law (as in the Sermon on the Mount). In his mission to redefine our vision of God, he regularly challenged or outright broke the traditions of the elders (what he called "the traditions of men"), whether oral or written (see also Matt 15:1–10 and Mark 7:1–24).[61] His listeners could never assume that Jesus meant what the other rabbis meant even when he used common terms like "temple" (John 2:19) or "kingdom" (Luke 17:21). Thus, we should not accept too readily that Jesus shared the other rabbinical teachers' definitions of Gehenna.

Third, when Jesus spoke of Gehenna, he was not merely acting as a rabbi engaging in debate. He opposed the scribes and Pharisees as a prophet in the vein of Jeremiah, whose temple rants paralleled, previewed, and perhaps prophesied those of Jesus:

> Jer 8:8–9—How can you say, "We are wise, for we have the law of the LORD," when actually the lying pen of the scribes has handled it falsely? The wise will be put to shame; they will be dismayed and trapped. Since they have rejected the word of the LORD, what kind of wisdom do they have?

In fact, Jesus raised the stakes when he confronted the teachers of the law as a prophet with his infamous woes, even calling them "sons of Gehenna" (Matt 23:15). Jesus might have been speaking of Gehenna as the teachers of the law understood it, but in accordance with his actions and his agenda during the Matthew 23 affront, it is more likely that Jesus was speaking of Gehenna as Jeremiah meant it.

2. The Historic-Prophetic Tradition (Jeremiah—Jesus)

Contrasting sharply with the Apocalyptic-Talmudic-Infernalist Gehenna tradition is the Historic-Prophetic Gehenna tradition, rooted in Josiah's actions, Jeremiah's oracles, and Jesus' warnings. To be strictly biblical, the Jewish prophetic tradition (climaxing in Jesus) points in a far more historically rooted and this-worldly direction than we find in 1 Enoch or the Talmud. In this tradition, Gehenna recalls the literal fire of destruction that came to consume Jerusalem for its sins and to cleanse the land and people of sin's defilement.

---

61. For a lively debate concerning Jesus and the rabbis concerning Gehenna, see W. Balfour, *Letter to Whitman on Gehenna.*

On first read, Jesus followed Jeremiah's straightforward use of Gehenna. He hearkened to God's forewarned, final scene of destruction for unrepentant rebels engaged in idolatry and injustice. For Jesus, Gehenna primarily retained Jeremiah's prophetic meaning for the wages of sin: death. Between death and resurrection, there may well be in an intermediate state of punishment or purification, but that would be Hades or Sheol, not Gehenna.[62] Likewise, after the Day of Judgment, there may be a lake of burning sulfur or a river of fire, but they are never called Gehenna either.

> The meaning of Gehenna must be established from facts furnished by the Scripture, not by falsehoods foisted by human tradition. To the reader of the Hebrew Scriptures themselves, Gehenna can only mean a verdict that, besides condemning a man to death, also ordains that, after death, his body should be cast into the loathsome valley of Hinnom. This being the sense of Gehenna in the Hebrew Scriptures, we may be sure that this is the sense in which Christ used it. . . . Gehenna is the capital punishment of the kingdom, without burial.[63]

Let us test, then, how Jesus' use of Gehenna intentionally referenced Jeremiah's prophetic use of the Valley of Hinnom (Jer 7, 19, 31–32) as an emblem of literal destruction. We shall see how Jesus recalled the fall of Jerusalem to Babylon in 587 BC as a warning of the impending fall of Jerusalem to Rome in AD 70.

Warning: Jeremiah 7

In Jeremiah 7, God sends the prophet to the gates of the temple (7:2). The people thought their temple was a sign of God's favor and a guarantee of their safety (7:4, 10), but it had actually become a den of thieves (7:11) in danger of demolition (7:14–15). Jeremiah lays out the indictment:

> Jer 7:20, 28–31 (NKJV)—Therefore this is what the Sovereign LORD says: "My anger and my wrath will be poured out on this place, on man and beast, on the trees of the field and on the fruit of the ground, and it will burn and not be quenched.[64] . . . So you

---

62. Cf. W. Fairweather, "Development of Doctrine in the Apocryphal Period," *HDB* (5:305). Cf. Stewart D. F. Salmond, "Hell," *HDB* 2:343–46.

63. James Coram, "The Fire of Gehenna," *Concordant Studies,* para. 14.

64. Apparently, this unquenchable fire is not eternal in duration, seeing as this particular prophecy was fulfilled in AD 587. Jeremiah used "unquenchable fire" again in

shall say to them, 'This is a nation that does not obey the voice of the LORD their God nor receive correction. Truth has perished and has been cut off from their mouth. Cut off your hair and cast it away, and take up a lamentation on the desolate heights; for the LORD has rejected and forsaken the generation of His wrath.' For the children of Judah have done evil in My sight," says the LORD. "They have set their abominations in the house which is called by My name, to pollute it. And they have built the high places of Tophet, which *is* in the Valley of the Son of Hinnom, to burn their sons and their daughters in the fire, which I did not command, *nor did it come into My heart*."

After verse 7, the warning really verges on verdict. Perhaps it is already too late, but if the people will "behold" (i.e., if they will see what Jeremiah sees and repent), then who knows? (see Jer 18:7–10) At this point it doesn't look good. It's not meant to.

Jer 7:32–34 (NKJV)—"Therefore *behold*, the days are coming," says the LORD, "*when it will no more be called Tophet,*[65] *or the Valley of the Son of Hinnom, but the Valley of Slaughter; for they will bury in Tophet until there is no room. The corpses of this people will be food for the birds of the heaven and for the beasts of the earth. And no one will frighten them away.* Then I will cause to cease from the cities of Judah and from the streets of Jerusalem the voice of mirth and the voice of gladness, the voice of the bridegroom and the voice of the bride. For the land shall be desolate."

Confronted with temple abominations and domestic injustice, Jeremiah foretold a day when the temple and the entire city of Jerusalem would be

---

17:27 to describe the destruction of Jerusalem's gates. The fire was unquenchable in that once started, it could not be put out. It would only end when all that was combustible was completely consumed. This is likely the same sense given in Matthew 3:12 and 9:43.

65. "In this valley of Hinnom was *Tophet,* concerning which Calmet thus writes. 'It is thought Tophet was the butchery, or place of slaughter at Jerusalem, lying south of the city, in the valley of the children of Hinnom. It is also said that a constant fire was kept here, for burning the carcasses, and other filth, brought hither from the city. Into the same place they cast the ashes and remains of the images of false gods, when they demolished their altars and statues. Isa 30:33 seems to allude to this custom of burning dead carcasses in Tophet. Speaking of the defeat of the army of Sennacherib, he says; 'For Tophet is ordained of old; yea, for the king it is prepared; he hath made it deep and large; the pile thereof is fire, and much wood; the breath of the Lord, like a stream of brimstone, doth kindle it.' Others think the name of Tophet is given to the valley of Hinnom because of the sacrifices offered there to the god Moloch, by beat of drum, to drown the cries of the consuming children." (Balfour and Skinner, *An Inquiry*, 121).

destroyed by Babylon's armies.[66] He envisioned a slaughter so horrible that Hinnom would become a mass burial site, the corpses scavenged by wild beasts and birds. For Jeremiah, Gehenna was not so much a metaphor for personal damnation in the afterlife but rather, a portrait of mass destruction whenever God's people rebel and make themselves a target for decimation by foreign armies. It is the Holy City under siege, her walls and temple demolished, her sacrifices and services ended, and her children left in mass graves or sent to exile. The prophetic warning is all too this-worldly and serves as an archetype for the repeatable, inevitable self-destructive consequences of betraying God's covenant in history. Most alarming of all, it presents the real possibility (for Jerusalem, for Judaism, for Christianity!) of a horrifying, "final discontinuity":

> The theologically abrasive nerve of this text confounds conventional notions of the Bible. Popular propensity is to stress the ultimate continuity of God's commitment to the religious community. When all else fails, God will still be faithful. But in this remarkable statement the text opts for a final discontinuity. We cannot of course claim that this notion is pervasive in the Bible. It is important to recognize, however, that the Bible dares this unthinkable notion . . . This text asserts something about the human prospect that we would prefer to be left unsaid.[67]

Verdict: Jeremiah 19

In Jeremiah 19, the prophet is told to return to the Postsherd Gate where he must smash a clay jar—a prophetic act that repeats and expands on the destruction of the city as punishment for burning her children in

66. "The rhetoric of the text is not 'realistic' in the sense that it describes what is known. Rather, it is an imaginative anticipation of what is as yet unknown and unexperienced, for which there is no precedent. But this future is boldly envisioned by the prophet. The judgment to come is so unprecedented that only such ominous images are adequate to communicate it . . . Poetic characterizations of God's new age of blessing and poetic scenarios of God's judgment are always extreme cases of imagination, in the NT as in the OT. Such extreme imaginations are to be taken seriously. But when treated as flat predictions or descriptions, they are sure to be misunderstood or distorted. In such a reductionism, poetic efforts are robbed of their imaginative power . . . Jeremiah seeks to penetrate and break open the imagination of the self-satisfied community so that it will see that the present circumstance is so extraordinary in its departure from torah that there can be no business as usual, not for Judah and surely not for Yahweh." (Brueggemann, *Jeremiah*, 84).

67. Brueggemann, *Jeremiah*, 85.

Hinnom.[68] I believe Jesus' act of overturning the temple tables and driving out the moneychangers should be seen as a prophetic echo of Jeremiah's mime. This time, however, Jeremiah was no longer giving a warning; this was a verdict.

> Jer 19:1–9—This is what the LORD says: "Go and buy a clay jar from a potter. Take along some of the elders of the people and of the priests and go out to the Valley of Ben Hinnom, near the entrance of the Potsherd Gate. There proclaim the words I tell you, and say, 'Hear the word of the LORD, O kings of Judah and people of Jerusalem. This is what the LORD Almighty, the God of Israel, says: Listen! I am going to bring a disaster on this place that will make the ears of everyone who hears of it tingle. For they have forsaken me and made this a place of foreign gods; they have burned sacrifices in it to gods that neither they nor their fathers nor the kings of Judah ever knew, and they have filled this place with the blood of the innocent. They have built the high places of Baal to burn their sons in the fire as offerings to Baal—something I did not command or mention, nor did it enter my mind. So beware, the days are coming, declares the LORD, when people will no longer call this place Topheth or the Valley of Ben Hinnom, but the Valley of Slaughter.
>
> "In this place I will ruin the plans of Judah and Jerusalem. I will make them fall by the sword before their enemies, at the hands of those who seek their lives, and I will give their carcasses as food to the birds of the air and the beasts of the earth. I will devastate this city and make it an object of scorn; all who pass by will be appalled and will scoff because of all its wounds. I will make them eat the flesh of their sons and daughters, and they will eat one another's flesh during the stress of the siege imposed on them by the enemies who seek their lives."

Jeremiah marked Jerusalem for the same desecration as the valley itself:

> Jer 19:10–13—Then break the jar while those who go with you are watching, and say to them, "This is what the LORD Almighty says: I will smash this nation and this city just as this potter's jar is smashed and cannot be repaired. They will bury the dead in Topheth until there is no more room. This is what I will do to this place and to those who live here, declares the LORD. I will make this city like Topheth. The houses in Jerusalem and those of

---

68. Note, however, that although God gives this instruction, the text does not say that Jeremiah actually carried it out. Cf. Brueggemann, *Jeremiah*, 178.

the kings of Judah will be defiled like this place, Topheth—all the houses where they burned incense on the roofs to all the starry hosts and poured out drink offerings to other gods."

Then Jeremiah, foreshadowing Jesus, re-entered the temple with his word of woe:

> Jer 19:14–15—Jeremiah then returned from Topheth, where the LORD had sent him to prophesy, and stood in the court of the LORD's temple and said to all the people, "This is what the LORD Almighty, the God of Israel, says: 'Listen! I am going to bring on this city and the villages around it every disaster I pronounced against them, because they were stiff-necked and would not listen to my words.'"

Jesus in the Jeremiah Tradition

Jesus identified himself strongly with the ministry of Jeremiah, especially through his Passion Week. With his symbolic enactment of the overthrow of the temple, he was consciously recapitulating the oracle of Jeremiah 7. In his famous "den of thieves" reference, Jesus quoted Jeremiah to deconstruct the security of the temple establishment (Jer 7:11 = Matt 21:13/ Mark 11:17/Luke 19:46; see also Isa 56:7 = Mark 11:17). His woes in Matt 23 to the scribes and teachers of the law no doubt echoed Jer 8:8 ("the false pen of the Scribes") and Jer 23:1 ("Woe to the shepherds who are destroying and scattering the sheep of my pasture!"). When Jesus cursed the fig tree's fruitlessness and it withered (Matt 21; Mark 11), he seemed to be drawing from Jer 8:13: "I will take away their harvest, declares the LORD. . . . There will be no figs on the tree, and their leaves will wither. What I have given them will be taken from them." Finally, that same week, Jesus consciously activated the New Covenant as a prophetic fulfillment of Jer 31–33 (esp. 31:31) with the Passover Cup (Luke 22:20).[69]

---

69. Other examples abound. The mystery of what Jesus wrote in the dust in John 8:8 might be solved in Jer 17:13, where we read the prayer, "O LORD, the hope of Israel, all who forsake you will be put to shame. Those who turn away from you [their names?] will be written in the dust because they have forsaken *the LORD, the spring of living water.*" The significance is not *what* Jesus wrote in the dust but *that* he wrote in dust. Note that Jesus had just referred to himself as *the streams of living water* in 7:37–38! Jesus uses Jeremiah 7 to shame the shamers but also to prophesy the destruction of those who reject him. (Thanks to Doug and Deana Brandt for pointing this out.)

Gehenna: Warning of Imminent Destruction

Seeing as Jesus consciously re-enacted Jeremiah's ministry, is it reasonable to identify his use of Gehenna as a reference to Jeremiah's warnings of Jerusalem's imminent destruction featuring the Valley of Hinnom? Whenever Jesus mentioned Gehenna, could he have been alluding to the judgments associated with Jer 7, 19, and 31 (e.g., Matt 24:28)? He may have been applying them specifically to the fall of Jerusalem once again for her rebellion or to individuals in peril of consequence for their own self-destructive rebellion. Thus, the Gehenna of the Gospels is understood as the earthly place where the wicked perish in fire in the temporal "last days" of historical events—not the mythical underworld of the Talmudic tradition.[70]

Building on N. T. Wright's work,[71] we can now see that Jesus' "Little Apocalypse" (Mark 13) functioned as an immediate prophetic warning concerning Jerusalem rather than an eschatological prophecy in the traditional sense.[72] Jesus was not describing the culmination of the universe. He was purposefully picking up the prophetic-historic tradition of Jeremiah, whose urgent warnings of coming desolation are repeated for his generation.

In Mark 13 and its parallels, Jesus envisioned the coming judgment in classic biblical terms:

> Invasion and destruction by foreign armies, allowed to do what they are doing because YHWH, having warned his people beyond patience and hope, has deliberately abandoned them to their fate. Assyria and Babylon had been the instruments of God's wrath before; now it would be the turn of Rome. . . . Israel's dreams and

---

70. See Nik Ansell, "Hell: The Nemesis of Hope?" para. 26 (online version).

71. N. T. Wright, *New Testament and the People of God*, 280–99.

72. "Mark 13:28 connects this apocalyptic discourse to the cursing of the fig tree in Mark 11:12–14. The reference to the passing away of heaven and earth in Mark 13:31, given the cosmic symbolism and significance of the temple, may be connected to Mark 13:1–2. These two references to the temple thus frame the chapter. In Wright's analysis, in *The New Testament and the People of God*, 390–96, the language about "the Son of Man coming in clouds with great power and glory" in Mark 13:26 (and parallels) refers in the language of Dan 7:13 to the coming of the Son of Man to God. This is enthronement language that signals vindication. If there is thus no reference to the "second coming" in the synoptic apocalypse (Mark 13; Matt 24; Luke 21), this coheres with the fact that there is nothing in these passages, or in the Synoptics' references to Gehenna, that would place the judgment referred to after the general resurrection." (Nik Ansell, "Hell: The Nemesis of Hope?" n. 39, online version / n. 40 in Afterword).

aspirations a heap of rubble, with Jerusalem as a whole turned into a large, smoking extension of Gehenna, her own rubbish-dump. In so far as Israel cherished nationalist ambition, it would end up on the fire. Those who took the sword will die by the sword.[73]

Sometimes we miss the immediacy of Jesus' warnings because we project his *parousia*[74] into the eschatological distance. When we read his parables that refer to a returning bridegroom, landlord, or king,[75] we usually assume that Jesus was foretelling his second coming and the judgments of hellfire. In fact, the surprise visit/return in most of these parables probably refers initially to Jesus' incarnation, his resurrection, or once he is rejected, to the resulting chain of events that bring down Jerusalem in AD 70. In other words, if the *parousia* refers to Jesus' own generation, rather than to the end of time, then Jesus' use of the historic destruction in Gehenna circa 587 BC is not a metaphor for John's eschatological lake of fire. Exactly the opposite. John's apocalyptic lake of fire is a visionary picture of Gehenna's historic pyres, prophesied by Jesus (reiterating Jeremiah) and fulfilled in AD 70. More simply, Jerusalem's destruction does not direct us to apocalyptic visions of fire; the heavenly visions indicate the earthly reality.

Jesus told us all of this as plainly as he could, "I tell you the truth, this generation will certainly not pass away until all these things have happened" (Matt 24:34). Some would not taste death until they had seen the "Son of man coming (*parousia* language) on the clouds" (Mark 8:38—9:1; Dan 7:13; Matt 24:30). What if Jesus was simply right about this and that it is we, not he, who have dislocated the fulfillment of the *parousia* and Gehenna passages?

That is not the whole story, but it is, in fact, how events played out. Josephus indicated that history repeated itself, and the same valley was heaped with dead Israelites following the Roman siege of Jerusalem:

> Now every one of these died with their eyes fixed upon the temple, and left the seditious alive behind them. Now the seditious at first gave orders that the dead should be buried out of the public treasury, as not enduring the stench of their dead bodies. But afterwards, when they could not do that, they had them cast down from the walls into the valleys beneath [i.e., Gehenna and Kidron].

73. Wright, *Jesus and the Victory of God,* 336.

74. E.g., Matt 24:3, 27, 37, 39. See also Wright, *Jesus and the Victory of God,* 341.

75. E.g., Matt 25:1–13; 25:14–28; Mark 13:34–36; Luke 12:36–38; 12:42–46; 19:12–27.

> However, when Titus, in going his rounds along those valleys, saw them full of dead bodies, and the thick putrefaction running about them, he gave a groan; and, spreading out his hands to heaven, called God to witness that this was not his doing; and such was the sad case of the city itself.[76]

But destruction is not the final word. Jesus' Gospel of the kingdom is that God would finally vindicate and redeem his exiled people (he will get the last word!), not by the carnal political or military means they had imagined but by his own self-sacrifice in solidarity with sinners outside the city. Jesus' resurrection reestablished the new temple with the Holy City built of living stones, living under the new law of the Holy Spirit and the New Covenant of his redeeming blood.

Promise: Jeremiah 32

In Jeremiah 32, God repeats this Gehenna message a third time, but now as part of the New Covenant oracle! First the bad news:

> Jer 32:34–36—But they put their detestable things in the house which is called by My name, to defile it. They built the high places of Baal that are in the valley of Ben-hinnom to cause their sons and their daughters to pass through the fire to Molech, which I had not commanded them nor had it entered My mind that they should do this abomination, to cause Judah to sin. Now therefore thus says the LORD God of Israel concerning this city of which you say, "It is given into the hand of the king of Babylon by sword, by famine and by pestilence."

To Jeremiah, this is worth repeating: Gehenna represents the slaughter, captivity, and oppression of God's rebellious people in history. This was Jesus' informing theology and the backdrop for his prophetic-historic use of Gehenna. Did his listeners understand this?

> Now, if Gehenna, and the "damnation of Gehenna," meant the vengeance of God which was then coming on the Jewish nation, as I believe it did, how stands this case both with Christ's disciples and the unbelieving Jews? As to the disciples, there was no way for them to escape this vengeance but by continuing as Christ's faithful disciples. Such of them as endured to the end should be saved from it (Cf. Matt 24). [In] Matt 3:7, "wrath to come" referred to the impending vengeance of God then coming on the Jewish nation.

76. Josephus, *Wars*, 5:12.3–4.

And this is expressly called *wrath*, (1 Thess 2:16. Luke 21:23). And
"the damnation of Gehenna." (Matt, 23:33)[77]

Thus, for Jesus, Gehenna referred primarily to the self-destructive consequences of rebellion, which give rise to bitter mourning and the worm of
regret ("weeping and gnashing of teeth") both for the pain we have caused
and the pain we must endure. Gehenna is also called "the outer darkness"
(Matt 8:12; 22:13; 25:30) where in each case, those sent there are "sons
of the kingdom," servants, and wedding guests who have been faithless,
fearful, or unrighteous. Gehenna is judgment to be sure—and may even
point secondarily to final judgment—but the picture is first of all about
the destructive wake left behind by our sin here and now, not an afterlife
of eternal, conscious torment. It is quite literally "the way of death."

When Jesus did extend his use of Gehenna metaphorically to include
postmortem disaster for the impenitent,[78] the picture he drew was more
akin to the smoking corpses outside the city in Jeremiah and Isaiah's visions (Isa 66:24, see also Mark 9:48) than the subterranean fire dungeons
of Jewish apocalyptic literature.

Gehenna: Metaphor for Spiritual Destruction

The foregoing established, Jesus also appears to add a realized, spiritual,
and personal dimension to his eschatology, more obviously in the Gospel
of John. He could use the term Gehenna (and its synonym, "condemnation") as a metaphor for spiritual lostness and the torment of alienation
from God. The metaphor includes both a current and an ultimate condition from which we can be saved.

In John 3, which the majority of scholars believe was written well after
the fall of Jerusalem,[79] Jesus explains to Nicodemus that God did not send

77. Walter Balfour, *Letter to Whitman*, 85. Note: Debates concerning Gehenna in the
nineteenth century focused on this impending wrath on Jerusalem for rejecting Jesus as
Messiah. Post-holocaust discussions, appropriately avoiding the politically incorrect (or
even anti-Semitic) language of earlier writers, resist the possibility that Jesus' Gehenna
echoed Jeremiah's indictments on his countrymen. Both eras seem forget that Jesus was a
Jewish prophet, not a Christian anti-Semitist. See also Thomas Baldwin Thayer, *Theology
of Universalism*, 378, Balfour and Skinner, *An Inquiry*, 126–27.

78. Cf. N. T. Wright, "Your Questions to N. T. Wright," para. 4.

79. Another point contested by Ansell: "Contrary to majority scholarly opinion, we do
not know that the fourth Gospel is late first century. This is assumed, often. But there is no
definitive evidence for this at all. N. T. Wright makes a few comments on this, including
in his *Judas and the Gospel of Jesus*. J. A. T. Robinson, *Redating the New Testament*, argued

him to deliver the world into some forthcoming condemnation but to deliver people from the condemned state in which they suffer already (John 3:16–18). It is about us, here and now—just as the kingdom of heaven is even now among us and within us, breaking into and flowing out through our lives in space and time, so too the awful reality of Gehenna. As the kingdom of God is with us, in us, and among us, so is the awful reality of Gehenna, manifesting in the tragic twists of our lives and the gnashing sorrow in our hearts. Andre Harden, a friend and lay-theologian, has this to say about Jesus' use of Gehenna as a spiritual metaphor:

> While Jesus was warning people against a real disaster (and the end/collapse/failure of the Mosaic/legal age), he was also trying to shift people away from the materialism that a ritual religion had spawned. Jesus personified spirituality, and that was what he tried to model—obedience to the living spirit that we (would) share, not to a priest-mediated law. He recognized Gehenna now—in the streets, in our minds—and taught that loving and respecting each other intently and courageously was what God wanted from us, more than any ritual observance.
>
> Jesus was pulling people out of the dump and steering them away from the path that leads back. The language is still metaphorical. While it's a place of desolation and despair and corruption, it's also the dump. It's good that there's a place where we can unload our desolation, despair and corruption. It's not only good, it's needful, and we can start in this life.[80]

Karl Rahner, careful to identify Jesus' use of threat-discourse as a current spiritual situation and a potential permanent outcome, says:

> The metaphors in which Jesus describes the eternal perdition of man as a possibility which threatens him at this moment are images (fire, worm, darkness, etc.) taken from the mental furniture of contemporary apocalyptic. They all mean the same thing, the possibility of man being finally lost and estranged from God in all the dimensions of his existence. Hence it can be seen that the question of whether the "fire" of hell is real or metaphorical is wrongly put, since "fire" and suchlike words are metaphorical expressions for

---

John was pre-70. . . . Personally, I don't see John as realized eschatology, spiritualized, etc. Try reading John-Revelation as a two-part work like Luke-Acts. The reason there is no 'synoptic apocalypse' in John is because this is worked through in Revelation." (Nik Ansell, email to me, May 29, 2009).

80. Andre Harden, email to me, Mar 2009.

something radically not of this world ... [that] can only be spoken of "in images."[81]

Gehenna: Hope for Purification unto Restoration

But even that is not the end. The cleansing aspect of God's fire in the Valley of Hinnom ought to be imported into our lives and forwarded into our eschatology as well. Just as Josiah's reforms and Babylon's siege were, on one level, a purification of the land from egregious sin, Jesus used the language of Gehenna as a backdrop to the salting by fire that purges sin and prepares us for the presence of God (Mark 9:47–49). First, he warned against the path that leads to Gehenna. Then he said that the salting by fire will happen to everyone in the unspecified future, but it is good, and we're to welcome it now internally.

What is the ultimate destiny of those exiles who experience defeat and dispersion? Jeremiah's final reference to Hinnom, embedded in the New Covenant kingdom prophecies, now takes a redemptive twist, rooted in God's solidarity with those who suffer and finally fulfilled in Christ!

> Jer 32:37–40 (NKJV)—Behold, I will gather them out of all countries where I have driven them in My anger, in My fury, and in great wrath; I will bring them back to this place, and I will cause them to dwell safely. They shall be My people, and I will be their God; then I will give them one heart and one way, that they may fear Me forever, for the good of them and their children after them. *And I will make an everlasting covenant with them,* that I will not turn away from doing them good; but I will put My fear in their hearts so that they will not depart from Me.

Why the change of heart when judgment was a forgone reality? Brueggemann sees the radical shift in 30:14, 17. When God hears his own verdict—"the nations care nothing for you"—on the lips of the nations—"Zion, for whom no one cares"—his heart is pricked. There is a pathos in God for his broken people.

> Yahweh is made freshly aware of deep concern for Israel. In the mocking voiced by the nations, Yahweh is driven to fresh saving action, becoming newly cognizant of a deep solidarity that Judah's guilt and Yahweh's indignation have not mitigated. It is as though in the depth of exile, in the bottom of Israel's terrible humiliation

---

81. K. Rahner, "Hell," 603.

before the nations, Yahweh found depths of love for Israel about which Yahweh did not heretofore know. It is the situation of Israel's hurt which evokes in Yahweh fresh measures of love and resolve.[82]

Perhaps what we see as the end, even when it was clearly spoken by God, is not always the very, very end. God's heart is big and free enough to imagine redemptive change, even in himself.

Gehenna's Terminus

In this same New Covenant context, we find another allusion to Gehenna in which the once cursed valley is reclaimed and consecrated:

> Jer 31:38–40—"The days are coming," declares the LORD, "when this city will be rebuilt for me from the Tower of Hananel to the Corner Gate. The measuring line will stretch from there straight to the hill of Gareb and then turn to Goah. *The whole valley where dead bodies and ashes are thrown, and all the terraces out to the Kidron Valley on the east as far as the corner of the Horse Gate, will be holy to the LORD.* The city will never again be uprooted or demolished."

The New Covenant promises that not only will Jerusalem be rebuilt; even the valleys of bodies and ashes (Kidron and Gehenna) will be reclaimed and sanctified as holy forever!

The NT describes and explains how this wondrous hope comes about in ways not expected (Luke 24:21; Acts 1:6). Christ's mission was not the literal rebuilding of the old temple in the old Jerusalem but the establishment of a new and living temple and a New Jerusalem. The restoration begins with Jesus' resurrection (John 2:9) and then continues with his church-temple of living stones (1 Cor 3:16; 1 Pet 2) as part of the spiritual city of Zion (Heb 12:22), and is then completed with the New Jerusalem to come in the new heaven and new earth (Rev 21–22).

The Irony of Apocalyptic Gehenna

Unfortunately, Christian tradition, theology, and translation followed the apocryphal reading of Gehenna rather than the biblical tradition of Jeremiah and Jesus. The Church zigged with Enoch, Esdras et al[83] when

---

82. Brueggemann, *Jeremiah*, 277.

83. Enoch's influence on the church is already evident in Jude 14. Even if the inter-testamental apocalyptic literature intended to describe historical cataclysm, this is apparently not how the Christian and Jewish infernalists read it.

Jesus zagged with Jeremiah, so to speak. Why? We can speculate: first, apocalyptic visions exert a strong magnetic pull on our imaginations so that we tend to fixate on the cosmic portrait instead of the earthly events they portray. Second, after the earthly events have passed (i.e., the fall of Jerusalem), interpreters often project the seemingly unfulfilled elements (like the end of the world, the eradication of evil) into the eschatological future. Thus, we embrace apocalyptic as a prophetic promise of the End of Days, consigning unbelievers to that Gehenna, but fail to see its warnings against our self-destructive idolatry for the here and now. Even those who believe that we now live in the last hour of this age can miss the admonitions against imperialism, nationalism, militarism, and consumerism—or the four horses they have let out of the barn (Rev 6). These principalities dash and demolish entire cities and nations into the local, temporal Gehenna about which Jeremiah and Jesus warned. One's individual afterlife aside, what happens to nations who continue to sacrifice their firstborn on Molech's altars of personal convenience or national security?[84]

If we were to be strictly biblical about Gehenna (in the conservative literalist sense) and let Scripture interpret Scripture, what would we find? If we allowed the Hebrew Scriptures to inform Jesus' use of the word Gehenna—rather than apocryphal works from before his time or rabbinical traditions that arose thereafter—would we still identify Gehenna with hell?

We ought to also note the irony and incongruence of the Church utilizing the very place where God became violently offended by the literal burning of children as our primary metaphor for a final and eternal burning of God's wayward people in literal flames. Thus, God becomes the very Molech who decrees that the angels must deliver his children to the flames, even though this was the very reason he ordered Hinnom to be desecrated in the first place!

The Good News about Gehenna

While the legacy of Gehenna stands as a genuine warning of destruction to those who persist in rebellion and idolatry, Jeremiah and Jesus forewarn us to avoid the consequential wrath. For those who experience the calamities of the "way of death," the invitation is extended to a New Covenant of restoration. Sin and its consequences are overcome by redemption and

---

84. See Ansell's Afterword below, n. 30.

restoration. Rather than terrorizing the world with eternal, conscious tor-ment in a literal lake of fire, the Church can hold out the New Covenant of Jesus in which even the Valley of Slaughter is sanctified, every curse of destruction is broken, and God's exiles find their way home.

In the Enoch version of Gehenna or apocalyptic hell we still have an image of God that includes, at least by permission or even design, a wrathful and unredemptive response to the unrepentant. Wickedness leads to unremitting condemnation by the divine Judge. Under the Jeremiah scheme, Gehenna describes a self-destructive trajectory that God not only intervenes to avert but also employs in ultimate redemption as our current condemnation exhausts itself and finds its terminus in a New Covenant, whereby even Gehenna is restored.

Ground Level Gehenna Evangelism: Here's an illustration of how this looks at the ground level of evangelism. My oldest son Stephen brought a friend by our home recently. Her life was spiraling into addiction and despair, so he set aside a day to encourage her. When she poked her head into my office to say hello, she saw me at the computer and asked what I was doing. I replied that I was writing a book on hell. I took her upturned eyebrow as permission to explain. "I'm studying how our traditional views of hell tend to be very . . ."

"Medieval?" she offered.

"Yes," I replied. "But I'm learning that when the biblical writers talk about hell, they are really addressing the self-destructive tendencies from which we already suffer. The good news is that God is not threatening to punish us with some future, fiery torture. Instead, he offers relief from the oppression we're under right now." That resonated with her, and she identified her hell as internal torment, chronic guilt, and self-destruction. Rather than try to convert her on the spot, I commissioned my son to be the Gospel of relief to her for the day. Later, Stephen shared that after assuring her that he would remain her friend no matter how badly she messed up, she made a full confession and commitment to turn her life around with his help.

What excited me about this was my son's incarnational message and the fact that he was able to witness the principle that the kindness of God—not our judgment or threats of punishment—leads to repentance (Rom 2). Further, I was heartened to see that his friend could grasp the Gospel: that "hell" is something God wants to save her from, not send her to. Now she stands at a fork in the road—healing and redemption on one side or more pain and suffering on the other. The choice is up to her.

This is the point of the biblical proclamation concerning heaven and hell. If we take these texts as true, as real and universal possibilities, then the warnings of judgment cannot be presumed as foregone descriptions of what must be. Rather, they stand as real warnings of a real path that no one ought to pursue alongside an assurance that God's love gets the last word. Without being crass literalists, we may face the realities conveyed by these ancient word-pictures with the Good News.

COMING UNDER THE TEXT

Having completed our survey of biblical terms used to describe "hell," it's time to move on, taking the same approach to the Bible's perspective on divine judgment. It's important to resist the urge to force-feed these passages into our favorite doctrinal mill lest their messages become unrecognizable when we are through with them. At least for now, let us allow the authors to say what they say without tampering, even if my headings appear to do so. My only intent is to group these verses according to what they appear to say upon first reading. The point of highlighting discrepancies is not to undermine the Scriptures as if they were flawed in their polyphony. Instead, we have an opportunity to exercise restraint by coming under the text without prejudging what it *must* mean according to our own conditions.

4

The Biblical Spectrum of Descriptions for Hell and Judgment

WHEREVER THE JUDGED ARE finally assigned, the spectrum of possibilities warrants pause to those who presume to know its precise nature. It's not that we have too little revelation on the matter. Rather, the Bible includes too many possibilities to allow for simplistic dogmatism. As I survey the range of descriptions, the reader will see overwhelming incongruities and may wonder at my motives. Is he trying to debunk what the Bible says about hell? Or is he trying to discredit the Bible itself? Most assuredly not! My agenda here is simply to stand under the Scriptures so earnestly that any shadow of hubris relating to our knowledge of perdition is swallowed in humility. Our habit is to dismiss the plain teaching of certain texts as not meaning what they say, because they don't fit the scheme upon which we have already settled. In that case, the Scripture bows to the authority of our hermeneutic. That topsy-turvy arrangement needs to continually be unsettled.

Much of what we might say about divine judgment finds support in one text (our pets) and contradiction in another (our gadflies). It is not dialectic; there is no unified synthesis of judgment in the Bible or even in the teachings of Jesus. It just is. So let us sample what is.

Besides Sheol, Hades, Abyss, Tartarus, and Gehenna, the Bible uses other designations and descriptions (whether literally or metaphorically) for the "abode of the damned": "lower hell" (2 Pet 2:4 Vulgate *tartarus*), "place of torments" (Luke 16:28), "pool of fire" (Rev 19:20), "unquenchable fire" (Matt 3:12), "exterior darkness" (Matt 7:12; 22:13; 25:30), "furnace of fire" (Matt 13:42, 50), "everlasting fire" (Matt 18:8; 25:41; Jude 7), "death" (Rom 6:21), "corruption" (*phthora*, Gal 6:8), "destruction" (*apōleia*, Phil 3:19), "eternal destruction" (*olethros aiōnion*, 2 Thess 1:9), "perdition" (*olethros*, 1 Tim 6:9), "mist" or "storm of darkness" (2 Pet 2:17; Jude 13), and "second death" (Rev 2:11).

In fact, the breadth of imagery spans everything from the positive pictures of a laundry tub and a refiner's furnace to the negative portraits of a garbage dump, a dungeon, and a sulfurous lake of fire. Each metaphor functions distinctly and deliberately, conveying specific truths as rhetorically necessary without, I would argue, demanding an exclusive literal interpretation. Once again, within and beyond this great symbolic landscape, note the range of potential outcomes.

ANNIHILATION

Some texts present the language of "damnation" in conclusive terms such as "perish" (John 3:16), "destroy" (Matt 10:28), and "the second death" (Rev 21:8). The implication is complete extinction:

> Ps 37—The wicked fade like grass and wither like the herb (2); they will be cut off and be no more (9–10); they will perish and vanish like smoke (20); and be altogether destroyed (38).

> Mal 4:1–4—The day of the Lord comes like a burning oven, burning up the wicked like stubble and leaving them reduced to ashes underfoot.

> Isa 66:24—In the new heavens and new earth, the unquenchable fire is visible in which we will view the dead bodies of those who rebelled.

> John 3:16—Those who believe receive eternal life; those who do not perish.

> Rom 6:23—The wages of sin is death; the free gift of God is eternal life.

> Heb 10:27—Judgment and raging fire will consume the enemies of God.

> Rev 19:19–21—While the beast and false prophet are thrown into the lake of fire, "the rest of them" are killed by the sword and then devoured by birds.

> Rev 21:4–8—Those thrown in the lake of burning sulfur die a second death, after which the old order of things passes away and all suffering and death ceases.

See also Matt 3:10–12; 13:30, 42, 49–50; 1 Cor 3:17; Phil 1:28; 3:19; 2 Pet 2:1–3; 3:7.

CONSCIOUS TORMENT

By stark contrast, other passages describe the damned in conscious torment. Regardless of whether the torment is temporary or eternal, pre- or post-final judgment, the souls in these verses are obviously not simply extinct.

> Matt 18:23–35—This parable describes the unforgiving servant as being delivered into the hand of tormentors until his entire debt is repaid (through punishment?).

> Luke 16:23—The rich man in torment is aware and in pain.

> 1 Pet 3:19–20—In whatever state, the spirits of the unrighteous were kept in a posthumous prison for a lengthy time.

> Rev 14:9–11—Whoever worships the beast or takes his mark must drink the wine of God's wrath and be tortured with fire and sulfur in the presence of the angels and the Lamb. They "will not rest day or night."

ETERNAL OR EVERLASTING DURATION

Other texts suggest that such torment is not only conscious but also everlasting (though this can literally mean "age-lasting," a terminable period which Christ brings to a close when "God is all in all") or eternal (though this may also mean either irrevocable or permanent, in harmony with the annihilation texts).

> Dan 12:1–4—Multitudes are raised from the dust, some to everlasting life, others to shame and everlasting contempt.

> Matt 25:46—Infernalists make the case that our interpretation of "eternal" must be consistent in both cases. If the life is everlasting in duration, so must be the punishment.

> 2 Thess 1:9—Those who do not know God or obey the Gospel of Jesus are "punished with everlasting destruction and shut out from the presence of the Lord."

POSTMORTEM SALVATION

Again, in direct contrast, the NT hints at postmortem salvation, whether through a purgative process (Mal 3; 1 Cor 3) or by a direct invitation to respond to the Gospel. These texts preclude a dogmatic *never* to the possibility of a second chance.

> 1 Pet 3:18–19—Jesus suffered death, the just for the unjust; then he preached to the spirits in prison who were rebellious to God (not merely ignorant!) in the days of Noah.

Subsequently:

> 1 Pet 4:6—lit. "Those now dead were evangelized." Those who had been judged in the body are made alive in the spirit. (Just like Jesus in 3:18!)

> Rev 22:17—The Spirit and Bride continue to invite the thirsty to come drink of the waters of life even after the final judgment in the new heavens and new earth.

DUALIST VERSUS UNIVERSAL

I dislike texts that divide humankind into two groups of people: righteous insiders who inherit eternal life and wicked outsiders who are punished (just as some folks enjoy them greatly, presuming of course that they are among the elect). We can employ a variety of ingenious ways to work around them, but when I do, I can feel myself manipulating the words to avoid . . . What? My discomfort? Their authority? Can we at least admit such texts exist?

> Matt 13:24–30, 36–52—Good seeds planted by God are children of the kingdom; the bad seeds are weeds planted by the devil. At the end of the age, the harvesters (angels) pull up the weeds and burn them in the fire. So too, the final judgment will be like sorting through a fishing net. Angels will keep the good fish (the righteous) and throw out the wicked like bad fish.

> Matt 25:31–46—The nations of the earth gather to be divided into sheep on the right and goats on the left according to how they treated Jesus in the least of these. The sheep inherit eternal life; the goats are dismissed to eternal punishment. (See also the wise and foolish virgins in Matt 25:1–13.)

John 5:28–29—. . . a time is coming when all who are in their graves will hear his voice and come out—those who have done good will rise to live, and those who have done evil will rise to be condemned.

Rev 20:12, 14—Again, two groups: those whose names are written in the Book of Life and those who didn't make the cut.

In these dualist texts, one group is welcomed to eternal life, the New Jerusalem, and the waters of life while the rest are dismissed, condemned, or thrown into the eternal fire, lake of fiery sulfur, or second death. At this stage, we are not concerned with the criteria, nature, or duration of this outcome, just that there are two groups of people with two very different fates.

In sharp contrast to these texts, a second group of passages shows us something very different. These passages forecast a universal judgment whereby everyone—righteous and unrighteous—will be salted by fire or pass through the flames:

Mark 9:42–50—This text is shocking in that Jesus starts by forecasting two possibilities—the Kingdom of God versus the fire and worms of Gehenna—but then immediately says, "For all [Greek *gar pas* or "yet everyone"] will be salted with fire [echoes of Sodom?], but salt is good! So have salt in yourselves."

1 Cor 3:10–15—Paul's version of this judgment explains that the day will test everyone's earthly works with fire, consuming what is worthless, manifesting what is precious, yet even those who suffer loss will be "saved, yet so as through fire."

Again, the question of the criteria, nature, or duration of the judgment is secondary.[1] The point in these texts is that everyone is subject to the cleansing fire, and everyone seems to pass through it. Neither the dualist nor the universalist evades the fiery trial. As my friend and intercessor, Adit Gamble, put it to me in a recent e-mail:

Although forgiveness happens the moment we ask Him, cleansing does not necessarily come at the same time, and in fact often it does not. This morning it looked like cleansing was a washcloth

---

1. "It is clear that we cannot calculate the "duration" of this transforming burning in terms of the chronological measurements of this world. The transforming "moment" of this encounter eludes earthly time-reckoning—it is the heart's time, it is the time of "passage" to communion with God in the Body of Christ." (Benedict XVI, *Spe Salvi*, 47).

dipped in salty water and dabbed against the burn of our sin. It looked very painful. It could be interpreted as punishment. But it was just the cleansing and removal of these offensive things and it was very good.[2]

BREADTH OF CRITERIA: FAITH VERSUS DEEDS

The biblical criteria by which one is judged either now or on the last day vary significantly. Many texts describe a judgment based on deeds done (or not done) in this life:

Matt 7:21–23—Criteria: those who do the Father's will versus "evildoers" even though they said "Lord, Lord," prophesied, cast out demons, and performed miracles in his name.

Matt 25:31–46—Criteria: acts of commission versus sins of omission to the least.

Rev 2:20–23—Criteria: everyone repaid according to the deeds of hearts and minds.

Rev 20:12—Criteria: judged according to what they had done recorded in the books.

In the synoptic gospels, and especially in Jesus' parables, the standard of judgment focuses mainly on how we have loved God and our neighbor or failed to do so. In other words, how we live determines whether we enter his Kingdom. The results are said to be a surprise to many. The specific deed being judged varies: e.g., motives, words spoken, forgiveness, readiness, treatment of others, faithfulness to calling, etc. Sometimes we see rewards for righteous acts; other times the issue is punishment or exclusion for wicked deeds.

By contrast, John's Gospel, Paul's epistles, and the preaching of the Gospel in Acts center most often on our faith-response to the person, message, and ministry of Jesus. Eternal life comes through belief in his name and reliance on his grace-gift of forgiveness and reconciliation.

John 3:16–18—Criteria: belief in the only Son sent by the Father.

Acts 10:42–43—Criteria: belief in the One whom God appointed as judge.

---

2. Adit Gamble, email to me, Mar 2009.

Eph 2:8–10—Criteria: by grace through faith; not by works.

Titus 3:4–7—Criteria: by God's mercy and grace; not by righteous deeds we have done.

We see these nearly opposing conditions highlighted in the NT's metaphor of "righteous robes," the mandatory garment for gaining entry into God's kingdom banquet and the New Jerusalem. On the one hand, the righteous robes represent "the righteous acts of the saints" by which "the Bride makes herself ready" (Rev 19:7–8). On the other hand, they express the washing of regeneration ministered through the blood of Christ alone (Rev 7:13–14; 22:14). And even though both the righteous and the wicked are invited to the wedding feast, in Matt 22:1–14 we hear of one who is bounced for showing up without wedding clothes. Could this represent self-righteousness?

The difficulty of integrating these passages and their obvious intent collude to strip us of false assurance. They leave us casting our hope upon the mercy of God. Only so washed and robed will we endure whatever trial by fire we ultimately face.

PUNITIVE VERSUS RESTORATIVE

Most troubling are those passages that portray God's judgment as punitive. For a God who describes himself as compassionate and gracious, slow to anger, abounding in mercy, and who does not harbor his anger forever, the imagery of judgment can sound very short-tempered, vicious, and vindictive. Eternal fire, gnawing worms, outer darkness, flaming garbage dumps . . . How does this square with "perfect love that casts out fear, because fear has to do with punishment"? Even allowing for the symbolism of the parables (and that some point to the pre-judgment day netherworld), the tone is still almost inescapably punitive. For example, in the parable of the rich man and Lazarus (Luke 16:19–31), the rich man seems to be stuck in unremitting agony and thirst in a place of fire despite his pleas for mercy. And in Matt 18:23–35, the formerly merciful king (who represents God) withdraws his mercy and delivers an unmerciful servant over to unnamed tormentors "until he should pay back all that was due him." Even if we imagine an eventual repayment and ultimate redemption, the means of that payment is torment. Compare that with the following passages:

Mal 3:1–6—We are purified like gold in a refiner's fire, washed clean with launderer's soap.

Mal 4:1–2—On the Day of the Lord, he rises like the sun with healing rays.

1 Cor 3:10–15—Our works are tested by fire so that only the good remains.

Malachi's Day of Judgment (fulfilled through the ministry of John the Baptist and Jesus in the Temple?) is restorative rather than punitive. The fiery presence of God acts as a furnace that removes dross from the gold in our character. He cleanses our robes with the launderer's soap, identified at the end of Revelation as the blood of Christ. In this category of verses, the consuming fire is God (see also Heb 12:28–29) burning away the chaff of our wickedness to reveal the pure image in which we were made. Such judgment is corrective, curative, and cleansing—crisis in the fullest sense (Gk. *krisis* = trial, judgment)—preparatory for paradise.

ACTIVE VERSUS PASSIVE

To defend God's character from charges of active tyranny, the Church has periodically argued for a passive judgment in which any exclusion from heaven is self-inflicted. We say that God sends no one to hell; that rejecting his love and departing from his presence is our own choice. It seems kind of us to let God off the hook for this,[3] and I wish that were the whole story. But this denies the fact that sometimes the Bible portrays God as a king, master, or judge who actively indicts the wicked, renders a verdict, and issues the sentence—sometimes with great relish. Recoiling from these descriptions solves as little as embracing them with excessive fervor. The way through is to first allow them to convey the revulsion that was intended to drive home their message, whatever that might be. Then we can return to the text to see God say, "And here is what I will do next."

Matt 24:45–51—The faithful and wicked servants

Matt 25:14–30—The parable of the talents

3. Bono nails this tension: "Stand up for hope, faith, love while I'm getting over certainty/Stop helping God across the road like a little old lady." (U2, "Stand Up Comedy," *No Line on the Horizon,* 2009).

In Matt 24, the master of the wicked servant, who is guilty of abusive leadership, dismembers him and then assigns his body parts to the place where hypocrites go, where there is weeping and gnashing of teeth. In Matt 25, the master reacts angrily, lashes out, and commands someone to throw the cowardly servant "outside, into the darkness, where there is weeping and gnashing of teeth." Who is this master? In the next paragraph, we read that it is "the Son of Man, coming in his glory" to sit as King to judge and separate the nations!

Meanwhile, the Jesus of John's Gospel refuses to judge or condemn at all. He simply allows our response to his word to speak for itself. Neither Father nor Son actively judge. Rather, those who do not believe the Good News of Jesus are *de facto* living in condemnation already.

> John 3:16–21—Jesus doesn't condemn; those who don't believe are already condemned.
>
> John 5:22–27– The Father doesn't judge; he gives the authority to judge to his Son.
>
> John 8:15–16—The Son passes judgment on no one; but if he did, he would be just.
>
> John 12:47–49—The only judge is the word that was spoken. That word will condemn the one who rejects Jesus and his words on the last day.

Those who believe appropriate the proffered life, and those who don't, refuse it. The judgment is entirely passive from God's perspective and entirely self-inflicted from ours.

OBJECTIVE PLACE VERSUS SUBJECTIVE STATES

Many passages, especially those that contain parables, visions, or symbolic imagery, describe hell as a place to which one is sent. Common images include that of a prison, abyss, lake of fire, Valley of Hinnom, etc. A few of many examples should suffice.

> Matt 8:12; 22:13; 25:30—a place of outer darkness
>
> Rev 21:8—their place will be in the lake of fiery burning sulfur
>
> Rev 22:15—the dogs are outside the gates of the city

Indeed, can you conceive of a way to talk about the state of the damned in terms that don't describe a location? Given their contexts, these places might be labeled *geogramorphic:* descriptions of that which is not technically a place in geographic terms but which attribute a symbolic "whereness" or "geographication" to a state of mind or being. For example, consider this missive from Pope John Paul II:

> Rather than a place, hell indicates the state of those who freely and definitively separate themselves from God, the source of all life and joy. . . . "To die in mortal sin without repenting and accepting God's merciful love means remaining separated from him for ever by our own free choice. This state of definitive self-exclusion from communion with God and the blessed is called 'hell'" (n. 1033).[4]

Thomas Merton concurred,

> Our God also is a consuming fire. And if we, by love, become transformed into Him and burn as He burns, His fire will be our everlasting joy. But if we refuse his love and remain in the coldness of sin and opposition to Him and to other men then will His fire (by our choice rather than His) become our everlasting enemy, and Love, instead of being our joy, will become our torment and our destruction.[5]

Meanwhile, the Eastern Orthodox Church has long regarded hell subjectively, as an existential experience. But rather than a question of inclusion and exclusion, they conceive of heaven and/or hell as two experiences of the same fire. To their way of thinking, God is the fire that we experience as either a blessing or a torment, depending on our spiritual state (Cf. Gen 19:24; Exod 3:2; 9:23; 13:21–22; 19:18; Num 11:1–3; 4:24; Neh 9:12; Ps 66:10; 104:4; Isa 66:15).

> Heb 12:29—Our God is the consuming fire.

> Isa 33:10–16—Who can dwell with the consuming fire? Not sinners, only the righteous.

> Exod 24:16–18—The glory of God was a cloud to Moses but a consuming fire to Israel.

> Mal 3:2–3; 4:1–2—God is a furnace. In him, the righteous are purified as gold and sinners are burned up as stubble.

---

4. John Paul II, "General Audience: July 28, 1999," 3.1.

5. Thomas Merton, *New Seeds of Contemplation,* 124.

Matt 3:11; Luke 3:16—John the forerunner announces the coming of one who will baptize with the Holy Spirit and with fire.

The Bible indicates that everyone comes before God in the next life, and it is because of being in God's presence that they either suffer eternally, or experience eternal joy. In other words, both the joy of heaven and the torment of judgment are caused by being eternally in the presence of the Almighty, the perfect and unchanging God.[6]

By way of analogy, when the children of Israel fled Pharaoh's army, the presence of God stood between them as a pillar of fire. To God's people, he was warmth, light, and comfort. To his enemies, he was darkness and terror. The same is true of the fiery furnace in the book of Daniel. To Daniel's friends, the fire served to burn only the ropes of their bondage. Meanwhile, it incinerated their captors. In the end, the glory and love of Christ is that fire. This was a major theme in the Patristics. St. Basil the Great taught that when the Psalmist says, "the voice of the Lord divides the flames of fire" (Ps 29:7), he means:

That this miracle happened to the Three Children in the fiery furnace. The fire in this case was divided into two, so that while it was burning those outside it, it was cooling the Children, as if they were under the shadow of a tree. In what follows he observes that the fire which had been prepared by God for the devil and his angels "is cut by the voice of the Lord." Fire has two powers, the caustic and illuminating energies, and that is why it burns and sheds light. Thus those worthy of the fire will feel its caustic quality and those worthy of lighting will feel the illuminating property of the fire.[7]

Modern Orthodox Christians still teach this. Jesus' parables emphasize two types of people going to two different places, but the references to the consuming fire of God (or the river of fire that flows from God's throne in Dan 7) portray two types of people experiencing one place (or Person) in two different ways.

6. Peter Chopelas, "Heaven and Hell in the Afterlife," para. 3.

7. Basil the Great, "On Psalm 28," *PG* 29, 297a. Gregory Palamas says, "Thus, it is said, He will baptize you by the Holy Spirit and by fire: in other words, by illumination and punishment, depending on each person's predisposition, which will bring upon him that which he deserves" (*EPE* 2, 498).

Consequently, paradise and hell are not a reward or a punishment (condemnation), but the way that we individually experience the sight of Christ, depending on the condition of our heart. . . . Man's condition (clean-unclean, repentant-unrepentant) is the factor that determines the acceptance of the Light as "paradise" or "hell."[8]

We have a sound biblical basis for this. In one of Isaiah's visions of God's Holy Mountain, Yahweh speaks to those who must endure the fire of his manifest presence:

> Isa 33:14–16—You who are far away, hear what I have done; you who are near, acknowledge my power! The sinners in Zion are terrified; trembling grips the godless: "Who of us can dwell with the consuming fire? Who of us can dwell with *everlasting burning?*"
> He who walks righteously and speaks what is right, who rejects gain from extortion and keeps his hand from accepting bribes, who stops his ears against plots of murder and shuts his eyes against contemplating evil—this is the man who will dwell on the heights, whose refuge will be the mountain fortress. His bread will be supplied, and water will not fail him.

"Everlasting burning"? Was Isaiah describing God or hell? In contrast to those instances where sinners are exiled to the valley of flames outside the city, Isaiah's sinners are feeling the terrifying heat of God's glory "in Zion." Lest we mistake Yahweh as a cruel warden afflicting sinners in lockdown, Isaak of Syria reminds us that the gnawing fire is our own reaction to God's omnipotent love, especially where we have spurned it:

> The pain that gnaws the heart as a result of sinning against love is sharper than all the other torments there are.

> The power of love works in two ways: it torments those who have sinned. . . . but to those who have observed it's duties, love gives delight. So it is in Gehenna: the contrition that comes from love is the harsh torment; but in the case of the sons of heaven, delight in this love inebriates their souls.[9]

8. Protopresbyter George Metallinos, "Heaven and Hell," 2.1.

9. *Isaak of Syria*, 83.

5

The Lake of Fire

THE BULK OF CHRISTIAN theology through the centuries has equated the Gehenna of the Gospels, the lake of fire (*limne tou puros*) in Revelation, and a post-resurrection hell. As we have seen, biblically, Gehenna represented this-worldly judgments of destruction with historical and geographic ties to Jerusalem's Valley of Hinnom. To enter the fires of Gehenna was to face the curse of immolation, individually or corporately, outside Jerusalem's gates. Now, turning our attention to the lake of fire, we shall see that it also signifies dramatic destruction rooted in earthly places and historic events, though distinct in both ways from Gehenna.

FIRE AND BRIMSTONE IN REVELATION

Our introduction to the fiery lake of burning sulfur is generally through the direct statements in the book of Revelation, where the most obvious reading places it as the place of final judgment for the wicked at the end of days. It appears to be a straightforward description of infernalism.

> Rev 14:9–11—A third angel followed them and said in a loud voice: "If anyone worships the beast and his image and receives his mark on the forehead or on the hand, he, too, will drink of the wine of God's fury, which has been poured full strength into the cup of his wrath. He will be *tormented with burning sulfur* in the presence of the holy angels and of the Lamb. And the smoke of their torment rises for ever and ever. There is no rest day or night for those who worship the beast and his image, or for anyone who receives the mark of his name."

> Rev 19:20—But the beast was captured, and with him the false prophet who had performed the miraculous signs on his behalf. With these signs he had deluded those who had received the

mark of the beast and worshiped his image. The two of them were thrown alive into the *fiery lake of burning sulfur*.

Rev 20:7–15—When the thousand years are over, Satan will be released from his prison and will go out to deceive the nations in the four corners of the earth—Gog and Magog—to gather them for battle. In number they are like the sand on the seashore. They marched across the breadth of the earth and surrounded the camp of God's people, the city he loves. But *fire came down from heaven and devoured them*. And the devil, who deceived them, was thrown into the *lake of burning sulfur*, where the beast and the false prophet had been thrown. They will be tormented day and night for ever and ever.

Then I saw a great white throne and him who was seated on it. Earth and sky fled from his presence, and there was no place for them. And I saw the dead, great and small, standing before the throne, and books were opened. Another book was opened, which is the book of life. The dead were judged according to what they had done as recorded in the books. The sea gave up the dead that were in it, and death and Hades gave up the dead that were in them, and each person was judged according to what he had done. Then death and Hades were thrown into *the lake of fire*. The lake of fire is the second death. If anyone's name was not found written in the book of life, he was thrown into *the lake of fire*.

Rev 21:8—But the cowardly, the unbelieving, the vile, the murderers, the sexually immoral, those who practice magic arts, the idolaters and all liars—their place will be in the *fiery lake of burning sulfur*. This is the second death.

Those who try to soften the impact of these passages by equating *theion, theiou, theito* (sulfur, brimstone) with *theos, theia, theion* (God or divine or divinize) so that we have a purification process[1] instead of retributive judgment are pressing too hard, and don't need to. The context simply doesn't allow it. This is a consuming fire of destruction rooted in wrath in absolute terms. It's ugly and it's meant to be. In the Bible, the language of fire and brimstone is used of disaster and calamity at the hands of God. And if these passages from John's Revelation were all that Scripture and Jewish history provided on the matter, we could well equate the lake of fire with eternal hell. But there is more to it.

1. Even if we acknowledge the Greek use of brimstone in religious purification practices. For example, Pliny (ca. AD 23–79) stated that houses were formerly hallowed against evil spirits by the use of brimstone.

FIRE AND BRIMSTONE IN BIBLICAL HISTORY

In *The Genesis Pursuit*,[2] author Stephen Spencer offers a chapter entitled, "The Lake of Fire—The Lost Hebrew Idiom." In it, he provides convincing evidence for identifying the lake of fire with the Dead Sea.[3] When I fact-checked his primary sources and others, especially from the centuries on either side of Jesus, a clear connection became apparent. But we begin in Genesis, with the location and then the catastrophe at Sodom and Gomorrah, where we find God using fire and sulfur (brimstone)[4] for the first time.

> Gen 14:3, 10—All these latter kings joined forces in the Valley of Siddim (the Salt Sea) . . . Now the Valley of Siddim was full of tar pits, and when the kings of Sodom and Gomorrah fled, some of the men fell into them and the rest fled to the hills.

> Gen 19:23–28—By the time Lot reached Zoar, the sun had risen over the land. Then the LORD rained down burning sulfur on Sodom and Gomorrah—from the LORD out of the heavens. Thus he overthrew those cities and the entire plain, including all those living in the cities—and also the vegetation in the land. But Lot's wife looked back, and she became a pillar of salt.

> Early the next morning Abraham got up and returned to the place where he had stood before the LORD. He looked down toward Sodom and Gomorrah, toward all the land of the plain, and he saw dense smoke rising from the land, like smoke from a furnace.

2. Stephen Spencer, *The Genesis Pursuit*, 185–212.

3. So did John Gill in his exposition of Rev 20:15: "There seems to be some allusion in the phrase [lake of fire], and in the preceding verse, and elsewhere in this book, to the lake Asphaltites, a sulphurous lake, where Sodom and Gomorrah stood, which the Jews call the salt sea, or the bituminous lake; and whatsoever was useless, or rejected, or abominable, or accursed, they used to say, to show their rejection and detestation of it, let it be cast into the sea of salt, or the bituminous lake; thus, for instance, 'any vessels that had on them the image of the sun, or of the moon, or of a dragon,' . . . 'let them cast them into the salt sea,' or bituminous lake{n}. n. T. Bab. Avoda Zara, fol. 42. 2. Vid. ib. fol. 49. 1. &. 53. 1. & 71. 2. & Nazir, fol. 24. 2. & 26. 1, 2." Bava Metzia, fol. 52. 2. Temura, fol. 22. 2. & Meila, fol. 9. 2. & 10. 1. (John Gill, *Exposition of the Entire Bible*, para. 4).

4. "Bitumen Sulphurea Terra is a fatty sap or exudition . . . There are many species of Bitumen: Liquid, like oil in appearance, and petroleum . . . There is the gross, black Bitumen, which takes its name from the Lake of Sodom; with this the Moors embalm dead bodies. There is the black, gross Palestine Bitumen, which is dug up like coal from the earth." (Martinus Rulandus [Physician and Alchemist, 1532–1602], *Lexicon of Alchemy*, 72–73).

The terrifying judgment of Sodom and Gomorrah, along with its desolate appearance, caused the Dead Sea to become associated with divine
retribution by fire and sulfur. Images of the Gen 19 incident fund future
threats, historical or eschatological, upon the wicked, as in these two
texts:

> Ps 11:6—On the wicked he will rain fiery coals and burning sulfur;
> a scorching wind will be their lot.

> Ezek 38:22—I will execute judgment upon him [Gog] with plague
> and bloodshed; I will pour down torrents of rain, hailstones and
> burning sulfur on him and on his troops and on the many nations
> with him.

The impact of the events that wiped out the cities adjacent to the Dead Sea
thus became embedded in history and theology, even beyond the Judeo-
Christian world, as the proto-type judgment that, in some way, still hangs
over the heads of the rebellious wicked. To share in the sin of Sodom was
to share in its destruction.

> The overthrow of Sodom and Gomorrah made a permanent im-
> pression upon the human psyche; all subsequent literature, pagan
> and divine, portraying hell as a place of sulfurous fumes and
> continuous burnings derives from this source. Fire and brimstone
> thus become synonymous with the fate of the wicked.[5]

THE LAKE OF FIRE IN HISTORICAL TESTIMONY

We can see this in the ancient sources that describe the Dead Sea and
remember its story. They note the ongoing evidence of subterranean fire
and smoke as a reminder of the reality of judgment. To some, it was not
merely a picture of the final place of judgment; the Dead Sea actually *is*
the fiery lake of burning sulfur *or* a perpetual warning that what happened to Sodom could happen to anyone, even beloved Jerusalem! (i.e.
Either you will end up in the Dead Sea/lake of fire too, or what happened
to the Dead Sea cities could visit your city as well). Consider this brief
catalog of early sources:

5. Kurt Simmons, "The Bottomless Pit," para. 5.

Wisdom of Solomon (2nd century BC)

Wisdom saved a man [Lot] from a destruction of the godless, and he escaped the fire that came down on the Five Cities,[6] cities whose wickedness is *still attested by a smoking waste*. (Wis Sol 10:7)

Diodorus Siculus (~60–30 BC)

The fire which burns beneath the ground and the stench render the inhabitants of the neighbouring country sickly and very short-lived.[7]

Strabo (63/64 BC—ca. AD 24)

Many other evidences are produced to show that *the country is fiery;* for near Moasada are to be seen rugged rocks that have been scorched, as also, in many places, fissures and ashy soil, and drops of pitch that emit foul odours to a great distance, and ruined settlements here and there; and therefore people believe the oft-repeated assertions of the local inhabitants, that there were once thirteen inhabited cities in that region of which Sodom was the metropolis, . . . and that by reason of earthquakes and of eruptions of fire and of hot waters containing asphalt and sulphur, the lake burst its bounds, and rocks were enveloped with fire; and, as for the cities, some were swallowed up and others were abandoned by such as were able to escape.[8]

Philo of Alexandria (20 BC–AD 50)

But God, having taken pity on mankind, as being a Saviour and full of love for mankind . . . extinguished [Sodom], . . . and that not by any ordinary chastisement, but he inflicted on them an astonishing novelty, and unheard of rarity of vengeance; for, on a sudden, he commanded the sky to become overclouded and to pour forth a mighty shower, not of rain but of fire; and . . . the flame poured down, with a resistless and unceasing violence. . . . And in one day these populous cities became the tomb of their inhabitants, and the vast edifices of stone and timber became thin dust and ashes. And when the flames had consumed everything that was visible and that existed on the face of the earth, they proceeded to burn

6. Sodom, Gomorrah, Admah, Zeboiim, Zoar/Belar (Gen 14:2, 8; Deut 29:23).
7. Diodorus Siculous, *LacusCurtius* XIX.98.
8. Strapho, *The Geography of Strabo* XVI.2.42–44.

even the earth itself, penetrating into its lowest recesses, and destroying all the vivifying powers which existed within it so as to produce a complete and everlasting barrenness, so that it should never again be able to bear fruit, or to put forth any verdure; and to this very day it is scorched up. *For the fire of the lightning is what is most difficult to extinguish, and creeps on pervading everything, and smouldering. And a most evident proof of this is to be found in what is seen to this day: for the smoke which is still emitted, and the sulphur which men dig up there, are a proof of the calamity which befell that country.*[9]

Flavius Josephus (AD 37–101)

It was of old a most happy land, both for the fruits it bore and the riches of its cities, although it be now all burnt up. It is related how, for the impiety of its inhabitants, it was burnt by lightning; in consequence of which *there are still the remainders of that Divine fire,* and the traces [or shadows] of the five cities are still to be seen, as well as the ashes growing in their fruits; which fruits have a color as if they were fit to be eaten, but if you pluck them with your hands, they dissolve into smoke and ashes. And thus what is related of this land of Sodom hath these marks of credibility which our very sight affords us.[10]

So we see each of these writers conjoining the story of Sodom with the firsthand sites and smells of desolation around the Dead Sea. The barren sickliness of the region stands as portent for those who lapse from covenant into the sins of Sodom.

FIRE AND BRIMSTONE FOR JERUSALEM'S DESTRUCTION

Ezek 16:46b–50—[to Jerusalem] . . . your younger sister, who lived to the south of you with her daughters, was Sodom. You not only walked in their ways and copied their detestable practices, but in all your ways you soon became more depraved than they. As surely as I live, declares the Sovereign LORD, your sister Sodom and her daughters never did what you and your daughters have done. Now this was the sin of your sister Sodom: She and her daughters were arrogant, overfed and unconcerned; they did not help the poor

9. Philo, *On Abraham* XXVI.137–41.
10. Josephus, *Wars of the Jews* IV.8.4.

and needy. They were haughty and did detestable things before me. Therefore I did away with them as you have seen.

What is God's response to Jerusalem's emulation of Sodom? When God's people abandon the covenant, they can expect calamity that will be like the destruction of Sodom and Gomorrah—a raining down of God's burning anger, wasting them with salt and sulfur:

> Deut 29:22–23, 27—Your children who follow you in later generations and foreigners who come from distant lands will see the calamities that have fallen on the land and the diseases with which the LORD has afflicted it. The whole land will be a *burning waste of salt and sulfur*—nothing planted, nothing sprouting, no vegetation growing on it. It will be like the destruction of Sodom and Gomorrah, Admah and Zeboiim, which the LORD overthrew in fierce anger . . . Therefore the LORD's anger burned against this land, so that he brought on it all the curses written in this book.

As it turned out, this threat did play out, but the fiery "destruction like that of Sodom" was figurative, not of hell but of military razing. They did not experience the hail of brimstone or fire from the sky . . . and yet they did.[11] The covenant curses were enforced through the siege-works of foreign enemies (formerly allies whose gods they had worshiped). Jerusalem's Sodom-like destruction is described with the analogy of an adulterous wife (and older sister of Sodom) prostituting herself out (cf. Hosea). Ezekiel described Jerusalem's forthcoming lake of fire/Dead Sea demolition in which she is ravaged by her "ex-lovers."

> Ezek 16:36—This is what the Sovereign LORD says: Because you poured out your wealth [or *lust*] and exposed your nakedness in your promiscuity with your lovers, and because of all your detestable idols, and because you gave them your children's blood [hints of Hinnom? See also v 21], therefore I am going to gather all your lovers, with whom you found pleasure, those you loved as well as those you hated. I will gather them against you from all around and will strip you in front of them, and they will see all your nakedness. I will sentence you to the punishment of women who commit adultery and who shed blood; I will bring upon you the blood vengeance of my wrath and jealous anger. Then I will hand you over to your lovers, and they will tear down your mounds

---

11. In Rev 16:21, hailstones that weighed one talent (approximately 100 pounds) fell from heaven. Josephus describes 100 lb. white stones coming from Roman catapults trashing Jerusalem (*Jewish Wars*, 5.6.3).

and destroy your lofty shrines. They will strip you of your clothes and take your fine jewelry and leave you naked and bare. They will bring a mob against you, who will stone you and hack you to pieces with their swords. They will *burn down your houses* and inflict punishment on you in the sight of many women. I will put a stop to your prostitution, and you will no longer pay your lovers. Then my wrath against you will subside and my jealous anger will turn away from you; I will be calm and no longer angry.

The prophetic-historic picture is developing for us. "Lake of fire" = "Dead Sea" = fate of Sodom and Gomorrah = cursed by God to fiery destruction and ultimate ruin. The lake of fire is thus an apocalyptic threat of being leveled by the fire of God's wrath, historically fulfilled through obliteration by foreign armies. In Revelation, the threat is specific to Jerusalem (as usual), "who is the great city, which is figuratively called Sodom and Egypt, where also their Lord was crucified" (Rev 11:8). When was she figuratively called Sodom?

> Isaiah 1:7–10—[to Judea and Jerusalem v. 1] Your country is desolate, your cities burned with fire; your fields are being stripped by foreigners right before you, laid waste as when overthrown by strangers. The Daughter of Zion is left like a shelter in a vineyard, like a hut in a field of melons, like a city under siege. Unless the LORD Almighty had left us some survivors, we would have become like Sodom, we would have been like Gomorrah. Hear the word of the LORD, you rulers of Sodom; listen to the law of our God, you people of Gomorrah!

FIRE AND BRIMSTONE FOR JERUSALEM'S ENEMIES

On the other hand, Jerusalem is not God's only target for the flaming scourge. In fact, when Babylon, Edom, Rome, or any of their leaders take part in incinerating Jerusalem, they can generally expect the same comeuppance, even if they were appointed God's instrument to begin with.

> Isa 34:8–10—For the LORD has a day of vengeance, a year of retribution, to uphold Zion's cause. Edom's streams will be turned into pitch,[12] her dust into burning sulfur; her land will become blazing

12. Note "pitch" in connection to sulfur/brimstone, Sodom and Gomorrah, and the Dead Sea. Gen 14:10 "Now the Valley of Siddim was full of tar pits, and when the kings of Sodom and Gomorrah fled, some of the men fell into them and the rest fled to the hills." The threat of burning pitch alludes again to the destruction of Sodom. Also called "bitumen."

pitch! It will not be quenched night and day; its smoke will rise forever [see also Rev 14:11!]. From generation to generation it will lie desolate; no one will ever pass through it again.

Jer 49:17–18—"Edom will become an object of horror; all who pass by will be appalled and will scoff because of all its wounds. As Sodom and Gomorrah were overthrown, along with their neighboring towns," says the LORD, "so no one will live there; no man will dwell in it."

Blazing fire (divine wrath) was also to be the fate of the "little horn" of Dan 7 (Antiochus Epiphanes, cf. 8:9). First, this is how his judgment looked in apocalyptic vision format:

Dan 7:9, 11—A river of fire was flowing, coming out from before [the Ancient of Days]. . . . Then I continued to watch because of the boastful words the horn was speaking. I kept looking until the beast was slain and its body destroyed and thrown into the blazing fire.[13]

So in apocalyptic terms, Antiochus is killed, then his body is consumed in the very fire that flows from the throne of God. Transposing this to the earthly reality, his tumultuous death looked like this:

2 Macc 9:8–12, 28 (NAB) Thus he who previously, in his superhuman presumption, thought he could command the waves of the sea, and imagined he could weigh the mountaintops in his scales, was now thrown to the ground and had to be carried on a litter, clearly manifesting to all the power of God. The body of this impious man swarmed with worms, and while he was still alive in hideous torments, his flesh rotted off, so that the entire army was sickened by the stench of his corruption. Shortly before, he had thought that he could reach the stars of heaven, and now, no one could endure to transport the man because of this intolerable stench. At last, broken in spirit, he began to give up his excessive arrogance, and to gain some understanding, under the scourge of

---

13. A similar passage occurs in 4 Ezra concerning the Messiah: "Behold, when he saw the onrush of the approaching multitude, he neither lifted his hand nor held a spear or any weapon of war; but I saw how he sent forth *from his mouth as it were a stream of fire, and from his lips a flaming breath, and from his tongue he shot forth a storm of sparks*. All these were mingled together, *the stream of fire and the flaming breath and the great storm,* and fell on the onrushing multitude which was prepared to fight, and burnt them all up, so that suddenly nothing was seen of the innumerable multitude but only the dust of ashes and the smell of smoke" (4 Ezra 13.9–11).

God, for he was racked with pain unceasingly. When he could no longer bear his own stench, he said, "It is right to be subject to God, and not to think one's mortal self divine." . . . So this murderer and blasphemer, after extreme sufferings, such as he had inflicted on others, died a miserable death in the mountains of a foreign land.

I am not sure which would be more amazing: that someone who is "slain, body destroyed, and thrown into the blazing fire" can still be truly broken and repentant or vice versa. But it is instructive that his apocalyptic demise and his earthly death appear quite different but in ways that interpret each other. The former clarifies God's hand in the latter, and the latter is the earthly fulfillment of the former.

FIRE AND BRIMSTONE IN JOHN'S REVELATION

In Revelation, the judgment is similar. Anyone worshiping the beast "will be tormented with burning sulfur in the presence of the holy angels and of the Lamb. And the smoke of their torment rises for ever and ever" (Rev 14:10–11). But now perhaps we have a vantage point from which to see what the prophets beheld. Visions of divine fire pouring out to destroy a beast and its worshipers or casting the wicked into a lake of burning sulfur must be interpreted or transposed into the earthly events they portray. We're not out of bounds to ask, "What is the beast in our age? Who is the horn now? What form does the destructive fire take this time?" But our first order of business in interpreting Revelation and its lake of fire is to look for the intended referents in John's day. The book of Daniel should have already trained us for this by walking us through that process several times. The tendency is to default into "last days" mode, because we think they refer to the final generation of humanity on planet earth. Rather, the last days are days of cataclysmic "transition" (think in terms of that stage of a mother's labor between contractions and pushing) between the old age and the new age whose birthing is prophesied in Joel 2:28 and began in Acts 2:17.[14]

This is what is happening in the book of Revelation. In his forthcoming book, *The Annihilation of Hell*,[15] Ansell concludes with "An

14. See Nik Ansell, "Hell: The Nemesis of Hope?" nn. 28, 35 (Online version).

15. "The Annihilation of Hell, refers to the overcoming of Hell as our eschatological hopes are realised, whilst at the same time alluding to Hell's own annihilative power in history—a power with which hope must contend. For Moltmann, Hell is the nemesis of hope. Yet hope clings to the certainty that God in Christ has embraced all things, even

Apocalyptic Appendix" with fresh insights and evidence that the focus of John's Revelation is on the fall of Jerusalem in AD 70, just as it had been for Jeremiah and Jesus.

THE LAKE OF FIRE AS PERSONAL JUDGMENT

With the imagery of Gehenna, Sodom and Gomorrah, and the Dead Sea echoing around the hearts of first century Jews, I want to acknowledge that Jesus spoke to the nation about recurring national disasters, but also addressed individual responsibility before God and the personal peril of judgment. Being thrown into Gehenna and winding up in the lake of fire did not have to wait for the ire of the next great empire any more than it did the final Day of Judgment. A glimpse over the south wall of Jerusalem would furnish whatever reminders one might need about the risk of a rebellious life. How might that have looked for an individual pondering the warnings of the prophets and rabbis? If we could step into the sandals and look through the eyes of a first century citizen of Jerusalem, we might experience something like this:

THE LAKE OF FIRE: AN IMAGINATIVE EXERCISE

Looking down from old Mount Zion or out from the Dung Gate, the infamous valley lies below, deepening to my left as it cuts toward its convergence with the Valley of Kidron. It will be a while until the rains come to wash the refuse out of Gehenna. For now, the smell of burning garbage and smoldering bodies wafts up and I shudder. The Romans have been at it again, their latest crackdown on insurgents has climaxed in too many crucifixions. Not what I would call freedom fighters exactly. Criminals? Who knows, the Sanhedrin's latest stoning may have contributed an adulterer or two to the pit. Whatever. If they were worthy of burial for the great resurrection, I suppose someone would have retrieved their corpses. Nothing worse for a Jew than to be burned with the garbage, reduced to ashes in the manner of heathen funeral pyres. Cursed are those who end up there. As the Rabbi said, "Better to enter the kingdom with one hand than to let the other hand find the kind of trouble that leads you to your end in Hinnom's pit."

---

death and Hell, so that creation may participate in the divine Life of the Age to Come." (Nik Ansell, *The Annihilation of Hell*, summary).

Squinting into the morning sun, I know I won't see the lake of fire from here, but I know it's out there ... Lot's wife still gazes longingly over its shores at Sodom's shadow with salty white eyes that would crumble if you squeezed them. Some fellow who can no longer urinate without pain will be out in a boat harvesting the asphalt. To each his own (his own curse). I imagine the final migration of Gehenna's human ashes, washing fifteen miles down the "ravine of fire" until they finally—very finally—disappear into the murky depths. I wonder if the remains will be encrusted before they sink to the fires below.

A centurion marches by leading his entourage. The occupation has swelled this month, with rumors that the new emperor has cast a dangerous eye this way. I coin a proverb: if the unrighteous don't go to the lake of fire, it will come to them. Today might be a good day to drop into the temple for some prayers. At least I'll be safe there.

SODOM AND GOMORRAH: THE ENDURING EXAMPLE

Everything we've seen so far in this chapter leads us to the apostles' (Peter and Jude) conclusion: Sodom and Gomorrah are examples of those whose wickedness demands punishment to the full extent of divine law:

> 1 Pet 2:6, 9—If he condemned the cities of Sodom and Gomorrah by burning them to ashes, and made them an *example* of what is going to happen to the ungodly ... then the Lord knows how to rescue godly men from trials and to hold the unrighteous for the day of judgment, while continuing their punishment.

> Jude 7—In a similar way, Sodom and Gomorrah and the surrounding towns gave themselves up to sexual immorality and perversion. They serve as an example of those who suffer the punishment (*dikēn*)[16] of eternal fire (*puros aiōniou*).

I confess that I am still so conditioned to reading through infernalist lenses that my first impression was that we have here two of the clearest cases of eternal, conscious torment in the NT (along with 2 Thess 1:8–10).

---

16. *dikēn* = punishment, payment of a penalty, justice personified. Used in 2 Thess 1:8–10: "He will punish those who do not know God and do not obey the gospel of our Lord Jesus. They will be *punished* with *everlasting destruction* (*olethron aiōnion*) and shut out from the presence of the Lord and from the majesty of his power on the day he comes to be glorified in his holy people and to be marveled at among all those who have believed." Also in Acts 28:4: "*Justice* has not allowed him to live."

Indeed, these parallel passages do belong to the lake of fire category with no hint of a cleansing or corrective trial by fire in sight. This is divine retribution plain, simple, and fatal, serving as a deterrent to all.

However, if we are to be true to the text, we ought not load too many traditional eschatological assumptions onto the front end of these verses. The punishment, first of all, is again *aiōniou*. Is it everlasting? Permanent? Age-lasting? Age-ending? Next-age? Or age-shifting? The debate continues. But we could at least say this: as the age of Sodom and Gomorrah ended in flames, so did the second-temple era of Jerusalem, just as it shall for anyone who scoffs at this warning.

Second, note that the wicked are punished with the "eternal fire" like Sodom and Gomorrah. The apostolic writers were not describing conscious torment in the netherworld. They were explicit: the unrighteous will perish as these cities did. They are destroyed, reduced to ashes. Annihilated by fire, *in history*. Traditionally, Sodom's fate was treated as an earthly *type* of the eschatological lake of fire (hell), but that is not what the Bible says. The cities around the Dead Sea are *samples* of destruction here and now, over and again, when God gives us over to the flames, whatever form they may take. The beastly empires and those who worship them have and will fall in succession into the lake of fire. Ultimately, even death and Hades will be swallowed up in a judgment that eradicates evil, births the new world, and extends salvation to all—even to Sodom!

THE LAKE OF FIRE HEALED AND RESTORED!

Most awesome to me is that even after the cinders of Sodom have long cooled, Yahweh prophesies about that city's final restoration:[17]

> Ezek 16:53–55—However, I will restore the fortunes of Sodom and her daughters and of Samaria and her daughters, and your fortunes along with them, . . . And your sisters, Sodom with her daughters and Samaria with her daughters, will return to what they were before; and you and your daughters will return to what you were before.

The profundity of that brief paragraph ought to extinguish any presumption in our infernalism. Yes, the fire and brimstone comes. Yes, there is judgment and destruction. Even a second death in the lake of

---

17. Ezek 16 details the allegory of Jerusalem the harlot (Rev 17), which shares Sodom's destiny, both bad and good (see also Rev 11:8; 18:18; Isa 1:10; Jer 23:14).

fire (Rev 20:15). Ashes, sulfur, annihilation. . . . And then—remarkably, miraculously—restoration.

As with Sodom, so with Israel. God is free to relent from what justice would otherwise demand. In Hosea 11, God reveals something of his nature that our own sense of the divine would not have fathomed. Yahweh is able to break his own promise of punishment, even without our repentance! God's own compassion stays that hand of wrath. He is able to say, "Peace. Be still," even to storms of fire. Watch the sudden shift in God's heart:

> Hos 11:6–9—Swords will flash in their cities, will destroy the bars of their gates and put an end to their plans. My people are determined to turn from me. Even if they call to the Most High, he will by no means exalt them.
>
> How can I give you up, Ephraim? How can I hand you over, Israel? How can I treat you like Admah? How can I make you like Zeboiim? My heart is changed within me; all my compassion is aroused. I will not carry out my fierce anger, nor will I turn and devastate Ephraim. For I am God, and not man—the Holy One among you. I will not come in wrath (or *against any city*).

Walter Brueggemann comments on verse 11:

> "I will not treat you like Admah and Zeboiim"[18]—are code words for Sodom and Gomorrah—and then the word that the NRSV translates "recoil" is the word in Genesis 19 (Sodom and Gomorrah) for "earthquake." And God says in verses 8 and 9, "I will take the earthquake of anger into my body so that it won't do you." And then it ends in verse 9 saying, "I am God and not man." Phyllis Trible says, "That doesn't mean 'I am not humankind'; it means 'guy.'" I'm not going to act with the violence of a guy. Now I think if you trace Hosea 11 through, it's the whole story of God's life as a recovering practitioner of violence in which God says, "I'm not going to do it anymore." . . . Now you may think that's too casual of an understanding of God but I think we have to struggle with the fact that God's got all this stuff buried in God's history the way we all do, so the issue is not to explain it. The issue is to ask, "What shall we do now?" I think that's God's question, too. Always. "What shall I do now?"[19]

18. Admah and Zebiim were two of the other cities destroyed with Sodom and Gomorrah.

19. W. Brueggemann, "Emergent Theological Conversation 2004." Brueggemann's challenge is to this type of courageous "first read" of the OT without auto-screening the

What does God do? He sends the Christ who takes the sin, death, and Hades, as well as the curse of a criminal destined for Gehenna and the lake of fire, and he swallows them, extinguishes their flames, and on the third day, rises to establish himself as the new temple from which springs of living water flow. Watch *where* the river of life flows and what it does:

> Zech 14:6–9—On that day there will be no light, no cold or frost. It will be a unique day, without daytime or nighttime—a day known to the LORD. When evening comes, there will be light. On that day living water will flow out from Jerusalem, half to the eastern sea [i.e., the Dead Sea] and half to the western sea,[20] in summer and in winter. The LORD will be king over the whole earth. On that day there will be one LORD, and his name the only name.

> Ezek 47:1–2—The man brought me back to the entrance of the temple, and I saw water coming out from under the threshold of the temple toward the east (for the temple faced east). The water was coming down from under the south side of the temple, south of the altar. He then brought me out through the north gate and led me around the outside to the outer gate facing east, and the water was flowing from the south side.

We need to picture this, understand where the water is flowing, and what this means prophetically. First, the water is flowing south from the temple (Christ), right out the doors, then out of the gates of the city (the New Jerusalem) where it washes directly into the valley below—Kidron and Gehenna! Then it heads east (south-east) through the "ravine of fire" and all the way down to the Eastern Sea: the Dead Sea, the Salt Sea, the Sea of Sodom—*the lake of fire!* It spills into the lake in such abundance that it accomplishes what four other inlets have been unable to manage:

> Ezek 47:8–12—He said to me, "This water flows toward the eastern region and goes down into the Arabah where it enters the [Dead] Sea. When it empties into the Sea, the water there becomes fresh. Swarms of living creatures will live wherever the river flows. There

---

text. On first read, God appears to be a recovering practitioner of extreme violence, as if learning by practice that violent punishment is not as effective as grace. That is how the Hebrew Scriptures present the situation. I wondered if John's Revelation (or our misread of it) represents a relapse.

20. Cp. to Joel 2:20 "I will drive the northern army far from you, pushing it into a parched and barren land, with its front columns going into the eastern sea and those in the rear into the western sea. And its stench will go up; its smell will rise." Surely he has done great things." Half these armies are being driven into "the lake of fire."

will be large numbers of fish, because this water flows there and makes the salt water fresh; so where the river flows everything will live. Fishermen will stand along the shore; from En Gedi to En Eglaim there will be places for spreading nets.[21] The fish will be of many kinds—like the fish of the Great Sea. But the swamps and marshes will not become fresh; they will be left for salt. Fruit trees of all kinds will grow on both banks of the river. Their leaves will not wither, nor will their fruit fail. Every month they will bear, because the water from the sanctuary flows to them. Their fruit will serve for food and their leaves for healing."

The River of Life flows into the Arabah Valley, the area between the Dead Sea and the Red Sea: the land of Edom. Note the fact that the Temple of God is supplying supernatural nourishment to Edom, the children of Esau, sworn enemy of Israel and one of the nations whom God had promised to destroy like Sodom. In this new world, even the estranged brother and his betraying descendants are given the birthrights once lost for a pot of soup. In Ezekiel's vision, all is restored in Christ; all are reconciled. When? Now, with the inauguration of Christ's kingdom and in the context of the church's mission in human history. And not yet, for we await the consummation of that kingdom when the river of life transforms even the lake of fire (divine judgment, demonic infestation, and human destruction). But more of that when we get to Rev 21–22 in Part Three.

SUMMARY: THE LAKE OF FIRE IN HINDSIGHT

As it turns out, the infamous lake of fire is a loaded historical reference to the Dead Sea, the scene of Sodom and Gomorrah's fire and brimstone destruction. When referring to "the lake of burning sulfur," the book of Revelation is not speaking of a traditional post-death hell. John was warning believers that Jerusalem is facing the end of the world as they know it.

21. Remembering to be sensitive to the imagery in this vision, Lyle Collie (a descendant of George MacDonald) suggested to me that the reference to fishers here may be a backdrop to Jesus'"fishers of men" (Matt 4:19; Mark 1:17). Imagine symbolically fishers of people on the banks of what had once been the lake of fire. This would parallel the invitation of the Spirit and the Bride saying, "Come" to those in the valley that had once been Gehenna (Rev 22). Others have noted a connection between Ezek 47:10 and John 21:11 (some *gematria* happening with En-eglaim [totals 153], En-gedi [totals 17, triangled = 153] and the 153 fish). Cf. Augustine and Jerome's theories in George J. Brook, *Dead Sea Scrolls*, 286–93.

Armageddon is coming (the destruction of Jerusalem in AD 70) for both Jerusalem and her attackers. Their judgment will be to share in the fate of Sodom and Gomorrah, as prophesied in the OT.

But that is only the penultimate word. The desolate waste places will be renewed as the river of life, flowing from Messiah's temple, floods and fills the lower parts of the earth. Whereas tradition has seen the fate of Sodom as a type of the final lake of fire, John's vision is a cosmic portrayal of fiery destruction after the pattern of Sodom. If there is an eschatological version to this, it's still about destruction (with interesting hints of hope) rather than literal flaming torture. But even then, the lake of fire will find its terminus in the New Creation.

"WHO THEN CAN BE SAVED?"

As we have seen, the Bible says volumes about the nature and possibility of divine judgment, so much so that we cannot boil its assertions down to single doctrinal system. The Bible's coherence is not found in static theological structures, but in the dynamic, Spirit-led storyboard of our journey with God. The same Western rationalism that infects evangelical hermeneutics with either/or literalism now bites on us on the proverbial behind. If we demand that every word of Scripture is literally true, *we make* Jesus and the Bible self-contradictory. E.g., Jesus says both, "I judge no one," and also "Depart from me you evildoers, into the lake of fire." But the Hebrew mind has long been able to hold a multitude of descriptions in open tension. What makes us dizzy—God is a punisher, God is not a punisher; I don't judge, I do judge—is less confusing if we start by just looking for the point in each case rather than trying to build an impermeable fortress of truth.

If we take all these descriptions into account, we have good reason to be agnostic about our ability to know the precise destiny of the lost. Still, the warnings are there. Are they to be taken seriously? Is their content to be taken literally? Do they represent real warnings of real possibilities? What truths do they convey? Taken seriously, the above passages curtail any grounds for presumption of an automatic, all-in universal salvation regardless of the state of one's life and soul. I do not like what I read in the Bible about divine judgment—especially from the mouth of Jesus. Frankly, I worry about those who do. But I am unwilling to discard biblical orthodoxy in favor of some fluffy, self-made spirituality that comforts me with lies. Reviewing these passages shakes me, leaving me wondering with the disciples, "Who then can be saved?" And yet, there's still more to the story . . .

Excursus 1

The Rich Man and Lazarus

Luke 16:19–31

A NIGGLING MATTER

AFTER COMPLETING THE FIRST draft of this work, I felt a disturbance in my heart. Even after all I'd written, I felt that the thoughtful reader would still ask, "What of the parable of the rich man and Lazarus?" I don't think I have satisfied that query—not even for myself. What we do know is that the parable follows the same cosmology of Hades that we once believed Josephus presented as the Jewish standard in his *Discourse to the Greeks Concerning Hades.*[1] In fact, it was actually an excerpt from Hippolytus' (d. AD 236 CE) work, *Against Plato, on the Cause of the Universe.*[2] A Christian work two centuries after Jesus is not terribly helpful as background, but we're at least getting an early Christian understanding that fills in some details in Jesus' parable. Jesus' first hearers may have assumed some of this.

> 3. For there is one descent into this region, at whose gate we believe there stands an archangel with an host; which gate when those pass through that are conducted down by the angels appointed over souls, they do not go the same way; but the just are guided to the right hand, and are led with hymns, sung by the angels appointed over that place, unto a region of light, in which the just have dwelt from the beginning of the world; not constrained by necessity, but ever enjoying the prospect of the good things they see, and rejoice in the expectation of those new enjoyments which will be peculiar to every one of them, and esteeming those things beyond what we

1. Josephus, *Josephus's Discourse to the Greeks Concerning Hades,* 3–4.
2. Hippolytus, *Against the Greeks and Plato on the Universe.*

have here; with whom there is no place of toil, no burning heat, no piercing cold, nor are any briers there; but the countenance of the [fathers], and of the just, which they see, always smiles upon them, while they wait for that rest and eternal new life in heaven, which is to succeed this region. This place we call *The Bosom of Abraham.*

4. But as to the unjust, they are dragged by force to the left hand by the angels allotted for punishment, no longer going with a good-will, but as prisoners driven by violence; to whom are sent the angels appointed over them to reproach them and threaten them with their terrible looks, and to thrust them still downwards. Now those angels that are set over these souls drag them into the neighborhood of hell itself; who, when they are hard by it, continually hear the noise of it, and do not stand clear of the hot vapor itself; but when they have a near view of this spectacle, as of a terrible and exceeding great prospect of fire, they are struck with a fearful expectation of a future judgment, and in effect punished thereby: and not only so, but where they see the place [or choir] of the fathers and of the just, even hereby are they punished; for a chaos deep and large is fixed between them; insomuch that a just man that hath compassion upon them cannot be admitted, nor can one that is unjust, if he were bold enough to attempt it, pass over it.

Does this represent reality? Does it even represent first century Jewish cosmology? How did the tradition Jesus used come to be? Was he endorsing it as a revelation of what is? Or was he merely borrowing it for his own purposes, even undermining it somehow? I've read copious interpretations that have left me discontented, so I suppressed the urge to run to my bookshelves or turn to Google for help. Instead, I chose to practice what I preach by doing theology on my knees. Following an Ignatian exercise, I entered the parable with Jesus as Rabbi to inquire about its meaning. What follows is the conversation of the Master leading his student with thought-provoking questions. I do not claim divine inspiration or authority for the words that I heard. Neither do I take credit for the thoughts that emerge in contemplative prayer. It is what it is for your discernment. As for me, it brought peace to my heart. I hope it will have the same effect on you.

THE CONVERSATION

DISCIPLE: Rabbi, before I go rushing to the wisdom of others, I want to make space for you to reveal your heart regarding the parable of the rich man and Lazarus. You promised your Spirit would lead us into all truth, and you enlightened those on the road to Emmaus. Would you teach me?

RABBI: All right, sit with me. We will walk through it together. What do you see in the story? What is the point?

DISCIPLE: I see that the point of the story is more important than the descriptions. I see this being a parable about kingdom justice where those in agony in this life receive their comfort in the next. The rich man represents those whose luxury in this life—whether spiritual or material (for the religious leaders were the target)—was marked, not by generosity but by opulence and willful disregard for the poor (Isa 1; Ezek 16:49). In death, they will have their time in agony. Things are evened out and even reversed. Isaiah says that high places are brought low; valleys are raised up (Isa 40:3–5), if not here and now then after . . .

RABBI: What are you noticing?

DISCIPLE: That Isaiah's vision of justice includes a prophecy concerning John the Baptist.

RABBI: And?

DISCIPLE: The first verse following this parable is about the Law, prophets, God's kingdom, and St. John the forerunner. John came to proclaim the arrival of this great reversal in fortunes and the need to prepare for it through repentance.

RABBI: What does this point remind you of?

DISCIPLE: It reminds me of your "Sermon on the Plain":

> Looking at his disciples, he said:
> "Blessed are you who are poor, for yours is the kingdom of God.
> Blessed are you who hunger now, for you will be satisfied.

Blessed are you who weep now, for you will laugh.
Blessed are you when men hate you, when they exclude you and insult you
and reject your name as evil, because of the Son of Man.
Rejoice in that day and leap for joy, because great is your reward in heaven.
For that is how their fathers treated the prophets.
But woe to you who are rich, for you have already received your comfort.
Woe to you who are well fed now, for you will go hungry.
Woe to you who laugh now, for you will mourn and weep.
Woe to you when all men speak well of you,
for that is how their fathers treated the false prophets."
(Luke 6:20–26)

And it reminds me of Mary's "Magnificat":

And Mary said:
"My soul glorifies the Lord and my spirit rejoices in God my Savior,
for he has been mindful of the humble state of his servant.
From now on all generations will call me blessed,
for the Mighty One has done great things for me—holy is his name.
His mercy extends to those who fear him, from generation to generation.
He has performed mighty deeds with his arm;
he has scattered those who are proud in their inmost thoughts.
He has brought down rulers from their thrones but has lifted up the humble.
He has filled the hungry with good things but has sent the rich away empty.
He has helped his servant Israel, remembering to be merciful
to Abraham and his descendants forever, even as he said to our fathers."
(Luke 1:46–55)

I am noticing that the Jesus of Luke's Gospel saw kingdom justice very much in terms of economic redistribution . . . not just equalization but the total reversal of fortunes. I have often thought that justice is about bringing those under the table and those on top of the table to equal positions around the table, but in the parable and these texts, they swap positions completely.

RABBI: Why would God do that?

DISCIPLE: My gut feeling is that it is not punitive but pedagogical.[3] Jesus' listeners are to learn what the rich man should be learning.

RABBI: What would God hope to teach the rich man?

DISCIPLE: It feels like God is taking him through the painful process of removing serious character defects that have to do with narcissism, arrogance, and the idolatry of wealth.

RABBI: Very painful indeed. And why flames?

DISCIPLE: I suppose the traditional use of flame imagery is no more literal than Abraham's bosom. The flames represent the burning agony of his thirsty soul. The rich man is experiencing the agony of thirst and deprivation that Lazarus had known throughout life. He is being taught the pain of empathy for the poor, but he is also in agony because he still can't apprehend his real problem. He's fighting the process rather than surrendering to it. He still wants Lazarus to be his servant. He is still self-consumed. Even when his request for reprieve fails, his agenda is to help his brothers avoid pain rather than concern for the poor and needy. There is nothing that resembles repentance. That's why he's still there.

RABBI: True, but his thirsty soul reveals something more than a mirror image of Lazarus' earthly poverty. Were not the rich man's worldly idolatry, greed, and selfishness birthed in his own unsatisfied cravings? His perpetual lust for more was never filled—nor could it ever be—to the point where he could ever welcome Lazarus in.

DISCIPLE: I am also starting to see how this was prophetic for your indictment of the religious elite—their hoarding of spiritual wealth within the storehouse of their temple. The "house of prayer for all nations," far from being a light and a blessing for all who are thirsty, all who are weak (Isa 55:1), and all who were afar off (Isa 66:19), had become an exclusive and compromised center of oppressive religious and

---

3. See also Josephus, *Discourse to the Greeks*, 1. "This region is allotted as a place of custody for souls, in which angels are appointed as guardians to them, who distribute to them *temporary punishments*, agreeable to every one's behavior and manners."

political power. Outside remained a Lazarus-class of the poor and disabled, sinners and strangers. The ruling Sanhedrin *were* the "rich man"[4] (the Pharisees in Luke 16:1) who stepped over this collective Lazarus as they begged daily outside the temple gate (e.g., Acts 3:2). Within a generation, the situation would be flipped around in drastic fashion.

RABBI: Now, what about that un-crossable chasm?

DISCIPLE: I don't know. We were always taught that it was about eternity and the impossibility of postmortem salvation. It appears that way still, but (i) if we are seeing the rich man not in hell but in Hades or the grave; and (ii) the final judgment has not yet come; (iii) if his experience is corrective chastisement rather than everlasting punishment . . .

RABBI: Then . . .

DISCIPLE: Then he is going through a refiner's fire that will purge him of his impurity and prepare him to sit at the banqueting table *with* Lazarus—or, even better, to serve Lazarus at the table in appreciation.

RABBI: Appreciation?

DISCIPLE: For freedom from the bondage and blindness of Self, whereby he could not even notice Lazarus; for freedom from the love of wealth and luxury that required him to exclude those who might threaten it; for finally knowing what it is to have one's own soul-thirst sated.

RABBI: Perhaps his isolation in Hades gave him not only a taste of Lazarus' loneliness and isolation but also awakened him to his own earthly isolation behind the gates of wealth and power.

DISCIPLE: He couldn't be filled until he saw that he was empty. The flames revealed his agony as much as caused it. Looking into the abyss of your own heart is a fearful, hellish prospect. In fact, that is the abyss

---

4. Although the "rich man" in the previous parable (Luke 16:1–13) represents God, while the manager refers to the religious power base.

in which he found himself . . . the black hole of his own spiritual bankruptcy. But therein is his salvation. When he understands that his luxury was an illusion and realizes his thirst . . .

RABBI: But there is more to this chasm. It is fixed, and he cannot cross it yet.

DISCIPLE: I feel that the chasm is a spiritual parallel in death to the social chasm fixed in life by the rich man's caste. By making it impossible for the poor or the sinner to cross that great gulf into their pseudo-kingdoms and religious enclaves, the spiritually privileged were unwittingly defining their own distance from God's kingdom. It seems a very painful chastisement. Yet I don't see many redemptive hints in the story. In fact, there's a sense of hopelessness to it. Acknowledging thirst isn't repentance; it is only the first step home, and the impossible gorge remains.

RABBI: That's true. The story was not meant to describe how redemption from Hades works any more than it was meant to describe how torment in Hades works. The point is that with the coming of the Baptist's prophesied kingdom, those in positions of spiritual or material wealth are in for the great upheaval. Not just in death—in their lifetimes. But they are still alive to hear and heed the warning of the law and prophets. The parable is a call to turn from the idolatry of Self and toward sharing the same cup of cold water now that they will otherwise crave in futility later.

DISCIPLE: So this story is obviously not about the eternal lake of fire?

RABBI: Of course not. It is death. It is Hades. And on the final Day of Judgment, death and Hades are thrown into the lake of fire (Rev 20:14). Then comes the great banquet to which all the thirsty are invited.

DISCIPLE: Even the rich man? Will he be able to come? Will he still be invited?

RABBI: It is possible. In the right robes, yes, all will be welcome.

Excursus 1: The Rich Man and Lazarus

DISCIPLE: Will those who did not want to come now—the ones who so offended the Master by declining the invitation—will they answer the call then?

RABBI: It is possible. When they are poor enough in spirit. When their parched hearts set themselves to pilgrimage for Zion's living waters (Ps 84).

DISCIPLE: How long?

RABBI: As long as it takes.

DISCIPLE: Even beyond Judgment Day?

RABBI: The gates of the Holy City will never be shut. The Spirit and the Bride will always say, "Come."

DISCIPLE: Then blessed are the poor in spirit,

RABBI: For theirs is the kingdom of heaven. You can become poor in spirit now by following me. The way to Zion follows me through the Beatitudes and the Sermon on the Mount. Obedience to that program empowers recovery from every addiction by systematically stripping the self of ego. It bankrupts you, leaving you powerless and thirsty enough to crave only God's table. For those who die and slip into Hades without completing the course, that process continues. This is where we find the rich man, and this is the peril against which I am warning. In other words, repent, for the kingdom of God is at hand.

DISCIPLE: It sounds like you are describing purgatory.

RABBI: Some call it that. And some who call it that are confused. Malachi the prophet calls God's cleansing day a "refiner's fire" or "launderer's soap" (Mal 3:2). All will be salted by fire (Mark 9:49), some in life, some in death, and others on the Day (1 Cor 3:11–13).

DISCIPLE: But as I read somewhere, "There is a deeper magic at work here," even deeper than Hades.

RABBI: Yes. I hold the keys to death and Hades (Rev 1:18). As it is written, "Since the children have flesh and blood, he, too, shared in their humanity so that by his death he might destroy him who holds the power of death—that is, the devil—and free those who all their lives were held in slavery by their fear of death" (Heb 2:14–15). I entered the depths of Hades, binding the strongman and plundering his goods (Matt 12:27–29). In life, death, and resurrection, I descended to the lower regions and led out a host of captives (Eph 4:8–10). Hades, even for the rich man, is not the last word. I AM. Does this satisfy?

DISCIPLE: Yes, Rabbi. For now.

6

The Biblical Possibility of Ultimate Redemption

THE WARNINGS OF REAL and actual judgment notwithstanding, another set of texts foretell ultimate and universal redemption in language that extends well beyond the limits of historic infernalism. Typically, we import the warning language of infernalist passages as caveats to limit these texts. The effect is that we largely diminish or negate their intended power. But what if we allowed them to have their full impact? What if we simply accepted them as truly meaning *all*?

BIBLICAL TEXTS ON ULTIMATE REDEMPTION FOR ALL

John 12:31–32—Now is the time for judgment on this world; now the prince of this world will be driven out. But I, when I am lifted up from the earth, will draw *all men* to myself.

Rom 5:18–19—Consequently, just as the result of one trespass was condemnation for all men, so also the result of one act of righteousness was justification that brings life for *all men*. For just as through the disobedience of the one man the many were made sinners, so also through the obedience of the one man the many will be made righteous.

Rom 11:32, 36—For God has bound all men over to disobedience so that he may have mercy on them *all*. . . . For from him and through him and to him are *all things*. To him be the glory forever! Amen.

1 Cor 15:25–28—For he must reign until he has put all his enemies under his feet. The last enemy to be destroyed is death. For he "has put everything under his feet." Now when it says that "everything" has been put under him, it is clear that this does not include God himself, who put everything under Christ. When he has done this,

then the Son himself will be made subject to him who put every-thing under him, so that God may be *all in all*.

Phil 2:9–11—Therefore God exalted him to the highest place and gave him the name that is above every name, that at the name of Jesus *every* knee should bow, in heaven and on earth and under the earth, and *every* tongue confess that Jesus Christ is Lord, to the glory of God the Father.

Eph 1:9–10—And he made known to us the mystery of his will according to his good pleasure, which he purposed in Christ, to be put into effect when the times will have reached their fulfillment—to bring *all things* in heaven and on earth together under one head, even Christ.

Col 1:15–19—He is the image of the invisible God, the firstborn over all creation. For by him *all things* were created: things in heav-en and on earth, visible and invisible, whether thrones or powers or rulers or authorities; *all things* were created by him and for him. He is before *all things*, and in him *all things* hold together. And he is the head of the body, the church; he is the beginning and the firstborn from among the dead, so that in *everything* he might have the supremacy. For God was pleased to have all his fullness dwell in him, and through him to reconcile to himself *all things*, whether things on earth or things in heaven, by making peace through his blood, shed on the Cross.

1 John 2:2—He is the atoning sacrifice for our sins, and not only for ours but also for the sins of the *whole world*.

1 Tim 4:9–10—This is a trustworthy saying that deserves full ac-ceptance (and for this we labor and strive), that we have put our hope in the living God, who is the Savior of *all men*, and especially of those who believe.

THE BREADTH OF REDEMPTION IN UNIVERSALIST TEXTS

Ultimate Redemption (Versus Either Infernalism or General Universalism)

If we take these passages seriously—not just as the flip side of judgment but as ultimate truth—then we may infer two convictions: First, God's mercy will trump all of his judgments to redeem all of creation. Second, his work of redemption is based not merely on his magnanimity but on the work of his Son. The death and resurrection of Christ will ultimately make all things well.

Universal Reconciliation (Versus a Remnant Elect)

These passages extend the work of forgiveness and reconciliation to all. Christ's atonement is unlimited and applies universally. All have already been reconciled through the Cross so that all will eventually be drawn into the life of Christ.

Inclusive Salvation (Versus Exclusion)

Christ is heralded as the Savior of all mankind, indeed of the whole cosmos. His reign will ultimately include the bowed heart and worshiping knee of every being on, above, and under the earth. This is presented not merely as the begrudging submission of defeated foes but rather the all-embracing confession that God is glorified through Jesus Christ.

Unilateral Grace/Jesus' Gift (Versus Conditional /our Faith-response to Jesus)

The above texts insist that Christ's saving, forgiving, reconciling work pre-dates any response on our part. A faith-response is not treated as a way to become saved but rather as a response of hopeful gratitude to Christ's saving work. Response matters greatly to our journey, for grace obligates us to receive the saving gift as prescribed. Even so, while faith, justification, sanctification, and glorification are real-life processes, Jesus alone authored the journey, and Jesus alone will bring it to perfect completion (Heb 12:2).

Instant (the Day of the Lord) or Inevitable (the Journey)

Some texts indicate either a virtually instant completion to our salvation process on a single Day of the Lord (whether we are first cleansed by fire or simply welcomed in). Others are more reminiscent of the journeys taken in C. S. Lewis' speculative novel *The Great Divorce*. In Rev 21–22, we see that the wicked may still begin outside the gates, wash their robes in blood, then enter the city, partake of healing leaves, and finally enjoy the waters of life. Such a process could conceivably take ages (e.g., "age-long correction," as taught by Gregory of Nyssa on Matthew 25). The point is that in the end, every spiritual pilgrimage is ultimately summed up in Jesus.

Our Journey Home (Prodigal Son) and His Journey to Find Us (Lost Sheep)

Whether the process of salvation looks like a lost son returning home to his father or a shepherd going out to pursue the lost sheep, God's commitment as Father is to welcome everyone into his house and to continue seeking and saving every lost soul until they are found (Luke 15:4). Again, these texts present that mission as incomplete until all are found and brought home.

As a young evangelical, I was taught that death interrupts God's saving mission for each individual, cuts short the journey of our lives. We did not see these passages as truly universal because, "It is appointed unto men once to die, and after that the judgment," with salvation only available to "them who look for him" (Heb 9:27–28). These two verses virtually swept away or negated the passages we've just pondered. Death, not God, gets the last word and determines our fate, whether or not we really apprehended the Gospel.

But don't these texts actually speak clearly of something grander and more enduring than death or judgment? We die, then judgment (in whatever form) . . . then God, then mercy. Or, just as simply, what if the last great judgment (verdict) of God is mercy? Each of these verses declares that possibility with the loud voice of a final trumpet. After all, is there any power greater than the flaming love of God?

> Song 8:6–7—Place me like a seal over your heart, like a seal on your arm; for love is as strong as death, its jealousy unyielding as the grave. It burns like blazing fire, like a mighty flame. Many waters cannot quench love; rivers cannot wash it away. If one were to give all the wealth of his house for love, it would be utterly scorned.

THE CROSSROADS OF TODAY'S CHOICES

If we take these texts as true, real, and universal possibilities, then the warnings of judgment cannot be presumed as foregone, conclusive descriptions of what must be. Rather, they stand as portents of a path that no one ought to pursue alongside an assurance that God's love gets the last word. As Rahner says, the NT passages that present an either/or dualism are to be read from the crossroads of today's choices, not as a preview or report of what's to come:

> Insofar as it is a report, it is rather a disclosure of the situation in which the persons addressed are actually found. They are placed before a decision in which the consequences are irrevocable. They can be lost forever if they reject God's offer of salvation. . . . We must maintain side by side, and unwaveringly the truth of the omnipotence of the universal salvific will of God, the redemption of all by Christ, the duty of all men to hope for salvation and also the true possibility of eternal loss. . . . [T]he emphasis on the possibility of hell as perpetual obduracy must be paralleled by insistent encouragement to rely with confidence on the infinite mercy of God.[1]

Open possibilities must be maintained in tension, because we insist that in this life, all are under the judgment of having to choose. All are in the valley of decision. Not that there must be two kinds of people (saved and damned) but that everyone has two kinds of options. There is no easy integration of infernalist and universalist texts precisely because they represent these options as truly optional.

ATTEMPTS AT HARMONIZING THE POSSIBILITIES

Still, the imagined need to defend the authority of the Bible through forced harmonization of infernalist and universalist (or dualist versus monist[2]) passages has led to at least three interpretive approaches:

1. Negate or Qualify One or the Other

Infernalists tend to qualify inclusive phrases like "all things," "all men," "everything visible and invisible," and so on, reducing their expansive promises to mean "all of the elect," "all who believe" or "all who remain after the great exclusion." The limits are inferred or implied not so much by the immediate context but by the broader scope of Scriptures that exclude the unbeliever, whether by annihilation or eternal punishment.

---

1. Karl Rahner, "Hell," 603–4.

2. In current discussions on divine judgment and hell, "dualism" refers to any eschatology that divides humanity into two groups (the saved and unsaved, elect or damned) and two destinies (heaven/hell). Monism in this context refers to an eschatology where all people are eventually redeemed to one place or state (eternal life with God).

Universalists make similar moves in reverse, capsizing the judgment texts into the deep ocean of God's love and thereby dowsing hell's flames. In essence, each group says to the other, my verse outweighs yours. Your truth is conditioned by mine.

2. Treat them as consecutive events

Traditional universalists acknowledge initially the possibility of divine judgment, but only as penultimate and restorative. Yes, there is a final judgment, and yes, some will be damned. But then after that, immediately or eventually, even the damned will finally come enter the New Jerusalem and join the Bride. Similarly, infernalists grant that universal salvation is initially offered to the whole world—then comes the end when humanity is divided into its respective compartments. The former view sees two groups of people (righteous and wicked) becoming one (the redeemed). The latter views sees one group (humans) being divided into two (the saved and the damned).

3. Treat Them as Hypothetical Possibilities

This group, represented by many in the early church and in modern Catholicism, insists in the real possibility that anyone can hypothetically choose for or against Christ. Thus, hell must potentially exist, but so too the hope that it might be empty. The final Day of Judgment has not yet come, so eternal damnation is purely provisional at this stage. An individual death may seal one's fate forever, but it remains to be seen what God's love and power might accomplish at the last. Dire consequences affirmed, we nevertheless insist that God is not a Medo-Persian monarch bound by ordinances bigger than the kindness of his heart.

TREMBLING BEFORE THE WORD

Thus ends our survey of the grand breadth of biblical words and descriptions for hell. Were you able to see some of the texts "again, for the first time?" Did you find yourself tempted to dismiss some of the texts too quickly as not really meaning what they say, just because they didn't align well with your tradition? Were you prone to prying difficult passages into doctrinal straitjackets along the way? Or were you humbled nearly to the point of agnosticism about it all? Maybe you just knew it all. Careful! Fixing the Scriptures into crossword-like patterns may just strangle them.

What is God's heart for us as we come to the text? It is written, "This is the one I esteem: he who is humble and contrite in spirit, and *trembles* at my word" (Isa 66:2b).

Great Christian minds—some trembling, others far too confident—have been sorting through this wealth of material throughout the ages. In the following section, we'll track some of the major historical trends, noting that when it comes to hell and judgment, the diversity of Scripture has made doctrinal uniformity very elusive indeed.

PART TWO

"Every Knee Shall Bow"

Presumptions and Possibilities
in Theological Tradition

7

Possibility and Hope in the Early Church

LITURGICAL HOPE

As I understand pre-Nicene Christianity, the Church at large believed in the reality of their options: that either heaven or hell were real possibilities, depending on how we respond to the Gospel of Jesus Christ. At the same time, they demonstrated their hope in God's mercy through their prayers for the salvation of all people. Scholars and pastors may believe that good theology begins with them and trickles down through lecterns and pulpits to the laypeople, who respond with worship and prayer. In truth, the best theology is a descriptive response to what God is revealing through the praying, worshiping church as it responds to the Scriptures and the Spirit. If the writers, preachers, and professors can keep up, so much the better. Thus, the history of early Christian theology concerning God's judgments and God's mercy might best begin with the liturgy (prayer in the context of community worship).

The Church powerfully embraced the apostles' assurance that God is not willing that anyone should perish but that everyone should come to repentance (2 Pet 3:9). They knew that God desires everyone to be saved (1 Tim 2:4) and that this begins with this urgent exhortation, that "requests, prayers, intercession and thanksgiving be made for everyone" (1 Tim 2:1). And so they did. Since its inception, the church has prayed for the salvation of everyone, both in this life and on Judgment Day, including the dead!

This begs the question: Why pray for the dead? And which dead? Up until the time of Augustine, the answer would have been rather simple: We cannot presume upon the damnation or salvation of anyone, so we pray mercy for ourselves and for everyone who stands before God.

The basis of our hope is the infinite mercy of the One enthroned on the judgment seat.

> From [our] position under judgment, the liturgy not only of the earliest centuries but of all Christian times can only repeat incessantly the prayer of supplication to be rescued, through God's grace, from becoming lost and to be led into heaven. It is important here that the word *"infernum"* was long able to signify, without further differentiation, not only the "netherworld," the "kingdom of the death" (Sheol) and its lost souls, but also the Christian "hell" in its narrowest sense. Without exception, the liturgical texts turn to God with the plea to be led out of the world of lost souls and into salvation and blessedness, whether they speak on behalf of those still living or of the deceased. They would like "to be rescued from eternal damnation" (*Gelasianum* III, 17, 1247), "free [his soul] from the place of punishment" (ibid., 91, 1621), "that we may suffer in time rather than undergo eternal torments" (*Gregorianum* 71, 1), "that the threatened vengeance may pass over into salvation" (vet. *Gelasianum* I, 43, 440), "whom you rescued from the abode of perpetual death" (*Gelasianum* I, 57), "(God) who redeemed both sexes from the destruction of everlasting death" (*Gelasianum*, ed. Cagin, 1850), "who wishes no one to perish" (*Gelasianum* I, 41, 413), "may you rescue the souls of your servants from the *flame* of your burning fire" (*Mozarabicus Liber ordinum* 427) and so on.[1]

This is not to deny the prolific use of fire and brimstone from early church pulpits. Justin Martyr, Tertullian, Chrysostom, and others were eloquent in their threats of eternal hell. Far from incinerating prayers of hope, such rhetoric intentionally fueled them with greater earnestness. They were unwilling to eradicate or minimize hell to avoid the horror of the thought. Instead, the idea of hell served to illustrate the seriousness of God's offer of love over the wrath we deserve. They did not consign others to hell but called on the faithful to carefully examine their hearts and lives, casting themselves upon the mercy of Christ.

Nor were the Fathers naive literalists. From Origen (*Peri Archon 2*, 10:4–5) to Chrysostom (*Matt Hom.* 23:7–8) to early Augustine (*De Genesi* 12:32, 61–62), they recognized hell's flaming sulfur and gnawing worms as spiritual afflictions or states of mind rather than an actual lake of fire, the chief torment being banishment from Christ's presence.

---

1. von Balthasar, *Dare We Hope?*, 48–49.

POSTHUMOUS SALVATION

Somehow, the early church was able to balance the dire warnings of its preaching with the passionate prayers of its liturgy, embracing hope for God's mercy even if it required posthumous rescue from judgment. They knew and preached the warning of Heb 9:27–28 ("We die once, and after that we face judgment"—"judgment" being more loaded, worrisome, *and* hopeful than a simple "verdict"). There was an urgency when they shared 2 Cor 6:2 ("Now is the time of God's favor. Now is the day of salvation"). But a good number of early Christians saw no contradiction in hoping that non-Christians could also be saved posthumously, if necessary.

This list may include both Peter and Paul, but we also see evidence of this belief in many other early authors: the writers of the *Apocalypse of Peter,* the second *Sibylline Oracle, The Acts of Paul and Thecla, The Life and Miracles of St. Thecla,* Clement of Alexandria, Perpetua, Origen, Gregory of Nyssa, Evagrius Ponticus, Jerome, the tow Aviti from Spain, Vincentius Victor, and pseudo-John Damascene. We also see this hope emerge in hagiography about of the efficacy of prayers of righteous people, as in the Gregory the Great/Trajan legends.[2] Many others believed that posthumous salvation, if at no other time, had at least occurred on Easter weekend with the descent of Christ into Hades.

Meanwhile, masses of regular Christians continued to pray expectantly for God's mercy for their lost loved ones who had gone to the grave unbaptized. The hope inherent in early church prayers for mercy naturally led to speculation that God is able and willing to finally answer them in every case, the reality of hell notwithstanding! Even the vilest offender who had never truly believed might become a candidate for redemption if God's heart for mercy were to conspire with our prayers for mercy. Is such speculative, universalist optimism rooted in genuine orthodox hope, or was it a manifestation of denial and presumption? That question has led to a long and winding trail of dialogue and debate that I will now summarize all too briefly at the risk of reductionism. Imagine a theological symphony in three movements: mercy proposed, judgment presumed, and hope dared.

---

2. Cf. Trumbower, *Rescue for the Dead,* ch. 8. Basically, Gregory the Great (Pope from AD 590–604) prays for the salvation of Emperor Trajan (who ruled Rome from 98–117 BC) after his death. Trumbower recounts other famous prayers for the dead, esp. Thecla's prayer for Falconilla (ch. 3), Perpetua's prayer for Dinocrates (ch. 4).

8

Mercy Proposed

Apokatastasis *in Clement, Origen, and Gregory*

WHEN DEALING WITH "THE redemption of all things" (*apokatastasis*, Acts 3:21) in the writings of the Church Fathers, some instinctively rush straight to Origen and Gregory of Nyssa,[1] bandying about the term "universalist" rather loosely. But, ultimate redemption (more accurately) permeated the thought of many of the Church Fathers, so much that the view was often taken for granted.[2] Origen and Gregory were two of only a few who dealt with the subject directly rather than only in passing. It is an infernalist mistake to separate Gregory and Origen from the rest, as if they were exceptions to the rule and atypical. Likewise, universalists may selectively quote the Fathers as if they all believed in ultimate redemption. In reality, no consensus won the day. The possibility of universal salvation was discussed in the most depth in Alexandria, beginning with Clement and Origen, whose influence extended to the great Gregory of Nyssa and his siblings.

Ironically, given the charge of universalism, neither man denied the existence of hell or the necessity that some should enter its gates. In fact, unlike the infernalists, they saw that *all* who would enter paradise must pass through the river or lake of fire as the Israelites had to pass through the Red Sea. They warned of the possibility that once the righteous passed through the waters, the unrepentant, like Pharaoh's armies, would be engulfed therein.[3] They heard in John the Baptist that in addi-

1. This is probably because they are the most famous proponents of *apokatastasis*, Origen in his undeserved infamy and Gregory because he was so highly regarded.

2. For an excellent survey of primary sources, see Hanson, *Universalism the Prevailing Doctrine*.

3. Origen, *Commentary on Luke*. Hom. 24. Cf. Le Goff, *The Birth of Purgatory*, 53–54 for citation and context.

tion to the baptism of water and the Spirit, entry to the coming kingdom requires a baptism of fire (Luke 3:16).[4] Yet as sensitive philosophers, they discerned that God is the consuming fire of pure spirit, not literal flames. God cleanses our hearts of impurity to prepare a suitable temple for his glory in each of us, both now and for the next life.

> But let us reflect that God does indeed consume and utterly destroy; that He consumes evil thoughts, wicked actions, and sinful desires, when they find their way into the minds of believers; and that, inhabiting along with His Son those souls which are rendered capable of receiving His word and wisdom, according to His own declaration, "I and the Father shall come, and We shall make our abode with him." He makes them, after all their vices and passions have been consumed, a holy temple, worthy of Himself.[5]

CLEMENT OF ALEXANDRIA: ON CHASTISEMENT VERSUS PUNISHMENT

Clement's importance, in my mind, is that he clarifies the NT language for "punishment."[6] Clement insists that God's "correction" (*paideia*—Heb 12:9) and "chastisement" (*kolasis*—Matt 25:46) is as a loving Father, only and always meant for the healing and salvation of the whole world. He denies that God ever inflicts "punishment" (*timōria*—Heb 10:29—vengeance) in the vengeful sense, a word Jesus never used. Watch how Clement ties judgment to correction with a view to universal redemption:

> For all things are arranged with a view to the salvation of the universe by the Lord of the universe, both generally and particularly. . . . But necessary corrections, through the goodness of the great overseeing Judge, both by the attendant angels, and by various acts of anticipative judgment, and by the perfect judgment, compel egregious sinners to repent.[7]

One way or another, God wills for all to be saved and executes perfect plans tailor-made to funnel each of us into God's redeeming love.

---

4. Origen, *Homily 3* on Ps 36. Le Goff, 53–54.

5. Origen, *De Princ.*1.1.1 (ANF 4).

6. Cf. esp. *Paed.* 1.5; 1.8 (ANF 2).

7. *Strom.*7.2 (ANF 2).

"And not only for our sins,"—that is for those of the faithful, is the Lord the propitiator, does he say, "but also for the whole world." He, indeed, saves all; but some [He saves], converting them by punishments; others, however, who follow voluntarily [He saves] with dignity of honour; so "that every knee should bow to Him, of things in heaven, and things on earth, and things under the earth;" that is, angels, men, and souls that before His advent have departed from this temporal life.[8]

One can see how Clement read God's corrective acts through the parental love emphasized in Heb 12:5–11, where we read that God disciplines those that he loves as dear children. For Clement, Providence uses corrections (*padeiai*) or chastisements (*kolasis*) when we fall away, but only for our good, only for our salvation. But God does not punish (*timōria*), which is retaliation for evil.[9]

God deals with sin through correction, not punishment. That's Clement, that's Hebrews, that's Hosea. The chastisements of God are disciplinary: not because divine justice demands satisfaction (Anselm, *Cur Deus Homo*), payback, or wrath (Calvin, penal satisfaction!), but because God is raising beloved children who tend to learn the hard way. The hardest lesson we learn is the lesson of the Cross: the horrible revelation that it was each of us who crucified perfect Love (Zech 12:10), yet in love God forgave us (1 John 4:9–10). This is more than learning by moral influence. The Cross is a revelation of God's love, our violence, and Jesus' power to forgive and redeem—all at once. Don't miss this point, because it marks a major fork in the theological trail. For centuries, I fear that we veered when Clement actually had it right.

Where Clement takes this to the nth degree is in suggesting that God's mercy extends the opportunity for revelation beyond the grave, since sinners released from the delusions of this life are more apt to comprehend the truth:

> If, accordingly, to all, then all who believe shall be saved, although they may be of the Gentiles, on making their profession there; since God's punishments are saving and disciplinary, leading to conversion, and choosing rather the repentance than the death of a sinner; and especially since souls, although darkened by passions,

8. *On 1 John* 2:2, Fragments, 1.3 (ANF 2).

9. *Strom.* 7.16 (ANF 2).

when released from their bodies, are able to perceive more clearly, because of their being no longer obstructed by the paltry flesh.[10]

ORIGEN OF ALEXANDRIA: *APOKATASTASIS/AIŌNIOS*

apokatastasis

For all of his theological brilliance and prolific writing as a distinguished church father and head of the catechetical school in Alexandria, Origen is infamous for being condemned as a heretic (much later under Justinian) for repudiating the doctrine of eternal hell. He was neither the first nor the last to propose ultimate redemption, but he became known for his teaching on *apokatastasis* from Acts 3:20–21: "And he shall send Jesus Christ, which before was preached unto you: whom heaven must receive until the times of restitution of all things (*apokatastaseos panton*)."

Apokatastasis is a theological extrapolation of the final phrase in verse twenty-one. It is the doctrine of ultimate redemption that believes a time will come when all things (the whole cosmos) will be saved by grace. This includes creation, the lost, the fallen angels, and for some, even the devil. It is a question of how far God is willing to extend restitution to "all things." The logic is simple and powerful: when God is finally "all in all" and everything is "summed up in Christ," evil will cease to exist. Finally, all free creatures will enjoy truly free will because every deception, delusion, and denial; every wound and every resistance to the love of God will be swept away by the light of truth. Who then would not freely bow in worship and adoration? Before the unveiled revelation of the Lord Jesus, even Satan could no longer deceive himself. In that moment, would he repent? Would he be forgiven?

In truth, while Alexandria provided an atmosphere of free and open speculation, Origen took care to approach *apokatastasis* hypothetically rather than dogmatically, offering Scripture-based proposals and leaving final judgment to the reader. Still, in *On First Principles,* he proposed that the "outer darkness" of the gospels (Matt 8:12) speaks metaphorically of spiritual ignorance, after which there comes a remedy:

> There is a resurrection of the dead, and there is punishment, but not everlasting. For when the body is punished the soul is gradu- ally purified, and so is restored to its ancient rank. For all wicked

---

10. *Strom.* 6.6. See also *Strom.* 6.14; 7.2; 7.16 (ANF 2).

men, and for daemons, too, shall be restored to their former rank. (Origen, *On First Principles* 146)[11]

aiōnios

Origen's universalism acknowledges, with Christ and Paul, that we shall all pass through the fire but that its punishments shall be curative[12] and complete "unto the ages of ages" (*eis tous aiōnas ton aiōnon*).

> Origen declares that Gehenna is an analogue of the Valley of Hinnom and connotes a purifying fire but intimates that it is not prudent to go further; showing that the idea of "reserve" controlled him from saying what might not be judicious. That God's fire is not material, but spiritual remorse ending in reformation, Origen teaches in many passages. He repeatedly speaks of punishment as *aiōnion* (mistranslated in the NT "everlasting," "eternal") and then elaborately states and defends as Christian doctrine universal salvation beyond all *aiōnion* [ages], suffering and sin.[13]

Although Origen was later condemned for his alleged doctrine of "the restoration of all things," others among the most influential Fathers were never condemned, even though they openly advocated the *apokatastasis*— as did Clement of Alexandria, Gregory of Nyssa, Didymus the Blind, and Jerome prior to his feud with Rifinus—or, more discreetly, propagated it as something that only mature Christians could accept, as did Gregory Nazianzen and Maximus the Confessor.[14]

GREGORY OF NYSSA AND THE CAPPADOCIAN FATHERS[15]

Gregory foresaw judgment as a potentially lengthy cleansing process, taking seriously the *kolasin aiōnion* of Matt 25, not as eternal punishment but

---

11. See also "Just as you do not punish a servant or a slave whom you punish simply out of a desire to torture, but so that, by means of his distress, he may change, so God also punishes, by making them suffer distress, those who have been changed by reason and have not been healed." (Origen, *Homily 12 on Jeremiah*, 183.

12. See also Origen, *Contra Cels.* 4.11–13; 5.15–16; 6.26, 44; 8.72; 10.17; 13.16; 47.14–15 (ANF 4).

13. Hanson, *Universalism*, 10.3 para. 1.

14. Cf. von Balthasar, *Dare We Hope?*, 63.

15. Gregory's siblings (Basil of Caesarea and St Macrina) and his colleague, Gregory of Nazianzus, collectively.

something more like "age-lasting correction," culminating in the ultimate salvation of all. Nor was he shy about his universalism.

> When death, and corruption, and darkness, and every other off-shoot of evil had grown into the nature of the author of evil, the approach of the Divine power, acting like fire and making that unnatural accretion to disappear, thus by purgation of the evil becomes a blessing to that nature, though the separation is agonizing. For it is now as with those who for their cure are subjected to the knife and the cautery; they are angry with the doctors, and wince with the pain of the incision; but if recovery of health be the result of this treatment, and the pain of the cautery passes away, they will feel grateful to those who have wrought this cure upon them. *In like manner, when, after long periods of time, the evil of our nature, which now is mixed up with it and has grown with its growth, has been expelled, and when there has been a restoration of those who are now lying in Sin to their primal state, a harmony of thanksgiving will arise from all creation, as well from those who in the process of the purgation have suffered chastisement, as from those who needed not any purgation at all.*[16]

This is striking, considering he is known as the "Father of the Fathers," "the Flower of Orthodoxy," and the great defender of the Nicene Creed. Unlike Origen, his bold teachings are far from condemned, and he is revered across the board. Because he was so cherished for defending orthodoxy against heretics like the Arians, I suspect he was given a measure of latitude in his boldness concerning *apokatastasis* that was not afforded to Origen.

Most remarkable are Gregory's dialogues with his older sister and teacher St. Macrina the Younger, whose deathbed wisdom he shares in his treatise *On the Soul and Resurrection*. As Macrina and Gregory mourn the death of their brother Basil and anticipate her own passing, their thoughts turn to life beyond the veil. Her confidence in God's relentless grace, even if it takes eons, is powerful:

> His end is one, and one only; it is this: when the complete whole of our race shall have been perfected from the first man to the last,—some having at once in this life been cleansed from evil, others having afterwards in the necessary periods been healed by the Fire, others having in their life here been unconscious equally of good and of evil,—to offer to every one of us participation in

16. *The Great Catechism* 26 (NPNF-2 5).

the blessings which are in Him, which, the Scripture tells us, "eye hath not seen, nor ear heard," nor thought ever reached. But this is nothing else . . . but to be in God Himself. [17]

Understand how privileged we are to overhear the hope of this tender moment. Imagine: one of history's greatest theologians—a central figure in deciding and defending what Christians believe—Gregory now sits at the bedside of this sister and teacher to whom he owes so much. With one foot and an eye already at the threshold of the life to come, she speaks quietly of the extent of *apokatastasis:*

> When evil shall have been some day annihilated in the long revolutions of the ages, nothing shall be left outside the world of goodness, but that even from those evil spirits shall rise in harmony the confession of Christ's Lordship. If this is so, then no one can compel us to see any spot of the underworld in the expression, "things under the earth"; the atmosphere spreads equally over every part of the earth, and there is not a single corner of it left unrobed by this circumambient air. [18]

Others, like Pseudo-Dionysius, regarded *apokatastasis* as one supreme act on the Day of the Lord, in harmony with passages like Mal 3, 4 and 1 Cor 3.

> [The Cause of All] is "all in all," as Scripture affirms, and certainly he is to be praised as being for all things the creator and originator, the One who brings them to completion, their preserver, their protector, and their home, the power which returns them to itself, and all this in the one single, irrepressible, and supreme act. [19]

HERE, THERE, OR IN THE AIR

Thus, we have a lineage of biblical prophets, Jesus, his apostles, and early church patristics who held forth the real expectation of a fiery judgment of purification—corrective, cleansing, and healing in nature—often identified as the glory and love of God himself. Among these, we note distinctions in conviction or emphasis over who, when, or how we might undergo the divine forge. By way of summary, to hear their voices in concert,

---

17. *On the Soul and Resurrection* (NPNF-2 5).

18. *On the Soul and Resurrection* (NPNF-2 5).

19. Pseudo-Dionysius the Areopagite, *On Divine Names,* 1.596c–597a.

1. We may endure fiery trials in this life.

2. We may experience a cleansing process in the intermediate state between death and resurrection.

3. We may be cleansed by fire in one glorious moment on the Day of Judgment.

4. We may undergo a period of purification after and as a result of the Day of Judgment.

Where these believers converged was on the hopeful prospect that the judgments of God are merciful acts purposed to cleanse what has already been forgiven, changing us from glory to glory for an eternity of union with God. As we shall see though, their speculative hope stirred up worries of presumption and the attending reactions.

9

Judgment Presumed

Infernalism in Augustine, Calvin, and Evangelical Tradition

One door and only one and yet its sides are two.
I'm on the inside, on which side are you?

—Sunday School Chorus

IN SPITE OF THE Early Fathers' clear warnings that redemption would include a fiery trial of judgment, their jump from hopes to hypotheses raised valid pastoral flags concerning potential presumption. For those who presume upon grace and give no thought to hell, what becomes of their belief in the Gospel (do they need to believe?), their place in the Church (is there a point?), or their behavior in this life (does it matter?)? Augustine to the rescue! Sort of. . . . As a highly concerned shepherd, Augustine let his hyper-commitment to guarding the flock against dangerous assumptions draw him into some of his own. Here was just one of his many worries:

> To the same purpose they [those who presume on grace] think the apostle said, For God has concluded all men in unbelief, that He may have mercy upon all, Romans 11:32 signifying that no one should be condemned by God. And yet they who hold this opinion do not extend it to the acquittal or liberation of the devil and his angels. Their human tenderness is moved only toward men, and they plead chiefly their own cause, holding out false hopes of impunity to their own depraved lives by means of this quasi compassion of God to the whole race. Consequently they who promise this impunity even to the prince of the devils and his satellites make a still fuller exhibition of the mercy of God.[1]

1. Augustine, *City of God,* 21.18.

Hans Urs von Balthasar describes Augustine's dilemma and how his reaction causes an inevitable stumble into excessive and unbiblical measures:

> It was part of his loving care for human souls that he saw himself forced to cast his warning of possibility of becoming lost in so extreme a mold. His campaign was directed not only against laxity but also, and quite rightly so, against the presumptuous hope of the great Church Fathers mentioned above that Christians, even when they were grievous sinners, would not need to have any fear of final condemnation. This had to be corrected. It is only regrettable that this great man, to whom posterity owes so much, did not do that within the limits laid down by the Gospel.[2]

The irony here is that the Alexandrians' hopeful speculations about how all might eventually be saved motivated Augustine's resistance and also provided him with the furnace for his own solution. He trumped one presumption with two others. His opposition to what he feared would become unbounded universalism led him to create an ironclad infernalism of (i) double-predestination and (ii) a doctrine of punitive purgatory.

Thus, Le Goff actually credits Clement and Origen as co-founders with Augustine of the doctrine of purgatory.[3] He sees in these Greek Fathers a fusion of Greek philosophy (chastisement as education and salvation) and the biblical imagery of fire as divine instrument. The difference comes down to the respective agenda of each side. In historical context, the Alexandrians were demonstrating how Christ was the ultimate answer to both the expectations of the Hebrew prophets and the questions of the Greek philosophers. They proclaimed Jesus as Savior of the world, fulfilling Israel's chosen purpose, and they integrated the OT imagery of the fire of God with the NT Gospel of Christ as Light of the Nations. It appears to me that their exegesis, their philosophy, their teaching—even their battles with the heretics—all served a ministry of evangelism at a pivotal point in history.

On the other hand, Augustine wrote, preached, argued, and theologized as a concerned pastor. His agenda was to guide and guard his flock from the real-life perils that he had escaped through his radical conversion from debauchery. He was not about to allow the worldliness that he experienced as a young man to take root in the church through seeds of

---

2. von Balthasar, *Dare We Hope?*, 71.
3. Le Goff, *Birth of Purgatory*, 52–53.

presumption or sentimentalism. In his warnings, perhaps Augustine also felt he was donning a prophetic mantle reminiscent of Jesus' warning letters to the seven churches in Revelation.

He devoted an entire book (*The City of God*, 21) to reinforcing the reality of hell, preaching its punishments,[4] and arguing that it is eternal.[5] He countered the broader hope for redemption of his forbearers with presumptuous claims to knowledge about eternal judgment for many specific groups of people. He claimed to be able to prove that human bodies may last forever, unconsumed and alive in a fire.[6] He renounced any possibility that purgatorial processes, treatment of the poor, or the intercession of the Church have any efficacy for redemption of the wicked (these are reserved for the elect).[7] His infernalist certainty marked a new and perilous stage in Church history insofar as Augustine's spiritual progeny (to this day) purport to plainly and simply *know* the outcome of divine judgment.

> In *The City of God* . . . every possible opening that might enable the "compassionate" to deny the fact of a hell populated not only by devils but also by people is fully plugged . . . the door was firmly closed and fitted with many bolts; and, for the theology of posterity, it has remained locked."[8]

But when you lock one door, another—arguably more dangerous—door swings open . . .

DOUBLE-PREDESTINATION

Upon his theology of original sin and irresistible grace, Augustine developed a doctrine of salvation by which no one is saved apart from the sovereign will of God (see also his works *On Original Sin, On the Predestination of the Saints, On the Gift of Perseverance* and *On Nature and Grace*). Only those whom God predestined to respond to the Gospel (the elect) are able to do so, and divine grace ensures that they will. Of course, if you believe that we are saved by God's sovereign and irresistible grace alone, then a loving God who wills that none should perish ought to extend saving grace to all. But to avoid presumption, Augustine has already renounced

4. *City of God*, 21.9.
5. Ibid., 21.19, 23.
6. Ibid., 21.2–4.
7. Ibid., 21.13, 18, 24, 26.
8. von Balthasar, *Dare We Hope?*, 65, 69; Augustine *De Civ. Dei*, 21.18.

universalism. His only option is that God must sovereignly elect some for eternal perdition. Why? Shrouded in the mysteries of God, this too is "for the praise of his glory" (Eph 1:6, 14). As a result, for some, the torment of the wicked even became an aspect of the believers' heavenly bliss![9]

Luther (*Bondage of the Will*) and Calvin (*Institutes*) later adopted this same line of logic. "[God] does not create everyone in the same condition, but ordains eternal life for some and eternal damnation for others."[10] This, the Catholic catechism rejects, reaffirming instead the call to prayers of hope in God's mercy:

> God predestines no one to go to hell; for this, a willful turning away from God (a mortal sin) is necessary, and persistence in it until the end. In the Eucharistic liturgy and in the daily prayers of her faithful, the Church implores the mercy of God, who does not want "any to perish, but all to come to repentance."[11]

INFERNALISM BEQUEATHED: EVANGELICAL PERDITION FROM CALVIN TO PACKER

Although the Vatican has inched snail-like away from Augustine's punitive purgatory, they formally abandoned his double-predestination and the certainty of infernalism some time ago. Meanwhile, the latter two doctrines were bequeathed from Augustine into the Reformation evangelical tradition, especially through John Calvin. In his *Institutes* (3.2 for example), Calvin defines faith, describes its properties, and divides the human race into "the elect" (chosen) and "the reprobate" (damned). The elect are known by their certain assurance of salvation (3.2.16), which is "the principle hinge on which faith turns." Without the surety of confidence in one's own salvation, one is not a true believer and has no place among the elect. The damned, however, "never go so far as to penetrate that secret revelation, which the Scripture confines to the elect" (3.2.12). They are completely unable to "apprehend the immutable will of God or embrace his truth with constancy" (3.2.12).

Ironically, he warns of those who "impiously profane faith by hypocritical pretensions to it . . . and presumptuously arrogate to themselves

---

9. Cf. Augustine, *De Civ. Dei*, 21; Aquinas, *Summa theologica*, Suppl. q. 94 art. I, Isaiah 66:24.

10. John Calvin, *Institutes*, 3.21–24.

11. "Hell," *Catechism of the Catholic Church*, 1.2.3.12.4.

what they possess not, and with their vain pretences, deceive others, and sometimes themselves" (3.2.12). One wonders how to discern between certain assurance and self-deceptive presumption, especially if the crucial sign of election is unwavering confidence!

Meanwhile, Calvin is as sure of the outcome for each group. He describes the imagery of damnation—its fire and worms—as metaphorical but genuine torment. [12] Here is his commentary on Matthew 3:12 (the winnowing fork and threshing floor):

> But let us now remember, that believers even now enter, by hope, into the *granary* of God, in which they will have their everlasting abode; while the reprobate experience, in their convictions of guilt, the heat of that fire, the actual burning of which they will feel at the last day.[13]

And in *Institutes:*

> Moreover, as language cannot describe the severity of the divine vengeance on the reprobate, their pains and torments are figured to us by corporeal things, such as darkness, wailing and gnashing of teeth, inextinguishable fire, the ever-gnawing worm (Matt 8:12; 22:13; Mark 9:43; Isa 66:24). It is certain that by such modes of expression the Holy Spirit designed to impress all our senses with dread, as when it is said, "Tophet is ordained of old; yea, for the king it is prepared: he has made it deep and large; the pile thereof is fire and much wood; the breath of the Lord, like a stream of brimstone, does kindle it." (Isa 30:33)[14]

While Calvin's double-predestination did not take hold in the long run among mainstream evangelicals, the baton of his infernalism was received as a dogmatic standard for revivalist preaching in America's first Great Awakening (1730s–40s). In his famous sermon, "Sinners in the Hands of an Angry God," Jonathan Edwards painted alarming word pictures for trembling listeners. Like prequels for today's horror flicks, Edwards' messages could titillate and terrify simultaneously. I once tried preaching several paragraphs of the infamous sermon in a church[15] but was forced

---

12. John Calvin, *Harmony of the Evangelists,* 1:200–21.

13. John Calvin, *Harmony,* 1:200.

14. John Calvin, *Institutes,* 3.25.12.

15. Making a point on the use of fear by the Church, the government, and the media.

to stop by the congregation. Rather than inspiring the "fear of the Lord," I accidentally triggered jeering laughter and irate demands to stop, both on the charge that something so opposed to the Father's heart should not defile a worship service! Here is a sample:

> The God that holds you over the pit of hell, much as one holds a spider, or some loathsome insect over the fire, abhors you, and is dreadfully provoked: his wrath toward you burns like fire; he looks upon you as worthy of nothing else, but to be cast in the fire; he is of purer eyes than to bear to have you in his sight; you are ten thousand times more abominable in his eyes, than the most hateful venomous serpent is in ours.[16]

Evangelicals revere Edwards, but most have learned that the Gospel of Jesus must come with love, that woeful indictments must come with tears, and that even infernalism must be preached sensitively.[17] Yet with few exceptions until the last few decades, to be evangelical was to be an infernalist.[18] The movement's doctrine of hell has largely been defined by the likes of Milton's poetry,[19] Bunyan's books (*The Groans of the Damned Soul*), and Arthur Pink and J. I. Packer's theology.[20] The exceptions prove the rule, with evangelicals like John Wenham, John Stott,[21] and Clark Pinnock taking heat for their defense of annihilation and Gregory MacDonald needing to write pseudonymously in favor of evangelical universalism. When

16. Edwards, "Sinners in the Hands of an Angry God," para. 26. Cf. also Jonathan Edwards, "The Justice of God in the Damnation of Sinners."

17. E.g., Billy Graham's famous euphemisms: "If your heart should skip a beat" and "Christless eternity."

18. Cf. Harry Buis, *The Doctrine of Eternal Punishment,* 1957.

19. At once as far as angels ken he views
   The dismal situation waste and wild:
   A dungeon horrible, on all sides round
   As one great furnace flamed, yet from those flames
   No light, but rather darkness visible
   Served only to discover sight of woe,
   Regions of sorrow, doleful shades, where peace
   And rest can never dwell, hope never comes
   That comes to all; but torture without end
   Still rages, and a fiery deluge, fed
   With ever-burning sulphur unconsumed.
   —John Milton, *Paradise Lost,* 1.59–69.

20. J. I. Packer, "Evangelicals and the Way of Salvation," 107–36.

21. Edwards and Stott, *Essentials,* 313–20.

not labeled with outright "liberalism," Augustine's old charge against sentimentalism is still put to use. Pinnock responds:

> How should I begin? Shall I treat the subject in the calm way one would when dealing with another issue? Would it be right to pretend to be calm when I am not? To begin calmly would not really communicate a full account of my response. I do not feel calm about the traditional doctrine of hell, and so I will not pretend. Indeed, how can anyone with the milk of human kindness in him remain calm contemplating such an idea as this? Now I realize that in admitting this I am playing into the hands of the critics, when I admit how disturbed the doctrine makes me. They will be able to say that I have adopted arguments on the basis of sentimentality and a subjective sense of moral outrage.
>
> In a recent paper, J. I. Packer has said that he dislikes the idea which critics of everlasting conscious punishment seem to have of their moral superiority, when it is not spiritual sensitivity, he says, but secular sentimentalism which motivates them (referring in the context to none other than his esteemed evangelical and Anglican colleague J. Stott). Nonetheless, I will take the risk of beginning at the point of my outrage and hope people will hear me and not put it down to sentimentality. To such a charge I would reply: if it is sentimentality which drives me, what drives my opponent? Is it hardheartedness and the desire for eternal retribution? Such recriminations will get us nowhere fast.[22]

Recriminations and accusations aside, the arrival of the book *Four Views on Hell*[23] heralded a shift in which the discussion legitimately broke beyond the walls of infernalism. Options were validated to some degree. Yet for the resounding and biblical word of "hope in mercy" to which the texts point, we do well to turn to twentieth century Catholic theologian, Hans Urs von Balthasar. But first, we must pause for a brief excursus on purgatory.

---

22. Clark H. Pinnock, "The Destruction of the Finally Impenitent," 7–8.

23. Crockett, William V., et al., *Four Views of Hell*. John Walvoord: Literal, Zachary Hayes: Purgatorial, Clark Pinnock: Conditional, and William Crockett: Metaphorical.

Excursus 2

Purgatory

From Punishment to Divine Gaze

PURGATORY: PUNITIVE VERSUS CURATIVE

C HRISTIAN HISTORY IN THE west tends to a reductionism that divides all of Christendom into either Roman Catholic or Protestant, the former believing in purgatory and the latter rejecting it. The truth is more complex than that. For one, both the Eastern Orthodox and the Anglican Communion pray for the dead and have theologies of an intermediate state. Yet they resist the term "purgatory," because they do not subscribe to Rome's old definition. Beyond that, Rome has changed its doctrine of purgatory substantially from the time of Augustine to Benedict XVI. We cannot do justice to the nuances of the teaching here, but we can survey four peaks along the journey.

1. A Punitive Purgatory

If the damned are irretrievably lost to an eternal hell (vis-à-vis a period of cleansing in God's presence), why pray for them? The double-predestinationist says, "We don't; we pray only for the elect who have passed away." But why pray if you already know the elect are not damned to punishment? In response, Augustine develops a full-blown doctrine of punitive purgatory that survived into and through the Middle Ages.[1] First he lays out the views of the Platonists (quoting Virgil but including the

1. He coins a load of special terms in his purgatorial theology: *poenae purgatorius* (purgatorial punishments), *tormenta purgatoria* (purgatorial torments), *ignis purgatorius* (purgatorial fire), *poenae temporariae* (temporary punishments), *poenae transitorius* (transitory punishments), and *poenae sempiternae* (eternal punishments). See also *City of God*, 21.13, 16; *Enchridion* 69; Jacques Le Goff, *The Birth of Purgatory*, 61, 63.

Alexandrians): "[They] maintain that no sins are unpunished, suppose that all punishment is administered for remedial purposes, be it inflicted by human or divine law, in this life or after death . . . They who are of this opinion would have all punishments after death to be purgatorial."[2] Augustine's response is surgical in cutting out hope for the reprobate and making purgatory exclusive to the saints:

> But temporary punishments are suffered by some in this life only, by others after death, by others both now and then; but all of them before that last and strictest judgment. But of those who suffer temporary punishments after death, all are not doomed to those everlasting pains which are to follow that judgment; for to some, as we have already said, what is not remitted in this world is remitted in the next, that is, they are not punished with the eternal punishment of the world to come.[3]

2. A Presumptuous Purgatory

In the West, Augustine's punitive purgatory dominated until the Reformers identified it as another, however distasteful, basis for presumption. Martin Luther, for Augustine's very reasons, rejected Augustine's answer without actually finding his way back to the Fathers:

> By the doctrine of purgatory they are brought to trust in a false security so that they think they can put in store their salvation and delay things until the day of their death; they try to assume repentance and sorrows and escape purgatory by means of covenants, masses for the soul, and testaments, but doubtless, they will then discover the truth.[4]

Thus the Protestant-evangelical tradition dropped the doctrine of purgatory for both the baptized and unbaptized. They also gave up the practice of praying for the dead. If the damned are irredeemable and the elect skip purgatory, why bother?

Excursus 2: Purgatory

3. A Projected Myth

Another perspective on purgatory is to see it as an allegory for our earthly purgative journey. Certainly mystics like Teresa of Avila and John of the Cross fixated on the purgations we suffer on the way to perfection now.[5] In fact, is that not exactly the point that Dante makes in the opening lines of his *Inferno?*

> Midway upon the journey of our life
> I found myself within a forest dark,
> For the straightforward pathway had been lost.[6]

Wright, writing now as Anglican Bishop of Durham, is unambiguous on the matter:

> Paul makes it clear here [Rom 8:33–39] and elsewhere that it's the *present* life that is meant to function as a purgatory. The sufferings of the present time, not of some postmortem state, are the valley through which we have to pass in order to reach the glorious future. . . . *The myth of purgatory is an allegory, a projection from the present onto the future.* This is why purgatory appeals to the imagination. It is our story, here and now. . . . this means that for millions of our theological and spiritual ancestors death brought a pleasant surprise. They had been gearing themselves up for a long struggle ahead, only to find it was already over.[7]

4. A Purifying Presence

Meanwhile, the Roman Catholic Catechism continues to teach purgatory as it was developed at the Councils of Florence and Trent. Purgatory is a cleansing fire that exists for friends of God who are still "imperfectly purified" at death. They are assured of eternal life after holiness is attained and they are heaven-ready.[8]

Under the last two popes (at least) the cleansing fire of purgatory has been identified with inner transformation through the glory of Christ rather than Augustine-style or Dante-esque punishments. Without ad-

---

5. Cf. Teresa of Avila, *The Way of Perfection and Interior Castles.* John of the Cross, *Ascent of Mount Carmel.*

6. Dante, *Inferno:* Canto 1.1–3.

7. Wright, *Surprised by Hope,* 170–71.

8. "The Final Purification, or Purgatory," *Catechism of the Catholic Church,* 1.2.3.12.3, para. 1030–31.

dressing the duration issue, Joseph Ratzinger, now Benedict XVI, counters a punitive purgatory:

> Purgatory is not, as Tertullian thought, some kind of supra-worldly concentration camp where one is forced to undergo punishments in a more or less arbitrary fashion. Rather it is the inwardly necessary process of transformation in which a person becomes capable of Christ, capable of God, and thus capable of unity with the whole communion of saints. Simply to look at people with any degree of realism at all is to grasp the necessity of such a process. It does not replace grace by works, but allows the former to achieve its full victory precisely as grace. What actually saves is the full assent of faith. But in most of us, that basic option is buried under a great deal of wood, hay and straw. Only with difficulty can it peer out from behind the latticework of an egoism we are powerless to pull down with our own hands. Man is the recipient of the divine mercy, yet this does not exonerate him from the need to be transformed. *Encounter with the Lord is this transformation.* It is the fire that burns away our dross and re-forms us to be vessels of eternal joy.[9]

Posterity will remember Benedict XVI as a great theologian and teacher. Though conservative socially, he is unafraid to take the Roman Catholic Church forward theologically[10] and move them into a deeper embrace with the Orthodox Church and the Eastern Fathers. I quote his papal encyclical *Spe Salvi* at length to illustrate both traits as they pertain to our topic. His context is Paul's description of the Day of the Lord in 1 Cor 3:12–15.

> Some recent theologians are of the opinion that the fire which both burns and saves is Christ himself, the Judge and Savior. The

9. Joseph Ratzinger, *Eschatology: Death and Eternal Life,* 230.

10. The puzzling continuance of *Plenary Indulgences* notwithstanding. Benedict's decree is instructive for what he perceives to be possible through Jesus' mandate to "bind, loose, forgive, or withhold forgiveness" (Matt 18:18; John 20:23). See also *On the Occasion of the Pauline Year,* para. 1. "Each and every truly repentant individual member of the Christian faithful, duly absolved through the Sacrament of Reconciliation and restored with Holy Communion, who devoutly makes a pilgrimage to the Papal Basilica of St Paul on the Ostian Way and who prays for the Supreme Pontiff's intentions, will be granted the *Plenary Indulgence* from temporal punishment for his/her sins, once sacramental forgiveness and pardon for any shortcomings has been obtained. The Christian faithful may benefit from the Plenary Indulgence both for themselves and for the deceased, as many times as they fulfil the required conditions but without prejudice to the norm stipulating that the Plenary Indulgence may be obtained only once a day."

encounter with him is the decisive act of judgment. Before his gaze all falsehood melts away. This encounter with him, as it burns us, transforms and frees us, allowing us to become truly ourselves. All that we build during our lives can prove to be mere straw, pure bluster, and it collapses. Yet in the pain of this encounter, when the impurity and sickness of our lives become evident to us, there lies salvation. His gaze, the touch of his heart heals us through an undeniably painful transformation "as through fire". But it is a blessed pain, in which the holy power of his love sears through us like a flame, enabling us to become totally ourselves and thus totally of God.... The pain of love becomes our salvation and our joy.[11]

In this comment on 1 Cor 3 and divine judgment, has Benedict written anything that any Christian would not willingly accept as truth? Could you? I believe I could read this portion in almost any evangelical church and get an enthusiastic "Amen!"—provided I waited until afterwards to reveal the author. Is Benedict talking about an interim purgatory or the final judgment? Following Paul's genius, he actually collapses them into one timeless moment—*"when we appear before the Judge."* Nodding briefly as he passes the old doctrine of purgatory, we find the Pope focused on the gaze of Christ (whenever) that transfigures us (2 Cor 3:18). That is the "fire" through which we must pass "to become fully open to receiving God and able to take our place at the table of the eternal marriage-feast."[12]

In short, purgatory is not a place or a punishment or a presumption. To Benedict, it is a transforming encounter with divine love in the face of Jesus Christ.[13] Judgment Day becomes a cosmic truth and reconciliation commission, addressing and redressing even history's most gruesome injustices.[14] With this historic statement, the Pope has finally expunged Augustine's purgatory of the toxins of presumption and punishment, rewinding the clock to remarry couples that never should have been divorced: judgment and hope, fire and glory, purification and encounter.

Finally, if purgatory is no longer acknowledged as an intermediate place of punishment, and instead merely describes the cleansing component of our first meeting with the Judge, why not avoid the fear, the confu-

---

11. Pope Benedict XVI, *Spe Salvi*, 47.
12. *Spe Salvi*, 46.
13. Cf. Dermot Lane, *Keeping Hope Alive*, 148.
14. Cf. Sharon Baker, "Hospitable Hell."

sion, and the division that the old moniker inspires by simply dropping it? Unless I'm mistaken, *Spe Salvi* is one significant step in that very process.

Evangelicals and Purgatory

All this talk of purgatory can be very unsettling for evangelicals, especially with its emphasis on the "finished work of Christ" on the Cross. All those classic stereotypes of the Catholic purgatory, with its flames and its torment—maybe those who roll their eyes in revulsion at purgatory can begin to empathize with the unbeliever who shudders to overhear our traditional views on hell! The real difference seems to be whether or not we think we'll be the ones being licked by the flames.

But seriously, are we forgiven or not? Wasn't Jesus' blood enough? Grace, faith, salvation—why the need for a cleansing fire? Believe me, I have more questions than answers, but it may help us to delineate between the act of forgiveness and the process of cleansing (1 John 1:9). The Cross of Christ is to forgiveness as the glory of Christ is to cleansing; both involve love and judgment. Our baptism in water is to forgiveness as our baptism in fire and the Spirit is to purification (Matt 3:11; Luke 3:16). The finished work of Christ stands alongside and behind the transforming process of Rom 8, where the apostle Paul describes the journey from justification through sanctification to glorification. That death (even suicide!) does not short-circuit life's voyage has been a conviction of much of the Church through the ages. The author and finisher of our faith honors our history, even into eternity. So Moltmann:

> Purifying fire, transmigration of souls, the soul's journey, an expiatory passage through the faults and omissions of this life are all images for this. If we leave aside the external ecclesiastical and political motives that were often bound up with ideas of this kind, and look simply at what is meant, we could after all say: I shall again come back to my life, and in the light of God's grace and in the power of his mercy put right what has gone awry, finish what was begun, pick up what was neglected, forgive the trespasses, heal the hurts, and be permitted to gather up the moments of happiness and to transform mourning into joy ... So I would think that eternal life gives the broken and the impaired and those whose lives have been destroyed space and time and strength to live the life which they were intended for, and for which they were born. I think this, not for selfish reasons, for the sake of my personal completion, and not morally, for the sake of some kind of purifica-

tion; I think it for the sake of the justice which I believe is God's concern and his first option.[15]

After all, "He who began a good work in you will carry it on to completion until the day of Christ Jesus" (Phil 1:6). What? Unless we die first? Or even thereafter? Notice: the day of Christ signals and coincides with the completion of our faith-history—personal and social—not its interruption. But how does it work? What really changes us? In our moralism, sometimes we forget that transformation is God's work in us, not our capacity to behave.

The Divine Gaze

Sometimes, Paul says we are transfigured (lit.) by beholding the glory of God in the face of Jesus Christ (2 Cor 3:18—4:6). Elsewhere, he talks about a purging by fire (1 Cor 3:13). What if they are the same thing? To gaze on Christ and receive his gaze: that is the glory that changes us from glory to glory, that is the fire of judgment that purifies me of dross. When I lift my eyes to his eyes, I find him gazing back at me, into me, seeing my heart, judging my heart, purging my heart, changing my heart, filling my heart.[16] The active ingredient in our glorification is the divine gaze of Jesus Christ, fire and love, both now and in the age to come.

To conclude, heaven and hell, purgation and transformation—all of these can be summed up by our experience of the divine gaze, though the various traditions differed on details:

1. For some, exclusion from the glory of the divine gaze is hell.

2. For others, proximity to the glory of the divine gaze is experienced as hell.

3. The glory of the divine gaze transforms us now to prepare us for God's glory.

4. The glory of the divine gaze will glorify us when we meet God face-to-face.

5. The glory of the divine gaze is heaven.

15. Jurgen Moltmann, *The Coming of God,* 116–18.
16. Cf. von Balthasar, *Prayer,* ch. 1.

10

Mercy Triumphs over Judgment

Eschatological Hope and von Balthasar's Dare

SINCE THE FOURTH CENTURY, via the Reformers and the Revivalists, the Western Church and its Evangelical wing have inherited Augustine's infernalism as the only biblical view of judgment and hell, typically writing off the early universalist Fathers as heretical and their modern proponents as liberal. But the infernalist doctrine that cured like concrete over the centuries has begun to crumble. Why?

First, writers like George MacDonald (esp. *Lilith*) and C. S. Lewis (esp. *The Great Divorce*) revived Origen's willingness to speculate about the afterlife. They pursued the theme of the cleansing journey whereby the pilgrim's odyssey is extended into the next life rather than being cut short into "perma-hell" or bypassed into "insta-heaven."[1] Unlike John Bunyan[2] and John A. Comenius,[3] whose pilgrims' journeys occur before death in allegorical visions, MacDonald and Lewis dwelt on the intermediate state where one progresses into the Kingdom of God. The trials can be painful and purgative but not retributive or punitive. Andre Harden, author of the forthcoming *Descensus* series, laid out the wherefore of their thoughts in a recent e-mail exchange:

---

1. See also the testimony of twentieth century Indian Evangelist Sadhu Sundar Singh on the "life after life," as recorded in his visions.

2. *Pilgrim's Progress.*

3. *Labyrinth of the Soul and Paradise of the Heart.* This testimony, like Bunyan's, features a character named Pilgrim but was written five years before Bunyan was born. Comenius (or Komensky in Czech) was the last Bishop of the Unity of Bohemian Brethren before he was forced to lead them into exile in 1620. The book, superior to Bunyan's in my view, is finally available in English.

For me the gut root of the problem is how we become ready to fully consummate our relationship with God?

Some believe our imperfections will be flashed away in a miraculous instant of transformation. While some accept that this is how the imperfect righteous will be cleansed for heaven, they tend to acknowledge that it would be unconscionable for God to perform such an instantaneous transformation on one of the unrighteous. It's thought to interfere with their free will—but of course—the whole reason a miraculous transformation is required is because the wholeness God desires from us seems to be beyond the free will of any who seek to follow him.

Our life in time, Jesus' entry into that life, and the alteration of the Faith from a genetic-based religion to a spirit-based way of thinking complete with a call to action suggests that we will only find transformation by choosing and living obedience over and over through the events we experience. The Gospel is not a Gnostic secret that, because we're aware of it, ensures that we'll be magically and effortlessly altered when the time is full. The Gospel is an invitation to live a life and to choose actions that express the chief commandments—to love God and others.

This life, even for the best of us, is probably not enough to bring us up to speed with God. He is too hidden here. Between this life and the next, wherein we are able not only to behold God in his fullness but also to reflect that fullness back to him, is a dark glass. It is in the passage through that dark glass that we must experience another sort of active life, wherein we can choose and obey and conform ourselves further to the increasing revelation of God.[4]

A second factor that is lengthening the evangelical tent cords is the arrival of evangelical annihilationism. This will come as a relief to those who were wondering why the Jehovah's Witnesses at their door were sounding more reasonable and biblical than their own pastors on the proportionality of God's judgments.[5] One wonders if the J.W.'s position did more to help or hinder evangelical openness to this view.

Even so, daring evangelicals like Clark Pinnock revisited the Scriptural alternatives to eternal, conscious torment. They found solid grounds biblically (Isa 66:24; Mal 4:3; Matt 10:28; John 3:16, etc.) and philosophically for annihilation or conditional immortality. Pinnock can

4. Andre Harden, email to me, Mar 2009.
5. Until Wright's *Surprised by Hope,* the J.W.s also sounded less Gnostic and more biblical than most in their reading of Rev 21–22.

sometimes be dismissed as a maverick for his avant-garde theology (e.g., "open theism"), but when someone so notably reliable and theologically solid as John Stott "came out" as an annihilationist . . . well! That gave many of us pause and permission to begin playing with ideas beyond the evangelical Sanhedrin's fold without losing our faith or our credentials. What if Stott truly was functioning as a John 10 porter who opened the door for the Good Shepherd to come speak afresh to the flock about God's ways and will in judgment?

Third, many in the "emerging church" movement, whether through its dissatisfaction with the Reformation or its attraction to liturgy and icons, have become reacquainted with older Eastern theologians like Gregory or Celtic radicals like Patrick. Along the way, they are discovering the possibility of ultimate redemption. Key leaders (e.g., Brian McLaren's, *The Last Word and the Word After That*) are communicating the wisdom of pre-Nicene teachers in popular forms to young people. Their parents and grandparents were raised on Luther, Calvin, Wesley, and Edwards. The upcoming generations will know Origen, Clement, Basil, and Gregory.

Fourth, mainstream evangelicals, such as the pseudonymous Gregory MacDonald (*Evangelical Universalism*), are challenging their colleagues on their own biblicist terms to accept ultimate redemption as a valid evangelical option. When we read truly evangelical scholars who talk our language, honor our values, and use our tools, change is possible, because it doesn't require us to compromise our non-negotiables.[6]

Fifth, the recent plethora of books espousing alternative theories to the violence of penal substitutionary atonement has left us asking, "If the Cross is about love and mercy rather than God's need to satisfy wrath with punishment, what becomes of hell? Is there a need? Is it punitive? Is it eternal? Or could even hell be swallowed up in the Lordship of God's eternal love?"

Finally, the laity, who know God intimately, sense that something is off about the infernalist Lord bequeathed to them by their traditions. They say, "The God I know is not like that. Does that make me a bad Christian?" Some might find it easy to write this off as mere sentimentalism. But could their hope in a greater mercy actually be Spirit-led insight? What if those aren't just weak-knees willing to be tossed about by every wind and wave of doctrine? Aren't they just as likely tenderhearted believers

6. I.e., Infernalism (not judgment) can be dropped from the evangelical set of core values. It was an accretion to the creeds in the first place.

whose lives in the real world protect them from the delusions that breed like bookworms in ivory towers and pastors' studies? What if the secret hopes of regular people are well founded? In my opinion, they are based in part on a revelation of the Father's heart that has gathered strength since the 1980s,[7] to the point where God's parental affection has become a given in many quarters. When congregations sing about God's loving heart week after week at church, in their homes and listen to CDs in their cars that affirm this truth, the strongman's house of fear and torment is inevitably devoured. The perfect love of God casts out fear of punishment as promised in 1 John 4:18, displacing it with godly hope.

VON BALTHASAR'S DARE

On this point, I believe our best resource is Hans Urs von Balthasar, arguably the twentieth century's sharpest Catholic theologian. Though controversial in his hope for ultimate redemption, John Paul II called him to become a cardinal. Von Balthasar passed away just prior to his ordination, but Cardinal Ratzinger (now Pope Benedict XVI), confirmed the Vatican's approval when he presided at Balthasar's funeral: "What the pope intended to express by this mark of distinction, and of honor, remains valid . . . No longer only private individuals but the Church itself, in its official responsibility, tells us that he is right in what he teaches of the faith."[8]

Taking seriously both the judgment and mercy texts, von Balthasar looked to Jesus (in John's Gospel) and dared us to hope for the salvation of all.

> In the case of John and his conception of God's judgment, the way that the two series of statements both intertwine and yet counter to one another becomes more obvious. Jesus says of himself both: "I did not come to judge the world but to save the world" (12:47), and "For judgment I came into this world, that those who do not see may see, and that those who see may become blind" (9:39). But the apparent contradiction is soon resolved: Jesus comes as the light of absolute love ("to the end" [13:1]) in order to save all men. But how will this be, if there are some who consciously draw back from this love and refuse it (3:19; 9:40–41; 12:48)? The question, to

---

7. Popularized through the teaching and worship of groups like YWAM, the Vineyard, and elements of the inner healing movement.

8. John L. Allen, Jr. "The Word from Rome," para. 8.

which no final answer is given or can be given, is this: Will he who refuses it now refuse it to the last?

To this there are two possible answers: the first says simply "Yes". It is the answer of the infernalists. The second says: I do not know, but I think it permissible to hope (on the basis of the first series of statements from Scripture) that the light of divine love will ultimately be able to penetrate every human darkness and refusal.[9]

The issue at this point becomes free will. We need, even with tongue in cheek, to preserve the possibility that in our humanity one can behold the love of Christ in all its fullness and still reject it. I say tongue in cheek, because it seems to me that absolutely everything in us that says "no" to perfect love and eternal salvation is not based in freedom but in bondage. When every deception and every wound and every worldly, fleshly, and demonic chain has been removed, I hope and expect that the truly free will shall always answer the call with a resounding "Yes!"

The point is that von Balthasar opposes presumption by integrating mercy and judgment texts as hypothetical possibilities that provide room for eschatological hope. Possibility is the operative word. In support, he cites this Confession of Faith:

> Neither Holy Scripture nor the Church's Tradition of faith asserts with certainty of any man that he is actually in hell. Hell is always held before our eyes as a real possibility, once connected with the offer of conversion and life.[10]

JURGEN MOLTMANN: THE UNIVERSALITY OF THE CROSS AND THE NECESSITY OF JUDGMENT

In many ways, Jurgen Moltmann takes up von Balthasar's dare with an even more confident theology of hope. He walks the line between the presumptive (or dogmatic) universalism that knows too much and the agnostic (or wishful thinking) universalism that knows too little. Moltmann's

---

9. von Balthasar, *Dare We Hope?*, 178.

10. *The Church's Confession of Faith*, 346. Similarly, Maurice Blondel, *La Philosophie et l'Esprit Chrétien*, 553: "Authentic Christianity speaks of [everlasting hell] in no other way than as a justly possible consequence, with the Church never, after all, having officially linked it to a particular person."

hope rests on the following three pillars,[11] summarized clearly in a lecture by Jon Stanley, on whose outline and analysis I am leaning.[12]

1. Moltmann's Critique of the Traditional Doctrine of Judgment

First, Moltmann critiques the traditional doctrine of judgment (the separation of believers and unbelievers into heaven and hell), under which umbrella he includes medieval and modern versions. The medieval version describes God as an actively wrathful Judge; the modern version (labeled above as "passive judgment") says that God predestines no one to hell, but those who persist in rebellion receive the just consequences of their own decision. Moltmann rejects both versions as being rooted in the Egyptian *Book of the Dead* and such non-Christian sources.[13] He argues that the traditional doctrine of judgment falls short of being "Christian theology" because it does not ultimately serve Life and actually bleeds terrible ecological, psychological, sociological, and political consequences into our world. As such, our doctrine of judgment needs to be Christianized. It needs to represent God as revealed in Jesus Christ. How so?

2. Moltmann's Universalism of the Cross

For Moltmann, salvation is not exclusive because it does not depend on a particular(ist) formula for relationship with God, but on what God in Christ accomplished effectually through the Cross event. Namely,

> Moltmann's universalism is a "universalism of the cross" because it is through Jesus Christ's descent into Hell in his death on the cross that God actually comes to fill "all things," beginning with Hell itself—first things first. This is why Moltmann can refer to the "theology of the cross" as "the gospel of Christ's descent into hell."[14]

This approach does not deny judgment, damnation, or hell—there is nothing minimal or cheap about such grace, based as it is in the profound suffering of the crucified God who descended there.[15] But by descending

11. Esp. in J. Moltmann, "The Final Judgment: Sunrise of Christ's Liberating Justice."

12. J. D. Stanley, "The Trouble with Judgment: Re-Christianizing the Final Judgment in Our Time."

13. Moltmann, "The Final Judgment," 569.

14. Stanley, "The Trouble with Judgment," para. 20.

15. Cf. Moltmann, *The Coming of God: Christian Eschatology*, 254.

into hell, Christ fills it, overcomes it, and annihilates it. "Through Christ's death and resurrection, God has entered the 'God forsaken space' of Hell for the first time, thus taking it up into his omnipresence and overcoming its deadly power."[16] By the destruction of hell, the foundation is set for God be all in all, resulting in the restoration of *all* things and the flourishing of *all* creatures.

> If death is no more and hell destroyed, the question of whether all or only a few shall be saved is irrelevant. The ground is then prepared for the healing and the new creation of all things. To put it philosophically: The negation of the negative constitutes a position of the positive, which cannot be destroyed.[17]

3. Moltmann's Cry for Justice and the Need for Judgment

While Moltmann rejects (i) the finality of a dual-outcome of judgment, (ii) the eternality of hell, and (iii) the conscious torment of the damned, he does not sacrifice humanity's cry for justice on the altar of compassion.[18]

> The expectation of a final universal judgment in which divine justice will finally triumph was originally a hope cherished by the victims of violence and injustice. It was their counter-history . . . They hoped for the final Judge who will establish justice for those who suffer wrong. . . . The victims must not be forgotten.[19]

For Moltmann, the universalism of the Cross would necessitate "The Day" foretold by Scripture where everyone must give an account and justice is truthfully established. Until that happens, "The victims who have suffered injustice and violence do not hold their peace. The perpetrators who have caused the suffering find no rest. The hunger for justice and righteousness remains a torment on both sides."[20]

As Jon Stanley explains, "Such a judgment isn't aimed at distinguishing between believers and unbelievers, the elect and the nonelect, or the righteous and unrighteous, but between the victims and perpetrators of actual interpersonal, familial, social, and political injustices."[21] God's judg-

16. *The Coming of God*, 252.
17. "The Final Judgment," 574.
18. Stanley, "The Trouble with Judgment," para. 29.
19. "The Final Judgment," 570.
20. Ibid.
21. Stanley, "The Trouble with Judgment," para. 35.

ments are a severe grace and a transforming fire in which perpetrators and victims must face the burdens they would rather not remember or else never want to forget in the presence of God and one another. This creative (versus retributive) judgment will save lives, heal wounds, restore dignity, and reconcile inequities, thus establishing God's just society where everything is made right.[22]

Thus, for Moltmann, the universalism of the Cross invites us to dare hope—hope with conviction—in the effective power of the Cross to eradicate hell; in the faithfulness of God be all in all for the restoration of all; and in the mercy of God whose just judgments will put things to rights. We don't merely hope: we hope in Christ and the power of his resurrection for a universal liberation from evil unto life.

SEGUE: FROM SCRIPTURE AND TRADITION TO THE VISIONS OF JOHN

When we study the Bible and tradition in any systematic or chronological manner, as we have just done, the act of dissecting or reorganizing data makes it feel like we're doing something scientific or objective (even though we might call our science "exegesis" or "theology"). But consider who and what we're studying. The fact that my nose is buried in heavy lexicons may obscure the fact that the content and the people (esp. the prophets, whose ministries span centuries) I am studying takes me into history's most mystical territory. We have really only been cataloging visionary experiences and testimonies that were received in dreams and trances then analyzing the interpretations of pre-medieval bishops whose opinions somehow matter. Incredibly, just because I call myself a Christian, I have chosen to believe their version of reality and accept it as my own. What I am getting at is that even the source and nature of our content lead us to the same conclusions as the content itself. Namely, that the diversity of sources, images, and opinions along with the obvious borrowing and evolution involved in biblical cosmology make presumption ludicrous. We are left, appropriately so, with possibilities and options, warnings and hope, all of which convey real openness and real truth. Like John before us, we are called to bear witness to what we have seen. Adrienne von Speyr, a twentieth century mystic and theologian, brings us back to the Apocalypse of John on the topic of God's judgment:

22. "The Final Judgment," 570–71.

John sees the condemned in the position of cast down, because he must bear witness to the possibility; this witness is part of his mission; he must be able to report that he has seen it, since it belongs, as a possibility, to the essence of judgment, and in order to be able to report it, he must have seen it. At this point, everything remains open; the hope that he leaves for all is not of such a nature that the fear of possibly being cast down might not also remain.[23]

Before diving into the grand possibilities of John's final vision, we need to prepare with a short primer on the relationship between visions, symbols, and reality.

23. Adrienne von Speyr, *Apokalypse*, 689–90.

EXCURSUS 3

Visions of Hell

Symbols and Reality

UPON HEARING OF MY hope in God's everlasting mercy, some will presume that I believe there is no hell (as they did with Clement, Origen, and Gregory) or that I am a closet universalist (as some suggest of Julian, Barth, von Balthasar, and Lewis). What I do have in common with the aforementioned saints is that love compels me to confident hope in the mercy of God. Human choice and divine mercy preclude presuming anything, but Christian love obligates me to pray fervently for all.

HELL ON EARTH

The truth is, I know hell exists, because I've been there. It's just west of Thailand. The horrors of Burma rival anything from Dante's tour of the netherworld. The apocalyptic fires, dismemberments, and everlasting tortures in Burma inspire belief in the reality of Gehenna—or worse, they evoke a bitterness that incites one to hope for it.

I have not yet recovered (*should I?*) from interviewing the victims of torture by gasoline, fire, and salt in the Karen refugee camps on Burma's borders. I remember my sacred visits to the thatched hospice for those whose limbs, faces, and eyes had been taken by the click-*boom* of land-mines. Testimonies of emergency amputations performed on-site amidst razed villages by amateur relief-workers wielding only a Leatherman tool. Abduction and rape of children by soldiers who were themselves kid-napped as children and crafted by others into instruments of horror. I can relive the late night conversations with aid-workers—eyes red with frustration, tears, and whiskey from the trauma. Yes, I've been to hell. And I feel the guilt of thanking God that I was only visiting.

And Burma is just one tiny corner of hell on earth. One has only to survey the historical landscape of the twentieth century to see how hell can reign on earth. The litany of hellfire's lament circles the globe: The genocides of African colonialism and tribalism; the holocausts of Nazi Germany, Stalinist Russia, and Maoist China; the killing fields and napalm saturation of Southeast Asia; the super-power driven civil wars of Central America; the disappeared of South America; from the war crimes of former Yugoslavia to the "extraordinary rendition" and suicide bombings of the Middle East. Well did Thomas Merton say,

> Hell is where no one has anything in common with anybody else except the fact that they all hate one another and cannot get away from one another and from themselves. . . . *If you want to understand the social and political history of modern man, study hell.* And history, however terrible, has another and a deeper meaning. For it is not the evil of history that is its significance and it is not by the evil of our time that our time can be understood. In the furnace of war and hatred, the City of those who love one another is drawn and fused together in the heroism of charity under suffering, while the city of those who hate everything is scattered and dispersed and its citizens are cast out in every direction, like sparks, smoke and flame.[1]

VISIONS OF HELL

I'm also one of those unfortunates who has had visions of being in hell, which, when you think about it, is the only source material for any scriptural or historical testimonies of the soul's torment. I.e., all those who have *seen* or *visited* hell—whether biblical authors or history's mystics—did so by way of a visionary (non-literal) experience. Allow me to illustrate from my own traumatic encounter.

One night, I found myself "in a vision, within a dream, in my head, on my bed" (to borrow a Dr. Seuss-like phrase from Daniel 7). Fully lucid, I realized I was confined in a prison and about to undergo the torments of my own tailor-made hell. A number of jailers restrained me. Then with an intimidating pair of pliers, one began to slowly extract my eyetooth (which I knew in the dream was actually my "I-tooth"). The pain was excruciating, and I screamed uncontrollably as they did their work. But I

---

1. Thomas Merton, *New Seeds of Contemplation*, 123–24.

knew without a doubt that struggling was futile and that no mercy was forthcoming. Eventually, they got the tooth out, and I began to bleed profusely from the enormous hole left behind in my gums. Finally, the men (?) left to go to work on their next "case" while I was left in agony to assess the damage. I picked up my orphaned tooth, thinking that I might jam it back into the cavity and thus cut off the flow of blood. Only then did I notice a giant nail was lodged lengthwise through the tooth, protruding up through the root by at least three inches. I couldn't imagine getting that back into my head and the pain, in any case, would not even allow me to begin to try.

At that point, the jailers deposited two more prisoners into my cell. They were writhing on the floor after having had their foreheads smeared with acid. Bubbling third degree burns and the remnants of the acid stained their brows. Their cries evoked my compassion, and it occurred to me that I might be able to offer relief by applying the blood from my mouth to their foreheads as a balm. To my surprise, this act of mercy supernaturally neutralized the acid, and they came to peace very quickly.

Then I awoke.

WAS THE VISION REAL?

If by real we mean, did I literally experience the extraction of my actual tooth? Then of course not. But equating reality with literalism is a failure of the modernist imagination. If by real we mean, did the images represent reality and convey truth? Then of course it was real, even though non-literal and entirely internal.

"The terms 'literal' and 'metaphorical' refer, properly, to the ways words refer to things, not to the things to which the words refer. For the latter task, the appropriate words might be 'concrete' and 'abstract.'"[2] Thus, many of the biblical images of hell are clearly metaphorical but nonetheless real.

Medieval visionaries and modern evangelicals historically have mistaken a commitment to belief in a literalized lake of fire as a crux of biblical faithfulness. Overheard in the coffee shop: two theology students agreeing that if heaven is real, then hell must be real, which they defined

---

2. N. T. Wright, *The Resurrection of the Son of God*, xix. I have been sloppier than this in my use of "literal" heretofore, but it may help to understand "literalize" as referring to transposing figurative language into literal descriptions.

as "an actual place with everlasting, literal flames." My impression is that by failing to perceive the nature and function of visionary experiences, these bright fellows conflated "real" and "literal" in a way that does not do justice to the biblical text. We might ask Malachi, at the final judgment, will I be refined in a literal oven and will the divine Launderer use literal soap? If Paul's wood, hay, stubble, gold, silver, and precious stones refer metaphorically to my character and deeds, are not the flames that purge them also metaphorical (yet still an accurate picture of real purification)? Why the metaphorical flames only for the believer but literal flames only for the unbeliever? A convenient dualism, is it not?

THE TRUTH OF SYMBOLIC LANGUAGE

After reflecting on my dream, I saw that the hellish extraction of my "I-tooth" represented the real way in which the fiery trials of life act to crucify (the nail) the demands and idolatry of my ego ("I"). Though painful and often bloody, struggling against this process only makes it more difficult. Dealing with the stubbornness of my ego is like "pulling teeth." Yet such a procedure is necessary. The pain is not retributive or punitive but redemptive and medicinal. The perceived prison is truly a clinic, and the torturers are really medics. As a result, the flow of God's mercy—the blood of the Gospel—can proceed from our own (non-literal but actual) wounds and mouths to bring healing to others.

We can infer from this dream what should be obvious: such visions of heaven and hell are symbolic descriptions of a state of mind and heart that we undergo, whether now or after death, not literal reports of what the afterlife will be like. The Church Fathers (esp. Origen and Ambrose, but Augustine and Calvin as well) knew and taught that the flames, the worms, the brimstone, the jailers, the chains, and the garbage dump (Gehenna) were symbols pointing to spiritual realities or states of mind. Further, their *function*—an urgent call to a change of heart and complete surrender now—is at least as important as the *content*, because their varying and often conflicting images are not meant as a travel-guide for the age to come. Rather, they remind us of the potential outcomes that proceed from this-world choices. They proclaim warnings but also hope and redemption that somehow ignites and influences outcomes.[3] These potential outcomes are treated as real possibilities in biblical tradition.

3. Brueggemann says it best in the case of Jeremiah's New Covenant promises: "This

Excursus 3: Visions of Hell

With this reminder that visions do correspond to reality and that symbols do convey truth, we are ready to launch into John's good news dream in Rev 21–22.

[Jeremiah's] entire collection of promises, and indeed the hope of Israel in every exile, depends upon the capacity to imagine reality beyond present circumstances. Moreover, that act of imagination is not simply inventive fantasy, but is linked to the power and freedom of God as known in Israel's memory . . . [Jeremiah] is voicing a dreamlike scenario of healing reality, not yet in hand, but already assured by the power of God. Hope is clearly understood as a dreamlike alternative imagination which accepts God's intent as more powerful than the present, seemingly intransigent circumstance." (Brueggemann, *Jeremiah*, 289).

PART THREE

"Her Gates Will Never Be Shut"
Hints of Ultimate Redemption in Revelation 21–22

11

Approaching Revelation

Bifurcation and Consummation

"Blessed is the one who reads the words of this prophecy, and blessed are those who hear it and take to heart what is written in it, because the time is near. . . . He who has an ear, let him hear what the Spirit says to the churches." (Rev 1:3; 2:29)

APPROACHING REVELATION

As we survey John the Revelator's final vision—the Christian Scriptures' last word on eschatology—we find strong hints of authentic hope for *apokatastasis*. But as we will see, there is no possibility of presumption for or against universal redemption. Before exploring these hints, we need to assess our approach to Revelation 21–22. Briefly, are these chapters about reality in the first century, today (this entire age), or was John writing about an age yet to come, pointing toward God's coming eternal kingdom?

THEN: PRETERIST FULFILLMENT

If we follow Wright's preterist interpretation of Jesus' "Little Apocalypse" (Mark 13)[1] and apply it to John's Revelation, we can make a case for some level of preterism[2] there as well. I.e., that in Revelation, the great tribu-

---

1. That Jesus' apocalypse is an imaginal description of the historical demolition of Jerusalem, whether prophetically or in retrospect.

2. Partial preterists believe that most biblical End Times prophecies were fulfilled in AD 70 with the fall of Jerusalem. They still await the return of Christ, final judgment, and his eternal kingdom. Full preterists believe that all biblical End Times prophecies were fulfilled in AD 70. Some deny the bodily return of Christ to earth, resurrection of the dead, and material re-creation of the heavens and the earth.

lation describes Vespasian's siege of Jerusalem (Rev 11:2; 13:5) and the destruction of the city and the temple in AD 70 under Titus. In light of Daniel's historically focused use of apocalyptic, such an interpretation seems likely. But some dare take it further, saying that even the battle of Armageddon also refers to the fall of Jerusalem in AD 70; the lake of fire judgment is a cosmic depiction of the actual carnage in geographic Gehenna after the massacre, as described by Josephus; the new heaven and new earth signify the New Covenant situation, where, by the Spirit's presence, God does truly live with the Bride; and the invitation to the nations to enter the open gates of the New Jerusalem is pictorial of the ongoing work of evangelism.

Instead of reviewing the critiques of preterism or its defenses, allow me one observation for each side of the question. Those who oppose preterism read John's vision of the new heaven and new earth in Revelation 21–22 as belonging exclusively to the next age, following Christ's glorious return—that is, until, I express my joy that the gates of the city are always open and that the Bride is still inviting the thirsty ones in. At this point, anti-preterists often cut and paste the text out of the next age into our evangelistic present. After all, it would not be biblical to posit the Gospel invitation after death, after final judgment, and after eternity has been launched. In response, I want to suggest that John made it biblical, and while it may not feel evangelical to leave the verses where John put them, perhaps John's vision is *more* than evangelical. What if we were allowed, biblically, to hope that Jesus is not willing to close the Gospel gates?

To the preterists, I want to say *yes*. I see that John was following in the footsteps of Daniel and Jesus by using the apocalyptic genre to address local churches of his day with a relevant, codified message that they could understand and apply to their current situation. Moreover, while preterists see biblical apocalypse anchored firmly in imminent events of the authors' space-time setting, they treat the symbolism with sensitivity and greater consistency. The preterists' historicism corresponds to a spiritual interpretation of earthly reality, while futurist interpretations incline more toward literalizing spiritual realities. This literalism is prone to be arbitrary more than futurists might realize.

Take the New Jerusalem and the temple as examples. For the preterist, the Holy City and the Bride both signify God's covenant people (Rev 21:2; Heb 12:22; Gal 4:21–31; cf. Acts 7:47–50). Paul and Peter affirm that we are the temple, with Christ as its cornerstone (1 Cor 3:16; 1 Pet 2:4–6).[3] These symbols—the Bride, the city, and the temple—represent an earthly reality (the Church) with spiritual pictures. There is a consistency to this approach. By contrast, as a futurist in my college days, the pretense of consistent literalism was challenged by Revelation's wild imagery. In any given verse, we might pivot from literal to figurative interpretations and back again. Using the Church in Revelation again as our example, it was easy to discern that the collective billions who constitute the Bride of Christ are not one literal female colossus in a humongous wedding dress waiting to consummate union with Jesus in actual lovemaking. We knew this was symbolic. Yet in the very same verse, we stumbled over our literalism into the New Jerusalem. Some of the popular futurist commentaries of the day quibbled over the Holy City's dimensions—whether it will be a pyramid or a cube and what the rooms, streets, and transportation will be like.[4] I tried to picture a city that was fifteen hundred miles tall and wondered what that would do to the earth's rotation. I also wondered what kind of oysters could produce pearls large enough to become the city's twelve gates (Rev 21:21).

Although I am more conscious of symbolism today, I continue to hold to the creeds, scanning the horizon for Christ "to return again, in glory, to judge the quick and the dead."[5] I confess an instinctual migration to literalizing the city, its gates, its river, and the flaming valley of Gehenna

3. Christian Zionists complain about Replacement Theology, but note: Preterists do not replace national Israel or the Jewish people with the Church. Rather, according to Hebrews, God replaces shadows with reality: the earthly temple, the law, and the priesthood give way to Jesus, the Spirit, and his Church—which includes both Jews and Gentiles. Specifically *Christian* support for a reinstituted temple-sacrificial system of fleshly heifers in a building of hewn stones (to hasten Christ's return!) defies adjectives.

4. "The cube . . . was the shape specified by God for the holy place, or the oracle, in Solomon's temple (1 Kings 6:20), where God was to 'dwell' between the cherubim. Both the language and the symbology thus favor the cubical, rather than the pyramidal, shape. Thus, it will as be easy for the inhabitants to travel vertically as horizontally, in the New Jerusalem. Consequently, the 'streets' of the city (verse 21) may well include vertical passageways as well as horizontal avenues, and the "blocks" could be real cubical blocks, instead of square areas between streets as in a present-day earthly city." (Henry M. Morris, *The Revelation Record*, 450, 451). Creation scientists, with an apologetic agenda to defend the truth of Scripture scientifically, continue to work on the new physics required for a literalist New Jerusalem. Cf. Hugh Ross, "The Physics of Sin."

5. First Council of Constantinople (AD 381).

outside its walls. It is tricky,[6] because I believe the Bible proclaims an actual resurrection of the redeemed after the fashion of Jesus as firstborn
from the dead. He was not a disembodied ghost but a glorified man in
an incorruptible human body (Luke 24:36–43). First John, countering
the proto-Gnostics, says that when we see him, we shall be like him (1
John 3:2). So on the one hand, John is sharing a highly symbolic dream.
But on the other, the symbols stand for a heavenly (spiritual) and earthly
(material) existence. This isn't difficult to accept if you consider that just
because the dreams you had last night are symbolic does not negate the
materiality of the situations and episodes they signify. In the same way,
calling the Church a city or a temple in no way denies that it consists of
living, breathing people who anticipate Jesus' real future return.

Still, I greatly appreciate the preterists' emphasis on the *already* aspect of Revelation's final chapters. In fact, importing that vision into my
current situation has revolutionized the way I understand and preach the
Good News. But to the full preterist, I want to ask, *Is that it?* First, is this
life the sum of my hope? As gracious and generous as God has been to
me, I am not satisfied that his vision is sufficiently fulfilled even in the
Spirit-filled church on earth, nor can it be without an intervention. I know
that Christians who are being persecuted in India or dying in poverty
and disease in Haiti and elsewhere aren't satisfied either. Personal dissatisfaction aside, is *now*—or even the very best version of now—all that
Revelation 21–22 promises?

NOW: BIFURCATION OF REALITY

We might also see John's vision proclaiming an ongoing message about
the Bride of Christ/Kingdom of God in contrast to the propaganda of any
prevailing Empire (Babylon = Rome then; fill in the blanks for today).
I.e., the vision pertains to the bifurcation[7] of reality as it was then and as
it is today, history seen from two points of view: the world's view versus

---

6. For examples of how arbitrary our interpretation is, ask yourself whether the following are symbolic or actual (from Rev 4–5): Jesus' throne, Jesus' horns, Jesus as king,
Jesus as Lion, Jesus as Lamb, the Spirit as lamps, the twenty-four elders as twenty-four
men, the bowls of incense full of prayers, the scroll in God's hand. By what criteria did
you come to each answer? It is as difficult as deciding whether having a dream about your
children is about your actual children or about something they represent to you.

7. Bifurcation: two opposing or co-existing ways of seeing and describing what is
real.

heaven's view. Like Toto in the *Wizard of Oz,* John tears back the imperial curtain to expose Almighty Rome the Savior of the World as Rome the Violent Beast, Rome the Whore, Rome the soon-to-be-vanquished Babylon.

> Revelation reveals a bifurcated universe in which "ordinary" life and "divine" life coexist at all times and places. Traditional interpretations of apocalyptic writings have misunderstood this bifurcated worldview in terms of an absolute separation between present and future. That is, they view Revelation as dividing time into two consecutive ages: a present evil age and a future blessed age. Others have understood Revelation as expressing a dualism between heaven and earth: the earth below is a place of evil whereas heaven above is a place of good.
>
> ...John's look behind the veil gave him a sense that reality was bifurcated. The word bifurcated means to divide into two branches. Apocalyptic discourse does this by arguing that there is not only the world constructed by those with social power but also another world hidden by empire's illusions. The world defined by those with power represents one branch. This is the one most people consider "reality" and which attempts to define our very being. The world where God lives and reigns is another branch. According to the apocalyptic worldview, this latter world is the "real" one, while the other is a parody or counterfeit vision of this reality.[8]

In other words, don't think of the world versus heaven in terms of now versus then (consecutive ages) or as here versus there (dual dimensions). Rather, Babylon (the world system) and New Jerusalem (the heavenly system) are two coexistent realities constantly competing for our allegiance. Second, apocalyptic writing reveals two competing visions of the same reality, the worldly point of view where Caesar/President/Empire is Lord versus the heavenly point of view where Empire is a vicious beast that Christ the Lord has already defeated and whose violence represents its death throes (Rev 12:10–12).

Think of the world and history, as we know it, projected onto a movie screen. From the front side of the screen, the emperor and his entourage appear to be world agents of peace and prosperity, godlike and glorious. But from the backside of the screen, the very same characters appear as monsters with gnashing fangs and clawed feet that shred and trample. From the front side, Christ and his followers appear weak, beaten, and ir-

8. Wes Howard-Brook and Anthony Gwyther, *Unveiling Empire*, 121.

relevant. From behind the screen, he is the Lord who has already defeated Satan, sin, and death through his crucifixion, resurrection, and ascension as King. Far from impotent and marginal, his people are kings and priests of God on the earth, co-reigning with him over the nations. The seven churches of Revelation 2–3 needed to hear this message in their time for their situation, just as we—especially our persecuted Christian brothers and sisters who face a real and present danger—need to hear it afresh for our generation.

YET TO COME: CONSUMMATION OF THE AGES

Bifurcation granted, Revelation says more than that. John also clearly indicates a coming Omega point in history where Babylon is fallen (Rev 14:8, cf. Isa 21:9; Jer 51:8), evil is defeated, and death is banished forever (Rev 21:4). It reflects our current need for radical redemption and reconciliation of heaven and earth. It points forward in hope to the end of this "present evil age" (Gal 1:4) and the arrival of eternity. Even though "the darkness is passing and the true light is already shining" (1 John 2:8), a day is coming when darkness must completely die—when the true light shines without shadows. In Rev 21, the final judgment and the lake of fire give way to the new heaven and new earth with God reigning as King over all. It marks the end of what was and the genesis of the eternal state.

To put things in economic terms, John's final vision describes more than a rapturous bailout package (dispensationalism) or an enlightenment-sponsored stimulus package (e.g., Eckhart Tolle's *A New Earth*[9]). And while a bifurcation persists now, Christ will break the impasse in a new world where God and his people manifest the eternal life for which all of creation groans.[10] We see the coming zenith of our hope in the last two chapters of our Bible.

9. "The inspiration for the title of this book came from a Bible prophecy that seems more applicable now than at any other time in human history. It occurs in both the Old and the New Testament and speaks of the collapse of the existing world order and the arising of "a new heaven and a new earth." We need to understand here that heaven is not a location but refers to the inner realm of consciousness. This is the esoteric meaning of the word, and this is also its meaning in the teachings of Jesus. Earth, on the other hand, is the outer manifestation in form, which is always a reflection of the inner. Collective human consciousness and life on our planet are intrinsically connected. 'A new heaven' *is the emergence of a transformed state of human consciousness, and 'a new earth' is its reflection in the physical realm.*" (Eckhart Tolle, *A New Earth*, 23).

10. Rom 8:18–28. Cf. Wright, *Surprised by Hope*, 105.

12

Eschatological Hope in Revelation 21–22

Rev 21:1—Then I saw a new heaven and a new earth, for the first
heaven and the first earth had *passed away* (*apēlthan*) . . .

THE FINAL CHAPTERS OF Revelation signal a new period. Though we
experience their truth in part already as "those upon whom the end
of the ages has come (*ta telē tōn aiōniōn katentēken*" (1 Cor 10), in Rev 21
we find that God will finally hit the restart button on the cosmos. Old is
gone (passed away); new has come. The redemption of all things visible
and invisible, earthly and heavenly has come to its *telos* (end/fulfillment)
at last through the blood of Christ (Col 1).

Traditional eschatology has rightly identified the new heaven and
earth as the eternal state of God's elect, permeated by God's presence
and devoid of any suffering or wickedness. Since the final judgment has
disposed of Satan, sin, death, and the damned once and for all, everlasting bliss can commence as God, his glorious angels, and the elect enjoy
the static blessedness of the New Jerusalem—at least that's what I was
taught.

But if we look carefully, this is not exactly what is in the text. Questions
and aporias arise defying easy answers. People and processes appear that
seem out of order—unless God continues to bring his Alpha purposes to
an inexorable Omega. Troubling anomalies surface, but then offer us a
possibility: Is the End just the Beginning? Perhaps the only thing that can
truly bring clarity is hope.

Rev 21:5—And the One seated on the throne said, "Behold, I am
making all things new (*kaina poiō panta*)."

Why *am making* (present active indicative)? Not in anticipation (I will) or
in retrospect (I have)? The One on the throne in the midst of his people

ESCHATOLOGICAL HOPE IN REVELATION 21–22

The Wicked Located

1. In a lake of fire	2. Excluded from the city	3. Outside the city gates
"But the cowardly, the unbelieving, the vile, the murderers, the sexually immoral, those who practice magic arts, the idolaters and all liars—their place will be in the fiery lake of burning sulfur. This is the second death." (Rev 21:8)	"Nothing impure will ever enter it, nor will anyone who does what is shameful or deceitful, but only those whose names are written in the Lamb's book of life." (Rev 21:27)	"Blessed are those who wash their robes, that they may have the right to the tree of life and may go through the gates into the city. Outside are the dogs … and everyone who loves and practices falsehood." (Rev 22:14–15)

The Invitation Opened

1. The river of life comes from the throne.	2. Those in the city partake freely.	3. The Spirit and bride say, "Come to waters."
"Then the angel showed me the river of the water of life, as clear as crystal, flowing from the throne of God and of the Lamb." (Rev 22:1)	"Then he said to me, 'Done. I am the Alpha and the Omega, the beginning and the end. I give freely to the one who thirsts from the spring of the water of life.'" (Rev 21:6)	"The Spirit and the bride say, 'Come!' And let him who hears say, 'Come!' Whoever is thirsty, let him come; and whoever wishes, let him take the free gift of the water of life." (Rev 22:17)

Gehenna Transformed

1. Remember Gehenna's location:	2. Remember Jeremiah's New Covenant promise:	3. Remember the Psalmist's forecast for the valley:
Gehenna is the loathsome place of fire and destruction in the valley just outside the city where the dead bodies are cursed and burned. (Isa 66:24)	"The whole valley where dead bodies and ashes are thrown … will be holy to the LORD." (Jer 31:40)	"While thirsty hearts journey to appear before God in Zion, the valley Baca (Gehenna to the 1st century rabbis) becomes a place of springs!" (Ps 84:5-7)

Entry into the City

1. Her gates are never shut.	2. To enter: wash robes in the blood of the Lamb.
"On no day will its gates ever be shut, for there will be no night there." (Rev 21:25)	"Blessed are those who wash their robes, that they may have the right to the tree of life and may go through the gates into the city." (Rev 22:14)

History of the Kings and Nations

1. Deception, immorality, and dominance	2. Rebellion and defeat	3. Surrender and submission	4. Homage and restoration	5. Honour and servitude
Rev 14:8; 17:2, 10-12, 15, 18; 11:2, 9, 18; 18:3, 9, 23	Rev 6:15; 16:12-14; 17:14,19; 19:18-19, 20:8; Isa 34:1-2; 60:12, 20	Rev 12:5; 15:3; 17:14; 19:15-16; Ps 2:8	Rev 15:4; Isa 60:3, 60:5-9, 11; Rev 21:24, 26; 22:2	Isa 60:10, 13; Rev 1:5; 2:26; Is 60:14, 16; Eph 1:18, 4:4

Destiny of the Nations

1. Isaiah's vision:	2. Kings and nations walk by the light into the gates:	3. The leaves of the tree of life are for the healing of the nations:
The nations gather at God's holy mountain with gifts of service and worship. Under the reign of the Prince of Peace, predators and victims reconcile where harm is abolished. (Isa 60; 65:17-25; 66)	"The nations will walk by its light, and the kings of the earth will bring their splendor into it … The glory and honor of the nations will be brought into it." (Rev 21:24, 26)	"And the leaves of the tree are for the healing of the nations. No longer will there be any curse." (Rev 22:2b-3a)

in the thick of the New Jerusalem is saying, "Watch. Behold the active processes of the new creation." And so we shall.

LOCATING THE WICKED

The first obvious anomaly is the stubborn reappearance of the wicked! Where are they located?

1. The Wicked are in a Lake of Fire

Initially, we find them where they "ought to be": consigned to the lake of fire (whether consumed or in torment):

> Rev 21:8—But the cowardly, the unbelieving, the vile, the murderers, the sexually immoral, those who practice magic arts, the idolaters and all liars—their place will be in the fiery lake of burning sulfur. This is the second death.

One may wonder philosophically where and how hell exists in the new order where suffering and death have already been expunged. A question for the ages, but not even half the problem, as we shall see.

2. The Wicked are Excluded from the City

Here, only a little more is revealed:

> Rev 21:27—Nothing impure will ever enter it, nor will anyone who does what is shameful or deceitful, but only those whose names are written in the Lamb's book of life.

The shameful and deceitful cannot enter the New Jerusalem. Of course not, but this should have gone without saying. It seems redundant to mention it when their exclusion was already established by their removal to the fiery lake. Why mention it? It's not as if they are waiting outside the city gates . . . Or are they?

3. The Wicked are Outside the City Gates

> Rev 22:14–15—Blessed are those who wash their robes, that they may have the right to the tree of life and may go through the gates into the city (*kai tois pulōsin eiselthōsin eis tēn polin*). Outside (*exō*) are the dogs, those who practice magic arts, the sexually immoral,

the murderers, the idolaters and everyone who loves and practices falsehood.

How is this? How did the wicked escape the flames to a location outside the city gates? Are they the same wicked we read about earlier? Or after the final judgment and lake of fire, were a new batch of wicked spawned somehow? Or is the lake of fire situated just outside the New Jerusalem? But how can this be if there is no suffering, death, or sorrow in the renewed creation? Or are the lake of fire and the place outside of the city different visions of the same realities? The text is not the problem; it simply resists propositional systems of eschatology in favor of narrative development. Remembering that John is having a series of visions that don't require consistent, mutual cross-referencing helps us realize that the book is not truly conflicted.

Seeing as the wicked here are still wicked and still exist outside the city, we cannot presume their eventual annihilation or salvation. John issues a very strange statement that seriously causes us to wonder whether their status is set in stone:

> Rev 22:11—Let him who does wrong continue to do wrong; let him who is vile continue to be vile; let him who does right continue to do right; and let him who is holy continue to be holy.

This is very odd in that up until the time of death, we are always exhorted and invited to repent and return. Once dead, it sounds like something has changed. If that were the last we hear of those outside the city, we would need to surmise their permanent doom. But as we continue reading, what we see is more than a growing ray of hope for these exiles: the invitation is renewed along with the rest of creation.

THE INVITATION OPENED

One argument for conditional immortality is the river of the water of life, from which one presumably must drink (literally or symbolically) to sustain and enjoy eternal life. While I imagine drawing water from a crystal clear stream, Jesus reminds us that this spring represents eternal life (cf. John 4), represents him (cf. John 7), and has been established in us (John 4:13; 7:38).

1. The River of Life Comes from the Throne

The river of life flows from the throne of God, who is now present in the midst of his people within the New Jerusalem (Rev 21:3–5). From there, God reigns over and generates the new creation. The life spring of Christ flows like a nourishing river to irrigate the whole city with pure water.

> Rev 22:1—Then the angel showed me the river of the water of life, as clear as crystal, flowing from the throne of God and of the Lamb.

God has dreamed this river through the prophets before. Ezekiel saw it spring from out of the temple to become an ever widening and deepening life-source:

> Ezek 47:6b–9, 12—Then he led me back to the bank of the river. When I arrived there, I saw a great number of trees on each side of the river. He said to me, "This water flows toward the eastern region and goes down into the Arabah, where it enters the Sea. When it empties into the Sea, the water there becomes fresh. Swarms of living creatures will live wherever the river flows. There will be large numbers of fish, because this water flows there and makes the salt water fresh; so where the river flows everything will live. . . . Fruit trees of all kinds will grow on both banks of the river. Their leaves will not wither, nor will their fruit fail. Every month they will bear, because the water from the sanctuary flows to them. Their fruit will serve for food and their leaves for healing. (Cf. Zech 14.)

Isaiah saw the New Jerusalem frequently, sometimes as a mountain city or a voluptuous valley or as an enormous tent. Note again the combination of city and river:

> Isaiah 33:20–21—Look upon Zion, the city of our festivals; your eyes will see Jerusalem, a peaceful abode, a tent that will not be moved; its stakes will never be pulled up, nor any of its ropes broken. There the LORD will be our Mighty One. It will be like a place of broad rivers and streams. No galley with oars will ride them, no mighty ship will sail them.

2. Those in the New Jerusalem Partake Freely

As in the Garden of Eden where our proto-parents could eat freely of the tree of life, the inhabitants of the New Jerusalem have free access to the eternal-life-giving river that flows down the middle of the street within the city (Rev 22:2).

> Rev 21:6—Then he said to me, "Done. I am the Alpha and the Omega, the beginning and the end (*telos*, fulfillment). I give freely to the one who thirsts (*egō tō dipsōnti . . . dōrean*) from the spring of the water of life. [my translation]

In visionary context, God is not relating the details of a populace tangibly lapping up water from a river. It is about appropriation of the eternal life of Jesus, and not as we quaff the Gospel in this life. We continue to partake of the life of Christ in the age to come, in the New Jerusalem. We are called to drink from the river, which is symbolic for the living waters that flow from Christ, our eternal fountain. The spring of eternal life (*zōē aiōnion*) that Jesus promised the woman at the well (John 4:10–14) gushes forth with living water (*hudatos zōntos*) (John 7:37–38) generously and eternally to anyone who is thirsty.

3. The Spirit and the Bride Say, "Come to Waters"

Now for the punch line: the Spirit and the Bride issue their invitation.

> Rev 22:17—The Spirit and the Bride say, "Come!" And let him who hears say, "Come!" Whoever is thirsty, let him come; and whoever wishes, let him take the free gift of the water of life.

Careful now, to what is the invitation? The eternal water of life. To where? The river that flows from the throne down Main Street, New Jerusalem. To whom? At first, we heard that it is only available as part of the inheritance of the overcoming ones (*ho nikōn*) (21:7). But in Rev 22:17, the invitation is thrown open: the Spirit and the Bride call "whoever is thirsty" and "whoever wishes" for a drink. But if the Bride is the city (21:2), who is left to invite?

The excluded, meanwhile, are at first seen in the lake of fire (21:8) and then later outside the city (22:15). Have the damned been relocated? Or more likely, are the two images synonymous? It comes time for us to remember three earlier points from our study:

GEHENNA TRANSFORMED

1. **Remember Gehenna's Location (Isa 66:24):** Gehenna is the loathsome place of fire and destruction in the valley just outside the city where the

dead bodies of the cursed are burned. The lake of fire (condemnation) is adjacent to the city walls.

2. Remember Jeremiah's New Covenant Promise (Jer 31:40): "The whole valley where dead bodies and ashes are thrown . . . will be holy to the LORD."

3. Remember the Psalmist's Forecast for the Valley of Baca (Ps 84:5–7): Pilgrims whose thirsty hearts are in journey to appear before God in Zion are met at the open gates. Even while the pilgrims are still in the valley (Gehenna, to the first century rabbis), Baca becomes a place of springs! It is as if the gates have been flung wide and the renewing river of God's love pours out into Gehenna. Jesus' great parable comes to its climax: "But while he was still a long way off, his father saw him and was filled with compassion for him; he ran to his son, threw his arms around him and kissed him" (Luke 15:16). The door is open, indeed.

ENTRY INTO THE CITY

1. Her Gates Will Never Be Shut

The simple math of the New Jerusalem Gospel is beautiful and powerful, even surprising: The wicked are outside the city + the gates of the city will never be shut + the Spirit and the Bride say, "Come" = hope! But I'm rushing ahead (it's difficult not to).

> Rev 21:25—On no day will its gates ever be shut (*hoi pulōnis autēs ou mē*[1] *kleisthōsin*), for there will be no night there.

This verse alludes to the new heavens and earth section of Isaiah 60, where we read: "Your gates will be open continually; They will not be closed day or night, So that men may bring to you the wealth of the nations, with their kings led in procession" (Isa 60:11 NASB). Those who were once outside now come in; those whom the Bride welcomes into the Holy City are entering, becoming part of it! How so?

---

1. *ou mē*—double negative for emphasis, as in *never ever*. Those outside the city will never ever find its gates locked. The door is open for the duration of their *kolasin aiōnion*, and then even beyond that.

2. *Only Entry: Washing Robes in Blood of the Lamb*

Rev 22:14—Blessed are those who wash their robes, that they may have the right to the tree of life and may go through the gates into the city.

It would be tempting to excerpt this verse from its context to make it read that we are blessed if we have washed our robes in the Gospel blood of Christ in this life so that we can be welcomed into the gates of the New Jerusalem in the next. In fact, to avoid any posthumous possibility of salvation, one *must* read it that way. But if we remain ardently biblical (now is not the time to waffle), the text says far more than that.

First, those who say *yes* to the Gospel in this life are already part of the Bride, adorned in righteous robes, coming down as the New Jerusalem and issuing the invitation to others to enter. I.e., those who are washed are already "in." The universal invitation is for those outside the city and needing to enter after the establishment of the new creation.

Lest the invitation be misunderstood as an *anything goes* pluralistic universalism, there is a hard pause. Anyone can come, but only if they have their robes washed in the blood of the Lamb. Only upon a specifically Christian redemption can one enter the gates and eat from the tree of life that grows in the city (another picture of Jesus). This vision declares the possibility and the hope that even in the next age, there are those whose thirst will finally bring them to say *yes* to the Lamb, even those who were unable to do so on this side of the grave.

Now just who are these who finally enter the New Jerusalem? Isaiah 60 and Revelation 21 call them "all the nations." In *Evangelical Universalism*, Gregory MacDonald calls us to track the progressive destiny of the kings and nations throughout the whole book of Revelation.[2] As we do so, note especially the chronology of events.

HISTORY OF THE KINGS AND THE NATIONS IN REVELATION

1. **Deception, Immorality, and Dominance:** The kings and all the nations are deceived by Babylon's sorcery. She gives them authority to rule, yet she rules over their kings. The kings and all the nations are in league with Babylon against God and his kingdom. They persecute God's people,

2. Gregory MacDonald, *Evangelical Universalism*, 93, 123–27.

city, temple, and witnesses (Rev 11:2, 9, 18; 14:8; 17:2, 10–12, 15, 18; 18:3, 9, 23).

2. **Rebellion and Defeat:** The kings and nations gather for war against God. They assemble for battle, but fire comes down to devour them, and birds devour their flesh. For a while, the nations are freed from the dragon's deception (Rev 20:3), after which they rebel against the Lamb a second time, only to be defeated utterly (Rev 6:15; 16:12–14; 17:14,19; 19:18–19; 20:8; Isa 34:1–2; 60:12, 20).

3. **Surrender and Submission:** Christ becomes King of Kings and rules all nations with a rod of iron (Rev 12:5; 15:3; 17:14; 19:15–16; Ps 2:8).

4. **Homage and Restoration:** The kings and all the nations come to worship the Lamb (Rev 15:4), to walk in God's light (Isa 60:3), and to bring their glory and riches (Isa 60:5–9, 11) into the city (Rev 21:24, 26). As they enter, the leaves of the tree of life are given to heal the nations (Rev 22:2).

5. **Honor and Servitude:** The kings and nations rebuild the city walls, serve God's people, and adorn her sanctuary (Isa 60:10, 13). God's people are given authority over kings, and the nations bow to honor them (Rev 1:5; 2:26; Isa 60:14, 16). This represents the hope of our eternal calling (Eph 1:18; 4:4).[3]

THE DESTINY OF THE NATIONS

1. Isaiah's Vision (Isa 60; 65:17–25; 66)

I do not doubt that John was both a genuine mystic and a literary genius. I believe that as immersed as he was in the prophetic tradition, what he saw in the spirit and by the Spirit brought to remembrance texts that would put language to the ineffable. He makes liberal use of Isaiah 60–66, particularly on the festive arrival of the kings and nations. The magi were mere hors d'oeuvres for what Isaiah imagined. We can see how the kings

---

3. Questions: How might this eternal call relate to the nature of God's calling on our lives, when it begins, or how it is fulfilled? How specific is it? What ramifications do eighty-plus years on earth have on that call? When does the process end? Or does it? Do we do for eternity what God has called us to do today? How do we prepare for the eternal nature of that calling? How does this influence how we pursue life in general? (Patrick J. White, email to me, Feb 2009).

and nations who congregate with outlandishly valuable gifts and willing servitude can symbolize the ingathering of the Gentiles to worship and follow Christ. Surely this is fulfilled through the global expansion of Christianity through world missions until the end of the age—or is it? For Isaiah and for John, this is a new heavens and new earth reality.

Reading through the final stretch of Isaiah in one sitting is overwhelming. I will dispense with a summary and draw your attention to one text for thought: "The wolf and the lamb will feed together, and the lion will eat straw like the ox, but dust will be the serpent's food. They will neither harm nor destroy on all my holy mountain," says the LORD (Isa 65:25). The parallel passage is found earlier in Isaiah: "The wolf will live with the lamb, the leopard will lie down with the goat, the calf and the lion and the yearling together; and a little child will lead them. The cow will feed with the bear, their young will lie down together, and the lion will eat straw like the ox" (Isa 11:5–7).

The literalist mind reels at the prospect of lions or wolves becoming vegetarians.[4] Of course, we knew that this must be so, for how could death have any place in the coming age? (Although Isa 65:20 is a real pickle.) In response, I propose that these verses have little to do with dietary preferences in the animal kingdom. Could they be, instead, symbols of peace and reconciliation in God's kingdom (both now and later)? Predators and victims come together in harmony through an exchange of repentance and forgiveness. This doesn't just happen between God's furry creatures but within and between the nations gathered. At Christ's table, former government death squad members and terrorist rebels embrace. The disappeared reappear, resurrected to speak the word of release to their torturers. Occupying forces bend the knee before those whom they sequestered in refugee camps. Holocaust victims, who went like sheep to the slaughter, make gracious eye contact with the wolves who gassed them. On God's Holy Mountain, all harm is abolished. From lime pits to extraordinary rendition to suicide bombing, humanity's nightmare is exposed and washed out like camera film in the sun's brightness.

---

4. Ansell: "The ongoing contrast is between wild and domestic animals. The domestic animals are within Israel's life, the wild are outside. Hence the connotations of the Gentiles—of violent enemies. By the way, salt water/fresh water strikes me as a similar contrast with parallel connotations." (Nik Ansell, email to me, May 29, 2009).

That's what Isaiah saw. The Prince of Peace will ensure it someday. Creation is groaning for it today. God's people were to model it as of yesterday.

2. Kings and Nations Come through the Light into the Gates with Their Glory

With our history behind us, the kings and the nations—vis-à-vis the Lamb and the Bride—make an incredible journey. Throughout the first twenty chapters of Revelation, there are only two groups of people: the kings and nations who are evil and the Bride, who has come from "out of the nations" (a synonym for "out of exile"; cf. Ezek 36:24; 37:21). So the nations begin in deception, idolatry, and violence, and then are destroyed in battle, devoured by fire, eaten by birds, and cast into the lake of fire. But in Revelation 21–22 (and Isaiah 60), we find them ultimately coming to submission, servitude, and salvation as they enter the city!

This cannot simply refer to a series of nations (the bad ones before, then the good ones since), because at the final battle and final judgment, *all the nations* are defeated and dispatched and only the Bride remains. From there we see the Bride touching down in the newly integrated heavens and earth, only to begin inviting in all the nations. From where did these nations come? Were a new litter of kings and nations spontaneously generated after judgment? Or did we retrieve the old batch from hell and relocate them outside the city? Or is "outside the city" a parallel image to the lake of fire? Or perhaps a remnant of repentant nations remains from their division into sheep and goats (in Matt 25). But then the "all the nations" label both before and after judgment seems nonsensical.

Again, the difficulty of a seamless harmonization of conflicting visions is probably impossible and unnecessary. John must speak of both universal judgment and universal conversion—juxtaposing images of the vintage of the earth (Rev 14:17–20) and the harvest of the earth (Rev 14:14–16)—because at any point up until judgment, either are bona fide potentialities.

> We do not take the images seriously if we allow either to qualify the other. The picture of universal judgment does not mean that the picture of the universal worship of God is not to be taken fully seriously, nor does the picture of the universal worship of God mean that the picture of universal judgment is not to be taken fully

seriously. Because Revelation deals in images, it does not make the kind of statements which have to be logically compatible in order to be valid. Each picture portrays a valid aspect of the truth. The two pictures correspond to the choice presented to the nations.... It is no part of John's prophecy to pre-empt this choice by predicting the degree of success the witness of the martyrs will have. One thing is certain: God's kingdom will come.[5]

This commentary highlights two critical revelations concerning the nations. First, in this age, the urgent message of hope that we who were once enemies and persecutors of God's people can now join as full heirs of the covenant, worshiping in the light of God and bringing wealth and splendor as gifts to the Savior-King. Second, in the age to come—however it works—all nations will come into this destiny. Here is God's end game:

> Rev 21:24, 26—The nations will walk by its light, and the kings of the earth will bring their splendor into it ... The glory and honor of the nations will be brought into it.

3. The Leaves of the Tree of Life Are for the Healing of the Nations; the Curse Is Lifted

> Rev 22:2b–3a—And the leaves of the tree are for the healing of the nations. No longer will there be any curse.

Bauckham explains the end of the curse as it applies to foreign nations:

> Revelation 22:3a recalls the judgment of the nations that worshipped the beast and opposed God's kingdom, but declares that, with the coming of God's kingdom, the nations which have been converted[6] to the worship of God and the acknowledgement of his rule need never again fear his judgment. In this way the vision of the New Jerusalem supersedes all the visions of judgment and

---

5. Richard Bauckham, *The Climax of Prophecy,* 309.

6. Potentially all the nations, though Bauckham is quick with a caveat. "This does not, of course, mean that Revelation expects the salvation of each and every human being. From 21:8, 27; 22:15, it is quite clear that unrepentant sinners have no place in the New Jerusalem. Attempts to see Revelation as predicting universal salvation (e.g., Maurice [1861] 400–405; Rissi [1972]) strain the text intolerably." (Bauckham, *Climax of Prophecy,* 318).

brings to fulfillment the theme of the conversion of the nations which was set out in 1:13; 14:14–16; 15:4.[7]

Supersedes all the visions of judgment? Is he suggesting that the previous judgment visions are not merely followed by this reconciliation scene, but that God actually provides a saving alternative that overtakes, supplants, or curtails the judgments altogether? Was this not exactly the experience of Nineveh in Jonah's time? I suppose that will largely be up to the nations as they stand at the crossroads of possibility.

Once into the New Jerusalem, the nations receive leaves for healing from the tree of life, which grows on each side of the throne-sourced waters. More questions arise: From what do they need healing in the new cosmos where suffering and mourning have been abolished? Would this not already have been taken care of through death and resurrection—or by having their robes washed in the blood of the Lamb on the way in? Without forcing answers into a particular eschatological system, let us accept once again the possibility of a next-world process of healing where the Lamb, himself, will shepherd us to the waters and will wipe away the last vestige of tears from this present evil age (Rev 7:17; 21:4).

The promise is that there will be no *katathema*. Once again, to Bauckham, who sees here an allusion to Zechariah 14:11 and the sacred ban of destruction, which Yahweh pronounced against his enemies, necessitating their utter destruction.[8]

> John has taken [Zech 14] to mean that the nations who dwell in the New Jerusalem, where they are healed of their idolatry and other sins by the leaves of the tree of life, will never again be subject to the destruction which God decrees for those nations who oppose his rule.[9]

THE ONE QUESTION: THE EMERGING VISION

What we know of the new heaven and new earth came completely in dreams. But they weren't just Isaiah's and Ezekiel's dreams or Daniel's and John's dreams. They are God's dreams, poured out by the Spirit into the hearts of old and young, women and men, even to the least of his king-

---

7. Bauckham, 318.
8. Baukham, 316.
9. Baukham, 317.

dom servants. And God is still dreaming of the world to come, sharing extravagant visions that make us thirsty for more.

My wife, Eden, dreams these dreams. In night visions, she sees a house on top of a mountain. A spring of water bubbles up from the floorboards and trickles across the floor. By the time it exits the door and crosses the deck, it is two feet deep. Running off the deck and toward the cliff, the stream becomes a powerful river. Then it plummets as a deafening waterfall, increasing in volume as it descends to the lush valley below. I believe such dreams come from the same Spirit who enlivened John's dreams, recounting spiritual truths in familiar ancient symbols, a foretaste of what is to come.

More than a foretaste—an inviting question: *Are you thirsty?* (cf. Isa 55:1–5). It's the question that opens the door of the city and leads the way into it as far as the river's source. It's the invitation-question of the Spirit and the Bride to the nations outside. It's the question that Rev 21–22 asks both then and now. Are you thirsty? As I've marinated in those chapters for the past two years, this vision has emerged for me . . .

Lost souls languish outside the gates of the great city, their thirst deepening as they fester in the smoking valley of Gehenna. Time has lost all meaning in this non-life of non-being. Lips and hearts are cracked with hopelessness like baked clay. Their time to choose has passed, their judgment just and certain, death eternal their lot. They cannot even make themselves care.

And then an intrusive question forms in their hearts. *Are you thirsty?* Beyond ludicrous—the question reawakens the exiles to their torment and intensifies their thirst. *Are you thirsty?* They recall the pointless supplication, "Have pity on me and send someone to dip a fingertip in water to cool my tongue, because I am in agony in this fire." Hopeless.

But the question has begun its work. Hearts gaze longingly at the city walls. The question has energized a plea. *What if we trudged out a pilgrimage to Zion's gates to seek an audience with the King? What if—hope against hope—someone opened the gates?* Even without hope or courage, the thirst itself drives them. *Are you thirsty?* There is no choice now. They must try.

Even as the damned set their hearts upon the journey, while still a good distance away, the heart of God is already turned toward them, for the question originated from his throne, amplified beyond the city walls by the voice of the Bride and the Spirit. The question and its answer gushes out with life-giving rivers of liquid love. Christ, the river of living water, pours out of the open gates and into the valley of death. Streams flow into Gehenna, where green shoots spring up on widening banks and moisture feeds the valley.

Parched for life and love, the outcasts rush to the river, falling on their faces to lap up the sparkling water. Tasting the goodness gives them a thirst for even more. They are drawn, freely yet irresistibly, to follow the river upstream. Its path welcomes them in through the gates, beckons them up the streets, a clear path to its mountain source—to God himself. As the rapids of Christ's love flow out of the city, so the nations stream into the city, joining the Bride, exalting the Bride, becoming the Bride, ready for the love of her King.

My vision . . . Isaiah's vision . . . John's vision . . . God's vision.

To what degree does this vision represent pure possibility—a choice we can pursue or reject? To what degree is it the eternally planned choice of God? How do our choices and God's plan intersect? And for how long will God pursue the dream?

13

The Alpha and Omega

"Done"

DONE?

So much of the activity we read about in Revelation 21–22 involves processes (invitation, cleansing, healing, entry) to which traditional theology has barred the door at death that it is tempting to either ignore or transplant these processes. If we don't treat them as already realized eschatology, the Bible forces us to consider the possibility that the lost who perish still have hope of eternal life after the Day of the Lord.

I use the term "forces" advisedly because of our reluctance to surrender old theological wineskins and neatly crafted temples of eschatology. What of my beautifully certain system? I say "forces" because such openness does not easily serve the interests and agendas of Christendom. Whither goes our leverage over the laity if we can't constantly remind them of the hellfire licking at their heels? Nor does it reflect accurately the less charitable dispositions of our own exclusive boundary building. How shall we define who is in and who is out? Us and them? I say "forces" for those who would avoid being marginalized as closet universalists. Is the contempt of the evangelical Sanhedrin worth the price of keeping your hope a secret? And even in the best case, I say, "forces," because Augustine's pastoral fears still haunt us. Won't such hope lead to presumption?

But at the end of the Book, at the End of Days, we are led not to presumption but to genuine Christian hope. The Bible has thoroughly warned us that a day of reckoning approaches where the destruction of the finally impenitent is possible. Acknowledging that, when literally all is said and done, we have Christ—the *telos*—fulfilling what he intended from the beginning, subsuming everything and everyone in himself for the glory of his Father. Only then will he conclude:

> Rev 21:6—He said to me: "Done! (*gegonan*[1]) I am the Alpha-intention and the Omega-reality, the Beginning-plan and the End-fulfilled." [my translation]

Julian of Norwich, the great mystic and doctor of the church, saw that end in her *Revelations of Divine Love,* through which she received this hope of assurance from Christ:

> There is a deed that the blessed Trinity shall do on the last day, and when that deed shall be done, and how it shall be done, is unknown to all creatures under Christ, and shall be until it has been done.... This is the great deed ordained by our Lord God from eternity, treasured and hidden in his blessed breast, known only to himself, and by this deed he shall make all things well; for just as the Holy Trinity made all things from nothing, so the Holy Trinity shall make all well that is not well.[2]

SURRENDER: A WORD FROM ANNE RICE

Could this possibly be true?

I sure as hell hope so.[3] That is to say, I am more hopeful of Jesus than I am sure of hell. What if there is a brand of surrender where hope is enough? What if God is so good that you could just trust him without really knowing? Anne Rice, famed author[4] and radical convert, thinks so. In *Called Out of Darkness,* Rice's spiritual autobiography, she describes the relief of exchanging certainty for hope.

> In the moment of surrender, I let go of all the theological or social questions which had kept me from Him for countless years. I simply let them go. There was the sense, profound and wordless, that if He knew everything I did not have to know everything, and that, in seeking to know everything, I'd been, all of my life, missing the entire point.

1. Verb: Third Person Perfect Active Indicative Plural. It could also be fun to translate this, "They became."
2. Julian of Norwich, *Revelations of Divine Love,* 33.
3. Catch the way that hell is sandwiched between surety and hope in that tiny phrase.
4. Esp. for her *Vampire Chronicles* and *Christ the Lord* series.

No social paradox, no historic disaster, no hideous record of injustice or misery should keep me from Him. No question of Scriptural integrity, no torment over the fate of this or that atheist or gay friend, no worry for those condemned and ostracized by my church or any other church should stand between me and Him. The reason? It was magnificently simple: He knew how or why *everything* happened; He knew the disposition of *every single soul.*

He wasn't going to let anything happen by accident! Nobody was going to go to Hell by mistake. This was His world, all this! He had complete control of it; His justice, His mercy—were not our justice or our mercy. What folly to even imagine such a thing.

I didn't have to know how He was going to save the unlettered and the unbaptized, or how He would redeem the conscientious heathen who had never spoken His name. I didn't have to know how my gay friends would find their way to Redemption; or how my hardworking secular humanist friends could or would receive the power of His Saving Grace. I didn't have to know why good people suffered agony or died in pain. He knew.

And it was His *knowing* that overwhelmed me, His *knowing* that became completely real to me, His *knowing* that became the warp and woof of the Universe which He had made.

His was—after all—the Divine Mind which had made the miracle of the Big Bang, and created the DNA only lately discovered in every physical cell. His was the Divine Mind that had created the sound of the violin in the Beethoven concerto; His was the Divine Mind that made snowflakes, idle flames, birds soaring upwards, the unfolding mystery of gender, and the gravity that seemingly held the Universe together—as our planet, our single little planet, hurtled through space.

Of course. If He could do all that, *naturally* He knew the answer to every conceivable question before it was formulated. He knew the worst suffering that a human soul could feel. Nothing was wasted with Him because He was the author of all of it. He was the Creator of creatures who felt anger, alienation, rage, despair. In this great novel that was His creation, He knew every plot, every character, every action, every voice, every syllable, and every jot of ink.

And why should I remain apart from Him just because I couldn't grasp all this? He could grasp it. Of course!

It was love that brought me to this awareness, love that brought me into a complete trust in Him, a trust that God who made us could not ever abandon us—that the seeming meaninglessness of our world was the limit of our understanding, but never, never the limit of His.[5]

> Despite the Church's curse, there is no one
> so lost that the eternal love cannot
> return—as long as hope shows something green.

> —Dante, *Purgatorio*, Canto III. 133–35

---

5. Anne Rice, *Called Out of Darkness*, 183–85.

Addendum

A Word to Fellow Evangelicals

As a born, bred, and reborn evangelical evangelist, I am keenly aware of the slippery-slope concerns over the rampant pop-universalism of our day. I hope evangelical readers catch my insistence upon the biblical possibilities, as employed by the Church Fathers, so they can distinguish hope from presumption. Even so, for their sake, I sense the need to press a bit harder on several points.

In our traditional defense of the Bible as the infallible Word of God, we have been so committed to proving that the Bible can never contradict itself that we have frequently forced agreement in ways that violate the text. As I hope this book has demonstrated, if we stand over the text rather than under it, we end up trying to force an abundance of puzzle pieces into fitting together, but we bend them badly in the process. People notice this and see us discrediting the very book we mean to honor. This plays right into the hands of atheists like Dawkins and Hitchens, allowing them to make a straw man of faith that is easily consumed by hell's flames.

We need to become even more biblical than that, allowing Scripture to trump our inherited ideologies even when we've invested so much of our hearts in those systems. Dare we let Scripture say what it says without reinterpreting what it "really means" into the margins of our Study Bibles?

Second, if we listen honestly, we will discern between pluralists who see every path leading to heavenly bliss without judgment and without Jesus vis-à-vis the ultimate redemptionists, who continue to say "no one comes to the Father except through Jesus" and "no one enters the kingdom without having his or her robe washed in the Lamb's blood." Yet the latter group proclaims with Revelation 21–22 that heaven's door never shuts, and the Spirit and Bride continue to say, "come." They hope that all may still ultimately respond to the Gospel with a "Yes!" They do not believe in a second-chance theology; it is a seventy-times-seven-and-beyond hope. The question is, is there a place among evangelicals for them? I hope so for the sake of the many who hold these beliefs in secret for fear of expulsion from the Holy City. But such hope does begin outside the gates, doesn't it?

Most grievously, I am troubled by those evangelicals (including ministers) who ask, "If hell doesn't exist (which I am *not* saying in this book), why bother being a Christian?" The envy of hedonism and need for fear is all too apparent in such remarks. To this, I would respond: If your only reason for being a Christian is to avoid hell, I wonder if you have ever encountered the love of our precious Savior. Have you met him? We follow Jesus because he loves us and we love him. We give ourselves to Jesus because he is Lord, because he purchased us with his own blood, and because our salvation is his reward as much as it is ours. In other words, Christian hope is to be Lamb-centered, not self-centered. If our only reason for being a Christian is to avoid hell, we will probably not only go there; we may be there already. Here's an irony: after the first decade of my own infernalism—vacillating between fear and haughtiness—another Bible camp counselor (of all things!) challenged me to follow Jesus just because I loved him, not because I needed his fire insurance.

A related question comes up often: "Why would a universalist share the Gospel? Why bother with missions or evangelism?" In reply I'd like to point out that one of the greatest missionary movements is history was the Moravian Brethren (my roots). They prayed for empowered missions 24/7 for over 100 years and then proceeded to go out into the world to preach the good news. "Earth holds not a sea or shore, unhallowed by [the Moravian missionaries'] dust."[1] Some sold themselves to slave ships to win the slaves, reasoning that, "the Lamb who was slain may receive the reward of his suffering."

> The simple motive of the brethren for sending missionaries to distant nations was and is an ardent desire to promote the salvation of their fellow men, by making known to them the Gospel of our Savior Jesus Christ. It grieved them to hear of so many thousands and millions of the human race sitting in darkness and groaning beneath the yoke of sin and the tyranny of Satan; and remembering the glorious promises given in the Word of God, that the heathen also should be the reward of the sufferings and death of Jesus;

1. From the poem "The Moravian Missionary" by L. B. Case.

and considering His commandment to His followers, to go into all
the world and preach the Gospel to every creature, they were filled
with confident hopes that if they went forth in obedience unto,
and believing in His word, their labor would not be in vain in the
Lord. (1791 Evangelical Report)[2]

With that backdrop of zeal, I was surprised to find that many of the
more radical Moravians were universalists![3] Included in the "Sixteen
Discourses" of Moravian literature is the statement,

> "By Christ's Name, all can and shall obtain life and salvation."
> A few hundred years later, Peter Boehler (1712–75) spread the
> Moravian faith to England and the American colonies, and in-
> cluded in his message the teaching of Universalism. He wrote that
> "all the damned souls shall yet be brought out of hell." Boehler was
> a German-born missionary who became a bishop in the Moravian
> Church.[4]

What drove them to lay down their lives if not the fear of hell? First, like
Jesus, the Moravians looked out on the masses and saw that people are ha-
rassed and helpless, in dire need of a Shepherd (Matt 9:35–38). They were
grieved by the grip that darkness had on the land. The compassion of the
Father rose inside them to see that broken people needed and freedom today, from every kind of bondage and oppression the world has contrived.
Christ saves us from a horrible reality—he called it "perishing"—both
present and future.

He also saves us to a glorious reality—namely, to himself—both
present and future. Having been freed, the prisoner exalts in that redemption and then falls at the feet of the Redeemer in gratitude. The Moravians
wanted people to know Jesus, because knowing the Savior is the greatest
privilege and blessing in the universe. They knew him as intimate Friend
and constant Guide—what could be sweeter? Why wouldn't we be com-
pelled to share such love?

Finally, in their mature love for Jesus, the Moravians' highest stated
motive for evangelism was so that the "Lamb would receive the full reward of his suffering." They were deeply convinced that we were the joy

2. Don Hawkinson, *Character for Life*, 303. See also Hamilton and Hamilton, *History of the Moravian Church*.

3. I wonder if they were reacting to the hellfire preaching of some of their Hussite forefathers of the generation after Hus.

4. "History of Universalism," para. 49.

Christ anticipated when he endured the Cross! What does that say about the value he has placed on us? And on how much he deserves to receive that joy? Is there any greater gift that we could give him than to present him with the pearls of great price for which gave his life?

Note: not a single one of their impressive motives for evangelism depended on the fear of infernalism.

I find myself more freely evangelistic now than at any other time in my life, and yet without any pressure or fear. It is wonderful. The sad thing is that some of my acquaintances, including many who lead entire churches, admit that if there was no hell, they would not follow Jesus and they would not bother telling others about him. I can't imagine a sadder state of affairs.

This is the negation of the negation[5]—where something that's supposed to represent the positive charge of a value produces the negative charge instead. It's the worst possible position to be in, in relation to any given value. Jesus describes the negation of the negation perfectly here: "But if your eyes are bad, your whole body will be full of darkness. If then the light within you is darkness, how great is that darkness!" (Matt 6:23).

In this instance, if my faith depends on fear of punishment, what will happen to my faith when perfect love (Jesus) comes to cast it out? (1 John 4:18) If God thinks that fear of punishment is something to be "cast out" like a demon, then our Gospel and our preaching better not rest on that foundation! Fear-based faith (a paradox) is the ultimate deception. We need to examine closely whether the devil has been hiding in plain sight—squatting within the very message that we've preached. Parasite and deceiver that he is, he found the ultimate host to help disseminate his terror campaign—the Church! If our faith message begins in fear, as it did for many evangelicals like me, it's in trouble. I am reminded of Jesus' warning, "Woe to you, teachers of the law and Pharisees, you hypocrites! You travel over land and sea to win a single convert, and when he becomes one, you make him twice as much a son of hell as you are" (Matt 23:15). The negation of negation. Does preaching on hell produce converts? Oh yes! But if in the process it also saddles someone with fear of punishment, then it has simultaneously reproduced a "son of hell."

Rather than wallpaper over these holes and renovate our theology in a vain attempt to mask or repair problems, perhaps it's time we considered

---

5. Thanks to my editor, Kevin Miller, whose experience in screenwriting led him to explain this phenomenon to me.

bulldozing the house and starting over, laying a new foundation in Christ, our blessed hope.

I conclude with this exhortation to examine our hearts on this question: What in us *needs* the traditional infernalist version of hell? What purpose does it fulfill? Is it our carnal sense of justice as payback or an even darker *Schadenfreude?* If anything needs purging, it is that. In exchange, I believe God has called us to surrender our self-assurance for a much broader and deeper hope. We return to the quote by Lauter that I used in chapter one, offering it as a summary statement.

> Will it really be all men who allow themselves to be reconciled? No theology or prophecy can answer this question. But love hopes all things (1 Cor 13:7). It cannot do otherwise than to hope for the reconciliation of all men in Christ. Such unlimited hope is, from the Christian standpoint, not only permitted but commanded.[6]

What think ye?

---

6. Hermann-Josef Lauter, *Pastoralblatt,* 123.

AFTERWORD

Hell: The Nemesis of Hope?

Nik Ansell

Abandon every hope, who enter here.

—Dante, *Inferno*, Canto III. 9

Despite the Church's curse, there is no one
so lost that the eternal love cannot
return—as long as hope shows something green.

—Dante, *Purgatorio*, Canto III. 133–35[1]

IF HELL IS THE nemesis of hope, can it be part of the Gospel? If Christ came to "free those who all their lives were held in slavery by their fear of death" (Heb 2:15[2]), should the fear of Hell keep the Church in business? If not, what on earth does "hell" mean in the New Testament?

TOO HOT TO HANDLE?

The central aim of this essay is to create an opening for a new understanding of the Final Judgment.[3] To that end, it will be helpful to first revisit a

1. *The Divine Comedy of Dante Alighieri, Inferno.* A Verse Translation with an Introduction by Allen Mandelbaum (New York: Quality Paperback Book Club, 1981) 20–21 and *The Divine Comedy Of Dante Alighieri, Purgatorio.* A Verse Translation with an Introduction by Allen Mandelbaum (New York: Quality Paperback Book Club, 1983) 26–27.

2. Because I am engaging with evangelical theology in particular in this essay, biblical quotations will be from the New International Version (NIV). Translations from the apocryphal/deutero-canonical work 2 Esdras (which includes 4 Ezra) will be from the New Revised Standard Version.

3. In the penultimate section, it will become clear that I do not accept this traditional way of referring to the judgment of the age to come. The correlate of creating an opening

controversy that came to a head twenty years ago concerning the theology of John Stott—a church leader who has been so influential and is so highly regarded world-wide that the New York Times recently referred to him as the "Pope" of Evangelicals.[4]

In 1988, David Edwards, an Anglican scholar long associated with the Student Christian Movement and SCM Press in the UK, published a respectful yet often probing analysis of Stott's theology entitled Essentials: A Liberal-Evangelical Dialogue. Predictably enough perhaps, one of Edwards' sharpest challenges concerned the traditional doctrine of Hell. Stott's response, in the space he was given at the end of the relevant chapter,[5] is now as famous as it is contentious. Forced to come clean about a topic he had largely avoided in his writings, he unambiguously rejected mainstream evangelical theology at this point, declaring himself to be an "annihilationist." While in traditional orthodoxy, the eternal souls of the saved and the damned experience either the blessing or the wrath of God forever, in Stott's "conditional immortality," the parallel (if not the contrast) is broken as those who fail to repent have no future in the age to come, thus passing out of existence. In the overcoming of evil, Hell itself will pass away.[6]

---

for a new understanding of the Final—better, eschatological—Judgment is that I will be arguing that it is inappropriate to read current notions back into the Gospels' portrayal of "hell."

4. See David Brooks, "Who Is John Stott?" New York Times, November 30, 2004, available online at: http://www.nytimes.com/2004/11/30/opinion/30brooks.html?_r=1. Brooks cites Michael Cromartie of the Ethics and Public Policy Center as saying that "if evangelicals could elect a pope, Stott is the person they would likely choose."

5. See "John Stott's Response to Chapter 6," in David L. Edwards, with John Stott, Essentials: A Liberal-Evangelical Dialogue (London: Hodder & Stoughton, 1988) 306–31.

6. Although Stott does refer to "annihilation," (Essentials, 315, 318, 320), he seems to prefer to speak of "conditional immortality" (ibid., 316). One of the merits of characterizing this position as "annihilationism" is that it captures how those who remain in their sins come to nothing (Latin nihil) to the point where they are not even "history." At the same time, it is important to note that for Stott, and for many others associated with this viewpoint, this is a misleading term because of what it could imply about God. A key tenet of Stott's position, in distinction from traditional orthodoxy, is that the soul is not inherently immortal. Consequently, those who reject the gift of eternal life are seen as either foregoing resurrection altogether or as being left to pass out of existence after the Final Judgment. God, in other words, does not "actively" destroy them. This is a more fundamental departure from the God of traditional orthodoxy than "annihilationism" might be imply.

Although reluctant to articulate his convictions in this area due to his concern for unity in the world-wide evangelical community, Stott nevertheless thanked Edwards for forcing the issue. He even went as far as to say of the traditional position, "[E]motionally, I find the concept intolerable and do not understand how people can live with it without either cauterising their feelings or cracking under the strain."[7]

Stott's reluctance to write on the issue of Hell and its annihilation because of the disunity it could create (or reveal) proved to be well founded. Soon afterwards, at a major conference set up in North America to discuss what it meant to be an evangelical, the question was raised as to whether Stott himself should now be excluded given these recent revelations.[8] This was put to a vote. The motion was only narrowly defeated. The Pope was almost excommunicated!

THE ANNIHILATIONIST ALTERNATIVE

Annihilationism or conditional immortality has since been widely discussed and debated.[9] If Stott's theology is as representative here as it is elsewhere, then perhaps in another twenty years, this view of Hell will no longer be confined to "open" evangelicals, but may come to characterize the evangelical "mainstream." Much will depend on whether there is widespread acceptance of Stott's two-fold conviction that the Bible "points

7. Ibid., 314.

8. The back cover of *Essentials*—hot off the press and on sale at the conference—introduced a summary of the dialogue to be found within its pages by posing the question: "What beliefs define an evangelical?" For an account of the Evangelical Affirmations consultation, see Walter Unger, "Focusing the Evangelical Vision" in *Direction* 20/1 (Spring 1991) 3–17, available online at: http://www.directionjournal.org/article/?692.

9. In *Essentials*, 320, Stott wrote, "I do not dogmatise about the position to which I have come. I hold it tentatively. But I do plead for frank dialogue among Evangelicals on the basis of Scripture." For examples of the dialogue that Stott was hoping for, see William Crockett, ed., *Four Views On Hell* (Grand Rapids: Zondervan, 1996) and Edward William Fudge and Robert A. Peterson, *Two Views Of Hell: A Biblical and Theological Dialogue* (Downers Grove, IL: InterVarsity, 2000). For additional evidence that annihilationism is increasingly perceived as a legitimate evangelical position, see David Hilborn, ed., *The Nature Of Hell: A Report by the Evangelical Alliance's Commission on Unity and Truth among Evangelicals (ACUTE)* (Milton Keynes, UK: Acute/Paternoster, 2000). For an Anglican case for annihilationism that included but was not confined to evangelical input, see *The Mystery of Salvation: The Story of God's Gift*. A Report by the Doctrine Commission of the General Synod of the Church of England (London: Church, 1995) 198–99.

in the direction of annihilation," and that "'eternal conscious torment' is a tradition which has to yield to the supreme authority of Scripture."[10]

Stott puts forward four main reasons for his position. *Firstly*, he proposes, we must take the biblical language of judgment-as-destruction far more seriously, and *secondly*, in the light of this extensive body of material,[11] we must interpret the imagery of eternal fire far more carefully. In this context, Stott argues that fire's main function "is not to cause pain, but to secure destruction, as all the world's incinerators bear witness."[12] It is the fire that is eternal and unquenchable, Stott insists, not what is thrown into it. The smoke that "rises for ever and ever" (Rev 14:11) is therefore to be seen as evidence that the fire has done its work. Eternal punishment, in other words, is not eternal punish*ing*.

Thus far, Stott has been claiming that the "imagery" of hellfire, addressed in his second argument, is to be understood within the "language" of destruction, addressed in his first argument.[13] His third and fourth arguments for annihilationism are similarly connected and concern the nature of justice as that is to be understood within God's victory over evil.

Stott's *third* point is that God's justice is surely a justice in which "the penalty inflicted will be commensurate with the evil done." Sin is indeed a grave matter, but in the traditional position there is a "serious disproportion,"[14] in Stott's judgment, between sins consciously committed in time and the torment that is to be consciously experienced throughout eternity as a result. Aware that traditional orthodoxy justifies everlasting punishment on the grounds that sinners will continue in their impenitence for ever, Stott develops his *fourth* point which involves an appeal to those texts that are taken by some to point to a biblical vision of universal salvation. It is not that Stott wishes to defend

10. *Essentials*, 315. One might explore the question of the future of evangelicalism by asking whether it will be the theology of John Stott or that of J. I. Packer that will endure. See n. 17 below.

11. In support of reading judgment as destruction, Stott, in *Essentials*, 315, initially cites: Matt 7:13; 10:28; John 3:16; 10:28; 17:12; Rom 2:12; 9:22; 1 Cor 1:18; 15:18; 2 Cor 2:15; 4:3; Phil 1:28; 3:19; 1 Thess 5:3; 2 Thess 1:9; 2:10; Heb 10:39; Jas 4:12; 2 Pet 3:9 and Rev 17:8, 11.

12. Ibid., 316.

13. Stott's distinction between "language" and "imagery" is explicit in ibid., 315 and 318 and frames the discussion of the first two points. His critics could presumably reverse this hermeneutically loaded distinction.

14. Ibid., 318.

universalism—far from it![15] But the biblical themes of God's final victory over evil and his becoming "all in all" (1 Cor 15:28) which are present in these texts[16] are incompatible, he insists, with the eternal existence of those who are damned and who would thus presumably continue to be in a state of rebellion against God.

Annihilationism, Stott proposes, solves these problems while doing justice to the biblical language about the judgment of the impenitent. His critics, however, accuse him of "special pleading" and of "playing fast and loose" with Scripture.[17] The questions this controversy raises are still very much alive. Which position can claim biblical support? Which viewpoint should we endorse? With whom should we side: the annihilationists or the traditionalists?

THE LAST WORD?

My own answer is: neither! Both positions, I suggest, must be rejected for at least two reasons, both of which call out for the development of a new theology in which Hell is no longer the nemesis of hope.

Firstly, both views allow evil to have the last word. As annihilationists have been quick to realize, the Hell of traditional orthodoxy cannot do justice to the vision of Hab 2:14 in which "the earth will be filled with the knowledge of the glory of the Lord as the waters cover the sea," or to the NT expression of this hope found in the promise that God will become "all in all" (1 Cor 15:28). The traditional claim that the eternal suffering of

---

15. See *Essentials*, 319. There is now some evidence that universalism is being considered as an evangelical possibility. See David Hilborn and Don Horrocks, "Universalistic Trends in the Evangelical Tradition: An Historical Perspective" in Robin A. Parry and Christopher H. Partridge, eds., *Universal Salvation? The Current Debate* (Grand Rapids: Eerdmans, 2003). This volume gives particular attention to the evangelical universalism of Thomas Talbott. Cf. Gregory MacDonald, *The Evangelical Universalist* (Eugene, OR: Cascade, 2006).

16. In addition to 1 Cor 15:28, he also cites John 12:32; Eph 1:10; Phil 2:10–11 and Col 1:20 in *Essentials*, 319. There is a parallel between Stott's first and fourth points and between his claim that the biblical texts that speak of judgment-as-destruction and the biblical texts that speak of the "universal" nature of salvation both need to be taken far more seriously. But the parallel is incomplete as Stott does not turn to the latter texts to define the contours of a paradigm.

17. See for example, J. I. Packer, "The Problem of Eternal Punishment," the account of Packer's response to Stott in Robert A. Peterson, *Hell On Trial: The Case for Eternal Punishment* (Phillipsburg, NJ: P. & R., 1995) 11–16, and Peterson's own response to Stott in ibid., 161–82. For Peterson's debate with Fudge, see n. 9 above.

the impenitent serves to glorify God by revealing his justice reduces the revelation of God's glory to the restoration of God's honor, thus separating the glory of God from the glorification of creation.[18] Justice conceived as retribution closes down redemption and blocks the dawn of the age to come. In traditional eschatology, sinners no longer have the power to sin after the final judgment, yet they remain sinners. If they are to be everlastingly punished for the sins of the past, and for their impenitent condition, how is evil not still present in the world?[19]

While the annihilationist attempt to find eschatological resolution beyond the confines of traditional orthodoxy is certainly justified, their counter-proposal has serious problems of its own. It is worth reminding ourselves, especially in this age of ecological violence and crisis, that the annihilation and destruction of God's good creation is precisely the aim and goal of evil, not evidence of its defeat. The destruction, including the self-destruction, of those made in God's image represents a victory for the forces of darkness. In the transformation of everlasting punishment into final judgment,[20] evil still has the last word.

Secondly, I would like to suggest that both traditional orthodoxy and annihilationism seriously misread the Scriptures. There are fourteen references to "hell" in the NT according to the NIV, eleven of which refer to a place where human beings may end up as a result of God's judgment. These eleven references all occur in the words of Jesus. Seven of the

18. Another way to put this is to say that traditional orthodoxy in unable to appreciate the biblical development in which God's rule over creation "makes way for" (even as it makes the way for) God's eschatological presence with creation. Cf. n. 19 below.

19. One might redefine good and evil in the light of a certain view of God's honor and imagine that provided God's justice is being revealed, there is no longer evil from God's point of view. But I do not see how God can be "all in all" in this perspective. Traditional orthodoxy can, in its own way, speak of God's eschatological presence. Thus God might be said to be present in terms of (a certain view of) justice towards the impenitent while being present in terms of a love beyond justice towards the saved. But the contrast— between justice and love, between a justice without love and a love beyond justice— points to an absence and thus to a limited view of God's full eschatological presence that cannot do justice to Hab 2:14 and 1 Cor 15:28.

It is important to stress that love beyond justice includes a justice whose nature is fulfilled in love. While there cannot be love without justice, there cannot be the fullest form of justice without love. This means that traditional orthodoxy cannot do justice to justice. On the notion of justice "making way for" love, see n. 18 above and the comments on "judgment unto salvation" below.

20. On the language of final judgment, see the section entitled "judgment unto salvation" below.

eleven are to be found in Matthew (5:22, 29, 30; 10:28; 18:9; 23:15, 33). The remaining four are all parallel texts: three in Mark (9:43–47) and one in Luke (12:5). These biblical references require closer attention than they have received in the current debate.

GEHENNA

The Greek word for "hell" in these texts is transliterated into English as "Gehenna."[21] In its earlier Hebrew form, Gehenna makes its debut in the Bible as a geographical place: the valley of (the son(s) of) Hinnom, or *gê hinnōm* (see Josh 15:8; 18:16).[22] According to archeologists, this is one of the valleys to be found close to the walls of Jerusalem.[23]

In Jer 7:30–34, this valley is no longer seen as a piece of real estate that anyone would wish to own.[24] Now it has become a place of judgment—an imminent judgment in history directed against Israel:

> The people of Judah have done evil in my eyes, declares the Lord. They have set up their detestable idols in the house that bears my Name and have defiled it. They have built the high places of Topheth[25] in the Valley of Ben Hinnom to burn their sons and daughters in the fire—something I did not command, nor did it enter my mind. So beware, the days are coming, declares the Lord, when people will no longer call it Topheth or the Valley of Ben Hinnom, but the Valley of Slaughter, for they will bury the dead

21. Gehenna is also the term in James 3:6, but this is not a reference to a place of judgment. To complete the survey of the fourteen references to "hell" in the NIV, Luke 16:23 refers to Hades as an intermediate state, while 2 Pet 2:4 refers to Tartarus, which is also intermediate and not associated with human beings.

22. To trace the journey of the term fully from Hebrew to English, there are four main steps: first, the Hebrew *gê hinnōm* takes on an Aramaic form as *gēhinā(m)*. This is then transliterated into Greek as *géenna*, before being transliterated into the Latin Gehenna, from which is derived the English term.

23. See Lloyd R. Bailey, "Gehenna: The Topography of Hell" in *Biblical Archaeologist* 49 (1986) 187–91. Cf. Stephen Von Wyrick, "Gehenna" in David Noel Freedman, Allen C. Myers, and Astrid B. Beck, eds., *Eerdmans Dictionary of the Bible* (Grand Rapids: Eerdmans, 2000) 489 and Richard A. Spencer, "Hinnom, Valley of" in ibid., 592. Cf. n. 25 below.

24. There is one other geographical reference, found in Neh 11:30, that does not carry the connotations of judgment to be explored below.

25. Brian P. Irwin, "Topheth," 1321, notes that Topheth was probably "at the lower end of Hinnom Valley close to the southern tip of the City of David." It is thought that the name may derive from the Aramaic word for "fireplace" combined with the vowels from the Hebrew word for "shame."

in Topheth until there is no more room. Then the carcasses of the people will become food for the birds of the air and the beasts of the earth, and there will be no one to frighten them away. I will bring an end to the sounds of joy and gladness and to the voices of bride and bridegroom in the towns of Judah and the streets of Jerusalem, for the land will become desolate.

Similar language occurs in Jer 19, where an imminent siege of Jerusalem is prophesied in response to Israel's idolatry. The references to burning sons and daughters in the fire (see Jer 7:31; 19:5 and 32:35) refer to atrocities associated with Judah's kings Ahaz and Manasseh (2 Kgs 16:2–3 and 21:1–6). That such sacrifices were conducted in the Valley of Hinnom is made explicit in 2 Kgs 23:10 and in the parallel account of their reigns found in 2 Chr 28:3 and 33:6.

The valley continues to be associated with idolatry and fire in the prophetic tradition, but now the fire is seen as coming from God. In Isa 30:33, God says:

Topheth has long been prepared; it has been made ready for the king [of Assyria, cf. v. 31]. Its fire pit has been made deep and wide, with an abundance of fire and wood; the breath of the Lord, like a stream of burning sulfur, sets it ablaze.

In this imminent, historical judgment, we have fire and sulfur, or fire and brimstone, which harks back to the destruction of Sodom and Gomorrah (Gen 19:24) and reappears in the Book of Revelation (see Rev 14:10; 19:20; 20:10 and 21:8).[26]

The same valley is also intended as the location for the judgment described in the final verse of the book of Isaiah. Thus Isa 66:22–23 reads,

"From one New Moon to another and from one Sabbath to another, all mankind will come and bow down before me," says the Lord. "And they will go out and look upon the dead bodies of those who rebelled against me; their worm will not die, nor will their fire be quenched, and they will be loathsome to all mankind."

During the rise and fall of Jewish nationalism—a period which includes the Maccabean revolt against the Seleucids (169–160 BCE), the Great War against Rome (66–70 CE) and the revolt of Bar Kokhba, also against Rome (132–135 CE)—it is not hard to see how these passages from Isaiah, taken

---

26. Imagery from Jer 7:30–34 shows up in Rev 18:23 and 19:21.

together with the portrayal of God's judgment of the nations in Joel 3,[27] could have fuelled the conviction that the dead bodies of Israel's enemies should be cast into this Gehenna.[28]

While a nationalistic agenda that would equate God's enemies with Israel's enemies is foreign to the prophetic tradition, it remains the case that for the OT prophets, Gehenna is understood as the place where the wicked will be punished with fire in the "last days." But as this is an earthly place outside Jerusalem and as the "last days" are clearly understood as taking place within history,[29] this is very different from the Gehenna of later rabbinic literature in which the Valley of Hinnom has become an underworld or otherworldly realm that has been in existence since the creation.[30] Such a place can indeed be identified with the Hell of traditional Christian theology. But these later Jewish texts all come from a time after the destruction of Jerusalem in 70 CE when the Jewish worldview was thrown into crisis, to be recast by the rabbis into a far less geograph-

27. While the valley in Joel 3:2, 12, 14 is symbolically rather than geographically named, its close vicinity to Jerusalem, as indicated in 2:9 and 3:16, means that it would have been associated, if not identified, with the Valley of Hinnom.

28. As Von Wyrick puts it in ibid., 489, "By the time of the Maccabees, the valley was the appropriate location in which to burn the bodies of one's enemies." Here he would seem to be echoing Bailey's claim, in "Gehenna," 188, about the use of the Valley of Hinnom in the Maccabean revolt. While 1 Maccabees itself is not considered an apocalyptic work, and while it makes no mention of the valley, the frequent references to the burning of Israel's enemies (see 1 Macc 3:5; 4:20; 5:5, 28, 35, 44, 65, 68; 6:31; 10:84, 85; 11:4, 61; 16:10; cf. 2 Macc 8:33; 10:36; 12:6) are significant, especially if this work influenced the way Joel 3 and Isa 66:23 were (mis)read. Cf. n. 33 below. The other texts that Von Wyrick refers to in this context are 2 Esdras 7:36 and 1 Enoch 27:1–2 on which see nn. 45 and 32 below.

29. If one were to read Isa 66 in the light of the reference to the "last days" in Isa 2:2, or if we were to interpret Joel 2:28 as referring to the "last days" (as this text is cited in Acts 2:17) and then read Joel 3:1ff. in that light, Peter's understanding of the "last days" as falling within history in Acts 2 underscores the point I am making. OT apocalyptic prophecy is not about the "end" of history. The transition between the two ages is a different matter. Cf. n. 36 below.

30. Although child sacrifice in the Valley of Hinnom was associated with Molech (2 Kgs 23:10), who was an underworld deity, the prophetic tradition does not seek to portray an "underwordly" reality. When later Christians saw this as a hellish realm ruled over by Satan (thus going beyond the underworld understanding of Gehenna found in the later rabbinic tradition, cf. n. 31 below), one might wonder whether Molech had found a place in the "Christian" imagination.

ically-rooted form.[31] By contrast, the Gehenna of the Gospels, I suggest, continues the OT tradition of imminent, this-worldly judgment.[32]

31. At this point, I find a crucial lack of precision in the articles by Bailey, Von Wyrick, Spencer, Kirk-Duggan and Reicke cited in nn. 23 above, 32 below, and in the present note. The projection of later texts back on to the Gospels is especially evident in J. Lunde, "Heaven and Hell" in Joel B. Green, Scot McKnight and I. Howard Marshall, eds., *Dictionary of Jesus and the Gospels* (Downers Grove, IL: InterVarsity, 1992) 309–11. For further details concerning the dating and evaluation of the relevant references to Gehenna, see my *The Annihilation of Hell: Universal Salvation and the Redemption of Time in the Eschatology of Jürgen Moltmann* (Carlisle, UK: Paternoster, forthcoming), chap. 7, esp. 7.1. There I argue that the eclipse of Jewish nationalism and its focus on land as the locus of God's promises after the destruction of Jerusalem, an eclipse which is so evident in the early rabbinic tradition, must be borne in mind when that tradition occasionally attributes belief in an "underworldly" Gehenna to Jewish teachers in the early first century. For, as Bo Reicke notes, in "Gehenna" in Bruce M. Metzger and Michael D. Coogan, *The Oxford Companion to the Bible* (New York and Oxford: Oxford University Press, 1993) 243, "In the Mishnah and later rabbinic texts, the name Gehenna ... has superseded the older terms for underworld (Sheol)." Cf. n. 32 below. (For the more general, methodological point of not reading the Mishnah back into the NT, see, e.g., Alan Segal, *Paul the Convert: The Apostolate and Apostasy of Saul the Pharisee* [New Haven: Yale University Press, 1990] xiv and Doron Mendels, *The Rise and Fall of Jewish Nationalism: Jewish and Christian Ethnicity in Ancient Palestine* [Grand Rapids: Eerdmans, 1992] 5.) Lunde's claim, in ibid., 311, that "there is ... no explicit distinction in Jesus' teachings between hades and gehenna" is especially misleading.

That Gehenna is effectively hellenized after 70 CE in the rabbinic tradition is a modest claim (cf. the analysis of the extent to which the Jewish worldview could be recast given the eclipse of Jewish nationalism after the failed Diaspora revolt of 115–17 CE in Carl B. Smith II, *No Longer Jews: The Search for Gnostic Origins* [Peabody, MA: Hendrickson, 2004]). But whatever we make of the relevant first century evidence outside the NT (cf. the comments on other non-rabbinic Jewish writings in n. 45 below), my main point below is that Gehenna is not seen as a postmortem underworld in the gospels.

32. This prophetic interpretation of Gehenna also makes good sense of the reference to the "cursed valley" in 1 Enoch 27:1–2 (contra Cheryl A. Kirk-Duggan, "Hell" in David Noel Freedman, Allen C. Myers, and Astrid B. Beck, eds., *Eerdmans Dictionary of the Bible* [Grand Rapids: Eerdmans, 2000] 572–73, which is misleading at this point). It is important to note that this valley is distinct from the underworld of 1 Enoch 22 (cf. George W. E. Nickelsburg, *1 Enoch 1: A Commentary on the Book of 1 Enoch, Chapters 1–36; 81–108* [Minneapolis: Fortress, 2001] 308).

Furthermore, the fact that the chapters that follow (1 Enoch 28–36) lack "explicit eschatological material" but "fill out the comprehensive tour of the ends of the earth" begun in 1 Enoch 17, as John J. Collins notes in *The Apocalyptic Imagination: An Introduction to Jewish Apocalyptic Literature*. Second edition (Grand Rapids: Eerdmans, 1998) 55–56, should (contra Collins) come as no surprise. This material, from what is usually considered the earliest (third century BCE) part of 1 Enoch, is in line with the geographically located portrayal of Gehenna in the OT prophetic tradition. I think that a good case can be made for discerning the same perspective when this valley is in view in later parts of 1 Enoch. See 1 Enoch 54:2 (cf. 53:1, 5 and the note on the displacement of 54:2 in George W.

But there is a twist. Whereas his Jewish contemporaries saw Gehenna as the place where the nations in general and the Romans in particular would get what was coming to them,[33] Jesus, standing in the tradition of Jeremiah, uses the language of the prophets to speak of God's wrath against Jerusalem.[34] Thus, in Mark 9:48, Jesus draws on the final verse of Isaiah, as cited above, to refer to a judgment that will soon fall not on the Romans as expected, but on his fellow Israelites:

> And if your eye causes you to sin, pluck it out. It is better for you to enter the kingdom of God with one eye than to have two eyes and be thrown into [Gehenna], where "their worm will not die, nor will their fire be quenched."[35]

APOCALYPSE THEN ... AND NOW

All of Jesus' references to Gehenna, which are widely thought by believer and non-believer alike to refer to a Last Judgment at the end of time, are actually about the coming judgment on Israel, Jerusalem and its temple. Here we should not be misled by the fact that Jesus' language is apocalyptic in character. It is no coincidence that the last of the seven references to Gehenna in Matthew's gospel (Matt 23:33) is so close to the long discourse about the "end of the age" (Matt 24:3; cf. 24:4—25:46). But to speak of this coming judgment of Jerusalem as "the end of the world," thus using apocalyptic language for the events of history, is a way of speaking that

---

E. Nickelsburg and James C. VanderKam, *1 Enoch: A New Translation* [Minneapolis, MN: Fortress, 2004] 68) and 90:26 (where the valley, seen as an "abyss ... south of that house" [i.e., Jerusalem], is distinguished from the "abyss" of vv. 24–25, as noted by Nickelsburg, *1 Enoch 1*, 403–4). In my view, the distinction between Gehenna and Sheol maintained in the work of VanderKam and Nickelsburg is to be preferred over against the strong inclination to identify them in Marius Reiser, *Jesus And Judgment: The Eschatological Proclamation in Its Jewish Context* (Minneapolis: Fortress, 1997), 66 (including n. 127) and 68.

33. It is easy to imagine how the success of the Maccabean revolt less than two hundred years earlier could inspire a certain reading of Joel 3 or Isa 66:22–23 in this context. Cf. n. 35 below.

34. It is most significant that seven of the eleven references to Gehenna in the synoptics occur in Matthew, for this Gospel is particularly steeped in allusions to Jeremiah. Cf. Michael Knowles, *Jeremiah in Matthew's Gospel: The Rejected-Prophet Motif in Matthaean Redaction* (Sheffield: JSOT, 1993).

35. Here we might contrast the nationalistic appropriation of Isa 66:23 in Judith 16:17.

is not as foreign to us as we might think. When we refer to certain events as "earth-shattering," for example, we know that there may be no literal geological upheavals or volcanic eruptions. But we also know that there are times when we need this kind of language if we are to even begin to capture the significance of what is happening. If we bear this language of cosmic upheaval in mind, then we can better understand the apocalyptic discourse that is found in Scripture.[36]

Contrary to popular belief, no Jew in Jesus' day was expecting God to bring about the end of the space-time universe.[37] But the destruction of the Temple, which was built to symbolize the creation and thus revealing God's presence within it,[38] would be seen as truly cataclysmic. For Jesus, this was God's judgment on Israel, signaling nothing less than what we might call the end of the Old World Order.[39] The only appropriate language was the language of de-creation. This is precisely how Jeremiah speaks in his day of the coming destruction of Judah and the Temple (Jer 4:23–28). God's judgment on Israel, carried out by the Romans, is acted out by Jesus in his "cleansing" of the Temple and his cursing of the fig-tree (see Mark 11:12–25 and 13:28–31). In the coming destruction, he said, the Son of Man would be vindicated (see Mark 13[40]). This judgment/vindica-

---

36. The nature of biblical apocalyptic is contested, but here and in what follows, I am indebted to what I take to be the extremely insightful analysis of N. T. Wright in his *The New Testament and the People of God: Christian Origins and the Question of God*, volume 1 (London: SPCK; Philadelphia: Fortress, 1992) 280–99 (though I differ from him in not developing this reading of apocalyptic in an annihilationist direction, for which see his *Surprised By Hope: Rethinking Heaven, the Resurrection, and the Mission of the Church* (New York: HarperOne, 2008) 175–83). In my judgment, biblical apocalyptic, in its fullest form, has as its focus the transition between the old age and the new age which I refer to below as "the death-throes of the old world order/ the birth-pangs of the new creation." Our contemporary language for the cataclysmic, though it does help us understand this kind of discourse, typically lacks a reference to the birthing of the new.

37. See Wright, *The New Testament and the People of God*, 333.

38. See G. K. Beale, *The Temple and the Church's Mission: A Biblical Theology of the Dwelling Place of God* (Downers Grove, IL: InterVarsity, 2004).

39. Using more traditional terms, this is the end of the old covenant. As references to the "old" covenant can easily be co-opted by anti-Judaism, it is worth pointing out that the language of the new (and by implication the old, first or former) covenant is found in the Hebrew Bible (see Jer 31:31 and cf. the contrast between new and former in Isa 65:17).

40. Mark 13:28 connects this apocalyptic discourse to the cursing of the fig tree in Mark 11:12–14. The reference to the passing away of heaven and earth in Mark 13:31, given the cosmic symbolism and significance of the Temple, may be connected to Mark 13:1–2. These two references to the Temple thus frame the chapter.

tion, which is described in terms of de-creation and enthronement, is also a main theme of the Book of Revelation.[41]

The Jewish leaders and those who followed them were destined for Gehenna, said Jesus. In refusing to be a Light to the Gentiles, in judging the world and in preparing to engage in "holy" war against Rome, Israel had become like her Gentile oppressors, caught in idolatry. It is a grim fact of history that when the Romans laid siege to Jerusalem and the temple, culminating in its destruction, one generation later, the dead who were thrown from the city walls literally piled up in the Valley of Hinnom, Gehenna, Hell.[42]

In Jesus' understanding, this was the "eternal" fire or destruction of God's judgment (Matt 18:8; 25:41; 25:46). When annihilationists claim that it is the punishment rather than the punishing that is everlasting, the argument is tenuous and tortured. But it is also unnecessary. The word translated "eternal" here literally means "of the age (to come)."[43] This is the judgment that ushers in the New Age as foreseen by the prophets who looked forward to the end of the exile.[44] According to the NT, God's judg-

In Wright's analysis, in *The New Testament and the People of God*, 390–96, the language about "the Son of Man coming in clouds with great power and glory" in Mark 13: 26 (and parallels) refers in the language of Dan 7:13 to the coming of the Son of Man to God. This is enthronement language that signals vindication. If there is thus no reference to the "second coming" in the synoptic apocalypse (Mark 13; Matt 24; Luke 21 [in contrast to the eschatological *parousia* that is not referred to until after the ascension of Acts 1:11]), this coheres with the fact that there is nothing in these passages, or in the Synoptics' references to Gehenna, that would place the judgment referred to after the general resurrection. This is an important difference between the gospels and 4 Ezra 7:36 (on which see n. 45 below).

41. I have explored the Book of Revelation in "An Apocalyptic Appendix" in *The Annihilation of Hell*.

42. For a contemporary account, see Josephus, *The Jewish War*, 5.12.3–4.

43. This understanding of *aiōnios* not only allows us to maintain the inverse parallelism of Matt 25:46, thus robbing traditionalists of their main "proof text" against universalists and annihilationists; it also helps us appreciate how the double reference to *ʿōlām* in Dan 12:2 is being intertextually developed within (Matthew's account of) Jesus' teaching (cf. n. 45 below). Biblical terms traditionally thought to refer to the eternal or everlasting need to be translated in a contextually sensitive way. Overlooking this mars the discussion in Alan E. Bernstein, *The Formation of Hell: Death and Retribution in the Ancient and Early Christian Worlds* (Ithaca: Cornell University Press, 1993) 232–33 despite his awareness that eternity is such a loaded term in Augustine's systematic control of the same biblical material in ibid., 318–21.

44. For the return from exile theme in the NT as far deeper than a geographical return to the promised land, see N. T. Wright, *Jesus and the Victory of God: Christian Origins and*

ment on Israel at the hand of the Romans is a judgment that Jesus suffers on the cross so that his followers may avoid it. The destruction of the Temple is the vindication of Jesus and his followers as the true Israel. It also marks God's judgment on the enemies of this true Israel; a judgment that marks the birth-pangs of a new world, heralding the true return from exile and the dawn of the New Creation.[45] Now, with the establishment

---

the Question of God, vol. 2 (London: SPCK; Philadelphia: Fortress, 1996) and Brant Pitre, *Jesus, The Tribulation and the End of the Exile: Restoration Eschatology and the Origin of the Atonement* (Tübingen: Mohr Siebeck; Grand Rapids: Baker Academic, 2005).

45. It is instructive to contrast this way of situating and understanding the fall of Jerusalem with the perspective of 4 Ezra which sees the fall as a punishment for Israel's sins that is unconnected to the transition between the old age and the new. In this Jewish apocalyptic work from the end of the first century CE (cf. "the thirtieth year after the destruction of the city" of 4 Ezra 3:1), part of the solution to this most traumatic of events is that the future Messiah will judge Rome (11:38–46 and 12:31–33) and set free the remnant of Israel "making them joyful until the end comes, the day of judgment, of which I spoke to you at the beginning" (12:34). This time of joy would seem to be the four hundred years referred to in 7:28 which precede the judgment described in 7:32–44.

Of all the texts that are seen as shedding light on the Gospels in this respect, the reference to Gehenna in 4 Ezra 7:36 (= 2 Esdras 7:36) seems to be in a unique category. While Gehenna is still distinguished from Hades in contrast to the rabbinic literature (see 4:7–8 and 8:53), 4 Ezra does parallel the rabbinic tradition in seeing Gehenna as having been created before the world, as Reiser notes in *Jesus and Judgment*, 123 with reference to 7:70. And while there are echoes of the prophetic tradition's judgment of the nations here (see 7:37, cf. the discussion in Michael Edward Stone, *4 Ezra: A Commentary on the Book of Fourth Ezra* (Minneapolis: Fortress, 1990) 222 and cf. the later 5 Ezra 2:28–29 [= 2 Esdras 2:28–29]), this judgment is now seen as taking place after a resurrection in the transition between the present age and the age to come.

This is a significant departure from the OT, where the vision (rather than the developed belief, cf. John E. Goldingay, *Daniel*. Word Biblical Commentary 30 [Dallas, TX: Word, 1989] 306–8) of postmortem, post-resurrection judgment/vindication, found only in Dan 12:2, is not explicitly associated with Gehenna. If we see 4 Ezra as developing an allusion to Gehenna that is implicit in Dan 12:2—based on a (plausible) linguistic connection between Dan 12:2 and Isa 66:24 established by the occurrence in only these passages of *dērā'ōn* (translated in the NIV as that which is "loathsome" or worthy of "contempt"), cf. Nickelsburg, *1 Enoch 1*, 319 and Goldingay, ibid., 281, 308—then this is very different from the development of Dan 12:2 that we find in Matt 25:46, on which see n. 43 above.

In my judgment, 4 Ezra 7:36 thus marks an important transition between the OT (and, I will argue, the NT) understanding of Gehenna and post-biblical conceptions of Hell. Other pre-Diaspora Jewish texts also from the first century CE (for current views of their dating and location, see Collins, *The Apocalyptic Imagination*) either give fleeting or confused attention to Gehenna (see 2 Baruch 59:10; *Apocalypse of Abraham* 15:6 [cf. the comments in James H. Charlesworth, ed., *The Old Testament Pseudepigrapha*, volume 1: *Apocalyptic Literature and Testaments* (New York: Doubleday, 1983), 686, 696]

of the people of God made up of Jews and Gentiles, God's promise to Abraham—that he would have offspring as numerous as the stars—is finally coming true.[46]

The decisive victory against evil, and thus against the idolatrous powers and principalities that humanity serves, has been won on the Cross, says Paul—a cross through which even the very powers and principalities that crucified Christ are reconciled to their Creator (see Col 1:20ff.). In the power of the Spirit, the Church is to live out this redemption, spreading the good news to the ends of the earth.

The future is far from dark. The non-human creation too will be healed and, according to the famous language of Rom 8, will experience a cosmic exodus and thus be set free from the oppression of our idolatry.[47] Evil will be completely eradicated. As Paul puts it in 1 Cor 15:24–25, 28,

> For as in Adam all die, so in Christ all will be made alive. But each in his own turn: Christ, the firstfruits; then, when he comes, those who belong to him. Then the end will come, when he hands over the kingdom to God the Father after he has destroyed all dominion, authority and power. For he must reign until he has put all his enemies under his feet. . . . When he has done this, then the Son himself will be made subject to him who put everything under him, so that God may be all in all.

and *Testament of Moses* 10:10 [cf. the rejection of R. H. Charles' textual emendation in ibid., 933]). By the time we get to the *Sibylline Oracles* 1.101–3, 2.293 and 4.106, later in the first century and written beyond the Promised Land, Gehenna and Tartarus have become synonymous (cf. the blending of Gehenna and Sheol in the rabbinic tradition in n. 31 above).

Of all the "extra-biblical" books thought to shed light on Gehenna in the NT, 1 Enoch and 4 Ezra are the most important both historically and theologically. The former (on which see n. 32 above) is considered canonical in the Ethiopian Orthodox tradition, while the latter (preserved as chapters 3–14 of 2 Esdras [1–2 and 15–16 being Christian additions]) also has this status in the Russian Orthodox and Coptic traditions. But even if 4 Ezra were considered fully canonical, and even if we were to overlook the fact that those who read it in the Vulgate Appendix knew a text that was actually missing 4 Ezra 7:36–140 (cf. Bruce W. Longnecker, *2 Esdras* (Sheffield, UK: Sheffield Academic Press, 1995) 110–12), it is still important to maintain on historical grounds that the post-resurrection Gehenna of 4 Ezra 7:36 should not be read into the gospels (see n. 40 above). Its perspective also differs from the Book of Revelation (see n. 60 below).

46. For a discussion in relation to Romans 9–11, see N. T. Wright, *The Climax of the Covenant: Christ and the Law in Pauline Theology* (Edinburgh: T. & T. Clark, 1991) ch. 13.

47. See Sylvia C. Keesmaat, *Paul and His Story: (Re)interpreting the Exodus Tradition* (Sheffield, UK: Sheffield Academic Press, 1999).

It is significant that here, in the most sustained discussion of the general resurrection in the NT, there is no mention of Hell, either as eternal torment or as annihilation. But this should come as no surprise, I suggest, as the Christian doctrine of Hell, for all the appeals to Scripture that have been made on its behalf, has no biblical basis.

HELL IN HISTORY

While Hell is foreign to the Gospels, Gehenna is another matter—its significance for the Church's own history having been completely overlooked. To briefly summarize the gospel setting in which the judgment of Gehenna is found, the Israel of Jesus' day is consistently portrayed as failing to be a light to the Gentiles, its election being (mis)understood not as a calling to reveal God's presence to the nations but as a sign that it is safe from the justice and wrath of God that would soon descend on the Gentile—and specifically Roman—world for its moral depravity and idolatrous ways.[48] Far from sharing God's love and wisdom, Israel's leaders, according to the Gospel writers, understood the way of holiness as purity from outside contamination.[49] Yet the very different spirituality and holiness of Jesus is vindicated when the judgment that he prophesied and enacted against the Temple comes to pass, marking the end of the old age (Matt 24:3, 14) and the birth-pangs (Matt 24:7) of the age to come.

Generalizations have their limits. But a good generalization is generally true. More often than not, I suggest, the Church has gone on to recapitulate the sins of Israel: calling God's wrath down on sinners, setting itself over/against the world, hiding its true light under a bushel.[50] The Roman Empire fell. Christendom was born. The "Holy Roman Empire," as it came to be known, ruled the world,[51] threatening all who would not toe

48. It is worth considering whether Paul in Rom 2:1 aims to expose not merely hypocrisy but the mindset that would say "Amen!" to the words found in Rom 1:18–31. Cf. the discussion in James D. G. Dunn, *Romans 1–8*. Word Biblical Commentary 38A (Nashville: Nelson, 1988) 78ff., including his comments on Rom 2:24 on ibid., 115–16. For further comment on Rom 1:18, see "judgment unto salvation" (including n. 57) below.

49. See Marcus J. Borg, *Conflict, Holiness, and Politics in the Teachings of Jesus* (Philadelphia: Trinity, 1998).

50. Here I allude to Matt 5:15/Mark 4:21/Luke 11:33 in its famous KJV form. These words have been interpreted individualistically but are best understood as referring to Israel in relation to the nations.

51. Here my generalizing is focused on "the world" of Western Christianity. For Christianity beyond Christendom at this time, see Philip Jenkins, *The Lost History of Christianity: The Thousand-Year Golden Age of the Church in the Middle East, Africa, and*

the line with the fires of eternal torment.[52] There is a place for nuanced historiography. But to those who were oppressed by the Church when it was at the height of its powers, this would not be seen as a caricature. The secular critique of Christianity, for all its one-sidedness, is not without foundation.

There are two biblical patterns, I believe, that can help us interpret this history. The first is a complex, two-part motif found in the prophets, while the second is a pattern found throughout Scripture in which judgment is understood as related to salvation rather than to damnation.

This first biblical pattern, evident in Isa 10:5–17, comes to the fore in the conviction that when God's people fall into idolatry and fail to respond to the warnings of the prophets, they are handed over to their enemies who act out God's wrath, to be judged in turn when God, responding out of his covenant love, judges Israel's enemies for the way they have judged his people! In this light, and in the light of the judgment revealed against Israel in the synoptic apocalypse (Matt 24/Mark 13/Luke 21), should we not ask ourselves whether history reveals God handing Christendom over to its enemies to face its hell, its Gehenna? If the Christian era came to an end with the dawn of the Enlightenment which, in is secular form, attacked the Church for its evils, not least for its cruel doctrine of Hell, then

Asia—and How It Died (New York: HarperOne, 2008). The first Holy Roman Emperor (Otto I) was crowned in 962, while the last (Francis II) abdicated in 1806. While the language of the Holy Roman Empire is striking, and should be alarming, in the light of Christianity's origins, the same ethos can be discerned whether we focus on the royal or papal throne. That the Church alone had the power to threaten damnation does not mean that it was separate from the Empire, but that it may be understood as its complement and quintessence.

52. For an illustrated history, see Alice K. Turner, *The History of Hell* (New York: Harcourt Brace, 1993). The social function of Hell also comes to light in the debates engendered by the growing opposition to Hell and damnation since the Protestant Reformation. D. P. Walker, in his *The Decline of Hell: Seventeenth-Century Discussions of Eternal Torment* (London: Routledge & Kegan Paul, 1964) 159–60, notes that even those who rejected eternal punishment distinguished between a secret esoteric doctrine for themselves and a vulgar exoteric doctrine (i.e., the standard view) which was to be presented to the masses in order to maintain the social order. Geoffrey Rowell, in his *Hell and The Victorians: A Study of the Nineteenth Century Theological Controversies Concerning Eternal Punishment and the Future Life* (Oxford: Clarendon, 1974) 83 n. 79, cites one anonymous nineteenth century critic of F. W. Farrar as saying, "Once remove the restraints of religion, teach the poor that future punishment is a fable, and what will be left to hinder the bursting forth with savage yells of millions of ravening wolves, before whom the salt of the earth will be trodden underfoot, Church establishments dissolved, and baronial halls become piles of blackened ruin?"

instead of condemning it, should we not, first and foremost, ask whether the dawn of the Modern age can be seen as God's judgment against the Church? Even as we may also ask whether, given the violence with which Modernity has dealt with people of faith, God has now handed it over to its post-modern critics?

JUDGMENT UNTO SALVATION

If we are open to God's revelation in the secular critique of Christianity, it will not be hard to see that for too long, a Church bent on control and motivated by fear has proclaimed that the Good News amounts to avoiding the Bad News. The self-critique of the prophetic tradition can further alert us to the fact that the Church, if it is to avoid being thrown into Gehenna yet again, will need to jettison its doctrine of Hell and the mentality that goes with it and recapture how the Gospel is the good news of life lived to the full in covenant with God, without whom there is no life.[53]

That said, if we are to find a deeply biblical orientation to our own history, this way of understanding the significance of Gehenna—the way of self-critique—needs to be related to the second biblical pattern to which I have alluded. Because justice conceived as retribution closes down redemption, we must be careful that we are not simply historicizing the traditional or annihilationist understanding of how God responds to evil. In a truly biblical redemptive-historical paradigm, I propose, judgment is not an end in itself, and is therefore not "final" in that sense, but is *always* a judgment-unto-salvation.

This understanding of justice and judgment calls for a fundamental rereading of many biblical passages. Elsewhere I have explored this in relation to the Book of Revelation.[54] Here I will mention just two examples, the first of which I think is paradigmatic for all of Scripture: the diversifying of the peoples and their ways of speaking that happens after the fall of Babel.[55]

---

53. For this emphasis on "Life," see Deut 30:11–20 which lies behind John 1:4 and 14:6.

54. See my "An Apocalyptic Appendix" in *The Annihilation of Hell*, esp. 9.5.

55. For a very helpful analysis of this narrative, see David Smith, "What Hope After Babel? Diversity and Community in Gen 11:1–9; Exod 1:1–14; Zeph 3:1–13 and Acts 2:1–13" in *Horizons in Biblical Theology* 18:2 (1996) 169–91.

In the light of God's self-maledictory oath, after the Flood, never to annihilate human life (Gen 8:21; 9:11), it is important to see how the judgment of Babel is not a punishment, but a blessing that intends to get history back on track in line with the emergence of the nations that are described as "spread[ing] out over the earth" in Gen 10:32 (cf. Gen 10:5). Viewed within Genesis as a whole, the diversifying of the peoples that is highlighted in emphatic detail just before the Babel narrative (see Gen 10:1–32) is seen as a positive response to the original benediction of Gen 1:28 to "fill the earth," even though this blessing, due to fear, is experienced as a threat in Gen 11:4. What the judgment on Babel reveals is that the attempt to resist history is itself a dead-end. It is a judgment-unto-salvation because the scattering allows the call to "fill the earth," misconstrued in a fallen world as the word of death, to once again become the word of life.[56]

The second example comes from the letter to the Romans. In Rom 1:18, Paul declares, "The wrath of God is being revealed from heaven against all the godlessness and wickedness of [those] who suppress the truth by their wickedness." In our traditional understandings of justice and judgment, we might assume that for the unrepentant, such wrath will mark the end of God's dealings with them. But to absolutize Rom 1:18 is to misconstrue what Paul is saying. If we connect this verse to Rom 11:32, we encounter one of the most striking examples of the judgment-unto-salvation dynamic when Paul says, "For God has bound all [people] over to disobedience so that he may have mercy on them all."[57]

Once again, God's Word is revealed as a Word of Life. The good news of Gehenna is that for those who have ears to hear and eyes to see, the attempt to invoke God's judgment as an end in itself, as "final," is revealed as a dead-end. Such a spirituality does not belong to, and cannot be a part of, the life of the age to come. Thus, in looking back over Church history at the rise and fall of fall of the doctrine of Hell, we may be set free to develop an eschatology in which hope is allowed to triumph over fear.

---

56. See the comments on Justice "making way for" love in n. 19 above.

57. James D. G. Dunn, in his *Romans 9–16*. Word Biblical Commentary 38B (Nashville: Nelson, 1988) 696, notes, "in a quite extraordinary way (extraordinary since only twelve [Greek] words are involved) the verse actually sums up the principal themes of the entire letter." See his discussion in ibid., 696–97.

OPEN ENDED

Rather than close by spelling out what this means for our theologies, or by articulating a theological position as such, I would like to end with an "open-ended" image from the Book of Revelation that is suggestive of a theology and a vision of the Church that does not yet exist.[58]

In the final chapters of John's vision, we might expect to discover that the sinners, who clearly do not escape the apocalyptic judgment described in 18:1—20:15,[59] are either in the lake of fire or have now been annihilated by it. But instead, we actually find them outside the city (Rev 22:15).[60]

Furthermore, this "exclusion" is one that must be read in the light of the fact that there is still a mission to the nations (Rev 21:24; 22:2). John's vision reveals that because sin has no future in God's world, the impure may not enter the city (Rev 21:27). Yet this provides no ammunition for those who want to preach the "final" judgment of hellfire and damnation as "On no day will [the] gates [of the New Jerusalem] ever be shut" (Rev 21:25).

Against the openness of God, the evil that would annihilate God's creation, close down history and shut the world off from its Creator, does not have a hope in hell.[61]

58. After writing these words, I came across, and immediately resonated with, what Brian D. McLaren writes in the Introduction to his *The Last Word and the Word after That: A Tale of Faith, Doubt, and A New Kind of Christianity* (San Francisco: Jossey-Bass, 2005) xxiii, "[C]larity is good, but sometimes intrigue may be even more precious; clarity tends to put an end to further thinking, whereas intrigue makes one think more intensely, broadly, and deeply."

59. This is announced in Rev 16:17–21 and reiterated in Rev 21:8. For further analysis of this judgment, including attention to the presence of OT language for the fall of Jerusalem in the fall of Babylon (such as the allusions to Jer 13:25–27 in Rev 17:1–16), see my "An Apocalyptic Appendix" in *The Annihilation of Hell.*

60. This is an important difference from 4 Ezra (and from the paradigm that results from reading 4 Ezra 7:36 into the Gospel references to Gehenna). Cf. nn. 40 and 45 above. For further discussion, see my "An Apocalyptic Appendix" in *The Annihilation of Hell.*

61. This essay is a revised version of a workshop presentation made at the "Crossing Thresholds, Blurring Boundaries: What Next for the Christian Community?" ICS worldview conference, Toronto, Ontario, October 30, 2004. It was subsequently expanded to appear online in *The Other Journal* 14 (April 2009). My thanks to all who participated in the original workshop and to all who have commented on this essay since then, especially Jon Stanley and Brad Jersak.

Bibliography

Abbott, Louis. *An Analytical Study of Words*. No pages. Online: http://www.savior-of-all .com/An%20Analytical%20Study%20of%20Words.pdf.

Aleghieri, Dante. *The Divine Comedy: Inferno*. Trans. Henry W. Longfellow. Online: http:// www.ccel.org/d/dante/inferno/infer02.htm.

———. *The Divine Comedy of Dante Alighieri, Inferno*. A Verse Translation with an Introduction by Allen Mandelbaum. New York: Quality Paperback Book Club, 1981.

———. *The Divine Comedy of Dante Alighieri, Purgatorio*. A Verse Translation with an Introduction by Allen Mandelbaum. New York: Quality Paperback Book Club, 1983.

Alfeyev, Bishop Hilarion. "The Descent of Christ into Hades in Eastern and Western Theological Traditions." No pages. Online: http://orthodoxeurope.org/page/11/1/5 .aspx.

Alison, James. *Raising Abel*. New York: Crossroad Publishing, 1996.

Allen, John L. Jr. "The Word From Rome." *National Catholic Reporter* 3/14 (28 November 2003). Online: http://www.nationalcatholicreporter.org/word/word112803.htm.

Ansell, Nicholas John. *The Annihilation of Hell: Universal Salvation and the Redemption of Time in the Eschatology of Jürgen Moltmann*. Milton Keynes, UK: Paternoster, forthcoming.

———. "The Call of Wisdom/the Voice of the Serpent: A Canonical Approach to the Tree of Knowledge." *Christian Scholars Review* 31/1 (2001) 31–57. Online: http://faculty .gordon.edu/hu/bi/ted_hildebrandt/OTeSources/01-Genesis/Text/Articles-Books/ Ansell-Serpent-CSR.pdf.

———. "Hell: the Nemesis of Hope?" No pages. Online: http://www.theotherjournal .com/article.php?id=746.

Aquinas, Thomas. *The Summa Theologica of St. Thomas Aquinas*. Second and Revised Edition, 1920. Translated by Fathers of the English Dominican Province. Online: http://www.newadvent.org/summa.

Augustine of Hippo, *The City of God*. Edited by Philip Schaff. Translated by Marcus Dods. NPNF, First Series, Vol. 2, Buffalo, NY: Christian Literature, 1887. Online: http:// www.newadvent.org/fathers/1201.htm.

Avila, Teresa. *Interior Castle or The Mansion*. Translated by Benedictines of Stanbrook. Online: http://www.ccel.org/ccel/teresa/castle2.html.

———. *The Way of Perfection*, Translated by E. Allison Peers. Online: http://www.ccel .org/ccel/teresa/way/formats/way1.0.pdf.

Bacchiocchi, Samuele. *Immortality or Resurrection? A Biblical Study on Human Nature and Destiny*. Berrien Springs, MI: Biblical Perspectives, 2001. Online: http://www

Bibliography

.friendsofsabbath.org/Further_Research/Bacchiocchis%20Research/Immortality%20or%20Resurrection.pdf.

Bailey, L. R. "Gehenna: The Topography of Hell." *Biblical Archaeologist* 49 (1986) 187–91.

Baker, Sharon. "Hospitable Hell." *Preaching Peace: Compassionate Eschatology Conference.* San Francisco Theological Seminary (26–27 September 2008).

Balfour, Walter and Otis Ainsworth Skinner. *An Inquiry into the Scriptural Import of the Words Sheol, Hades, Tartarus, and Gehenna: Translated Hell in the Common English Version.* Boston: A. Tompkins, 1854. Online: http://books.google.ca/books?id=6XHhFJ4YfJwC.

Balfour, Walter and Bernard Whitman. *A Letter to the Rev. Bernard Whitman, on the Term Gehenna, Rendered Hell in the Common Version.* Boston: T. Whittemore and B. B. Mussey, 1834. Online: http://books.google.ca/books?id=cMkUAAAAYAAJ.

Barnhart, Robert K. *The Barnhart Concise Dictionary of Etymology.* New York: HarperCollins, 1995.

Batiffol, Pierre. "Apocatastasis." *The Catholic Encyclopaedia.* Vol. 1. New York: Robert Appleton Company, 1907. No pages. Online: www.newadvent.org/cathen/01599a.htm.

Bauckham, Richard. *The Climax of Prophecy: Studies on the Book of Revelation.* Edinburgh: T. & T. Clark, 1999.

———, editor. *God Will Be All in All: The Eschatology of Jurgen Moltmann.* Minneapolis, MN: Fortress, 2001.

———. "Descent into the Underworld." *Anchor Bible Dictionary,* edited by Bruce W. Winter and Andrew D. Clarke, 105–52. Grand Rapids: Eerdmans, 1993.

———. *The Theology of the Book of Revelation.* Cambridge: Cambridge University Press, 1993.

Beale, G. K. *The Temple and the Church's Mission: A Biblical Theology of the Dwelling Place of God.* Downers Grove, IL: InterVarsity, 2004.

Benedict XVI (Joseph Ratzinger). Encyclical Letter: *Spe Salvi,* 2007. No pages. Online: http://www.vatican.va/holy_father/benedict_xvi/encyclicals/documents/hf_ben-xvi_enc_20071130_spe-salvi_en.html.

Bernstein, Alan E. *The Formation of Hell: Death and Retribution in the Ancient and Early Christian Worlds.* Ithaca: Cornell University Press, 1993.

The Bible—Latin Vulgate. Vatican. *Online:* http://www.vatican.va/archive/bible/nova_vulgata/documents/nova-vulgata_nt_evang-lucam_lt.html#16.

Bietenhard, Hans. "Gehenna." *NIDNTT.* 2:208–9.

Blondel, Maurice. *La Philosophie et l'Esprit Chrétien,* 2 vols. Paris: Presses Universitaires de France, 1946.

The Book of Enoch. APOT. No pages. Online: http://www.heaven.net.nz/writings/thebookofenoch.htm.

Borg, Marcus J. *Conflict, Holiness and Politics in the Teachings of Jesus.* Philadelphia, PA: Trinity Press International, 1998.

Brook, George J. *The Dead Sea Scrolls and the New Testament.* Minneapolis: Fortress, 2005.

Brooks, David Brooks. "Who Is John Stott?" *New York Times* (30 Nov 2004). Online: http://www.nytimes.com/2004/11/30/opinion/30brooks.html?_r=1.

Brown, Colin, editor. *New International Dictionary of New Testament Theology,* 4 vols. Grand Rapids: Zondervan, 1975–1985.

Bibliography

Brown, F., et al., editors. *A Hebrew and English Lexicon of the Old Testament*. Oxford: Oxford University Press, 1907.

Brueggemann, Walter. *A Commentary on Jeremiah: Exile and Homecoming*. Grand Rapids & Cambridge: Eerdmans, 1998.

———. *2004 Emergent Theological Conversation*. Decatur, GA: All Souls Fellowship (13–15 September 2004).

———. *Genesis: Interpretation*. Atlanta: Knox, 1982.

———. *Theology of the Old Testament: Testimony, Dispute, Advocacy*. Minneapolis: Fortress, 1997.

Buis, Harry. *The Doctrine of Eternal Punishment*, Grand Rapids, MI: Baker, 1957.

Bunyan, John. *Sighs from Hell or the Groans from the Damned Soul*. Whitefish, MT: Kessinger, 2003.

Case's Bible Atlas. Harvard: O.D. Case & Company, 1878. Online: http://books.google.ca/books?id=7TcAAAAAYAAJ.

Catechism of the Catholic Church. Online: http://www.vatican.va/archive/ENG0015/__P2O.HTM.

The Catholic Encyclopaedia, 18 vols. New York: Robert Appleton Company, 1913. No pages. Online: http://en.wikisource.org/wiki/Catholic_Encyclopedia_(1913).

Calvin, John. *Commentary on a Harmony of the Evangelists: Matthew, Mark, and Luke*, 3 vols. Trans. William Pringle. Grand Rapids, MI: Eerdmans, 1949. Online: http://ia310133.us.archive.org/0/items/harmonyrevelatio01calvuoft/harmonyrevelatio01calvuoft.pdf.

———. *Institutes of the Christian Religion*, 2 vols. Trans. John Allen. Philadelphia: Westminster, 1844.

Case, L. B. "The Moravian Missionary." *The Universalist Miscellany* 3 (1843) 428–29. Edited by O. A. Skinner and E. H. Chapin. Boston: Alfred Mudge. Online: http://books.google.ca/books?id=SFIUAAAAYAAJ&printsec=toc&source=gbs_summary_r&cad=0#PPA1,M1.

Charles, R. H., editor. *The Apocrypha and Pseudepigrapha of the Old Testament*, 2 vols. Oxford: Clarendon, 1913.

Charlesworth, James H. editor. *The Old Testament Pseudepigrapha*, volume 1: *Apocalyptic Literature and Testaments*. New York: Doubleday, 1983.

Childs, Brevard S. *Introduction to the Old Testament as Scripture*. Philadelphia: Fortress and London: SCM, 1979.

Chopelas, Peter. "Heaven and Hell in the Afterlife, According to the Bible." No pages. Online: http://aggreen.net/beliefs/heaven_hell.html.

The Church's Confession of Faith: A Catholic Catechism for Adults. Catholic Church Deutsche Bischofskonferenz, edited by Mark Jordan and Cardinal Walter Kasper. Trans. Stephen Arndt. San Francisco: Ignatius Press and Communio Books, 1987.

Collins, John J. *The Apocalyptic Imagination: An Introduction to Jewish Apocalyptic Literature*. 2nd ed. Grand Rapids, MI: Eerdmans, 1998.

Coram, James. "The Fire of Gehenna." *Concordant Studies*, Santa Clarita, CA: Concordant Publishing Concern, n.d. Online: http://www.concordant.org/expohtml/DeathAndJudgment/TheGehennaOfFire.html.

Crockett, William V. et al., *Four Views of Hell*. Grand Rapids: Zondervan, 1997.

Crossan, John Dominic. *God and Empire*. New York: HarperCollins, 2007.

"Descriptions of Hell in Islam." *Shariah Program Articles Library*. Online: http://www.shariahprogram.ca/articles/hell-devil-description.shtml.

Bibliography

Diodorus Siculous, *LacusCurtius* XIX.98. Cited in William Smith, *Dictionary of Greek and Roman Geography*, 2 vols. Harvard: Little, Brown and Co., 1857. Online: http://books .google.ca/books?id=aysbAAAAYAAJ.

"Diyu." No pages. Online: http://www.viswiki.com/en/Diyu._Chinese original: http:// big5.xinhuanet.com/gate/big5/news.xinhuanet.com/school/2005-07/12/ content_3202514.htm.

Dunn, James D. G. *Romans 1–8.* Word Biblical Commentary 38A. Nashville, TN: Nelson, 1988.

———. *Romans 9–16.* Word Biblical Commentary 38B. Nashville, TN: Nelson, 1988.

Edersheim, Alfred. *Life and Times of Jesus the Messiah,* 2 vols. Grand Rapids: Eerdmans, 1953. Online: http://www.ccel.org/ccel/edersheim/lifetimes.html.

Edwards, Jonathan. "Sinners in the Hands of an Angry God." No pages: Online: http:// www.jesus-is-lord.com/sinners.htm.

———. "The Justice of God and the Damnation of Sinners." No pages. Online: http:// www.biblebb.com/files/edwards/JE-justice.htm.

Edersheim, Alfred. *The Life and Times of Jesus the Messiah.* London: Longmans, Green & Co., 1883. Online: http://books.google.ca/books?id=VJUHAAAAQAAJ.

Edwards, D. L. and J. R. W. Stott. *Essentials: A Liberal/Evangelical Dialogue.* London: Hodder & Stoughton, 1988.

Erasmus, Desiderius, *and* Martin Luther. *Luther and Erasmus: Free Will and Salvation.* The Library of Christian Classics: Ichthus Edition. Translated by E. Gordon Rupp, A. N. Marlow, Philip Watson, and B. Drewery. Philadelphia: Westminster, 1969.

Fairweather, W. "Development of Doctrine in the Apocryphal Period." *HDB* 5:305. Online: http://books.google.ca/books?id=Rxt3f6fbHGgC.

Farrar, F. W. *Mercy and Judgment.* London and New York: MacMillan, 1904. Online: http:// tentmaker.org/books/mercyandjudgment/mercy_and_judgment_ch13.html.

Fudge, Edward William and Robert A. Peterson. *Two Views of Hell: A Biblical and Theological Dialogue.* Downers Grove, IL: InterVarsity, 2000.

Gill, John. "Commentary on Revelation 20:15." *The New John Gill Exposition of the Entire Bible.* No pages. Online: www.studylight.org/com/geb/view.cgi?book=re&chapter=0 20&verse=015.

Goldingay, John E. *Daniel.* Word Biblical Commentary 30. Dallas, TX: Word, 1989.

Gomes, Alan W. "Evangelicals and the Annihilation of Hell." *CRIJ.* No pages. Online: http:// www.iclnet.org/pub/resources/text/cri/cri-jrnl/web/crj0137a.html.

"The Gospel of Nicodemus, or Acts of Pilate." *The Apocryphal New Testament.* Translated by M. R. James. Oxford: Clarendon Press, 1924. Online: http://www.earlychristianwritings .com/text/gospelnicodemus.html.

Green, Joel B., Scot McKnight, and I. Howard Marshall, editors. *Dictionary of Jesus and the Gospels.* Downers Grove, IL: InterVarsity, 1992.

Grimsrud, Ted. *Triumph of the Lamb: A Self-Study Guide to the Book of Revelation.* Scottdale, PA, Kitchener, ON: Herald, 1987.

Hamilton, J. Taylor and Kenneth G. Hamilton. *History of the Moravian Church: The Renewed Unitas Fratrum, 1722–1957.* Bethlehem, PA: Interprovincial Board of Christian Education, Moravian Church in America, 1967.

Hanson, J. W. *Universalism: The Prevailing Doctrine of the Christian Church During Its First Five Hundred Years.* Boston and Chicago: Universalist, 1899. Online: http://www .tentmaker.org/books/Prevailing.html.

Bibliography

Harris, Maurice H., editor and translator. *Hebraic Literature: Translations from the Talmud, Midrashim and Kabbala*. Washington, London: Walter Dunne, 1901. Online: http://www.archive.org/details/hebraicliteratur00harriala.

Hawkinson, Don. *Character for Life*. Green Forest, AR: New Leaf, 2005.

Healy Jr., Nick. "On Hope, Heaven and Hell." *University Concourse* 2/96 (6 May 1997). No pages. Online: http://www.theuniversityconcourse.com/II,9,5-6-1997/Healy.htm.

Hershon, Paul Isaac, editor. *A Talmudic Miscellany*. Translated by Paul Hershon. London: Trubnic and Company, 1880. Online: http://books.google.com/books?id=dqXAUrGjV-oC.

Hesiod. *The Theogony of Hesiod*. Translated by Hugh G. Evelyn-White (1914). Online http://www.sacred-texts.com/cla/hesiod/theogony.htm.

Hilborn, David, editor. *The Nature of Hell: A Report by the Evangelical Alliance's Commission on Unity and Truth among Evangelicals (ACUTE)*. Milton Keynes, UK: Acute/Paternoster, 2000.

Hilborn, David and Don Horrocks. "Universalistic Trends in the Evangelical Tradition: An Historical Perspective." *Universal Salvation? The Current Debate*, edited by Robin A. Parry and Christopher H. Partridge. Grand Rapids, MI: Eerdmans, 2003.

Hippolytus, *Against the Greeks and Plato on the Universe*. Online: http://www.earlychristianwritings.com/text/hippolytus-dogmatical.html.

Hirsch, Emil. "Sheol." *The Jewish Encyclopedia*, 12 vols. Edited by I. Singer. New York: Funk and Wagnalls, 1906. Online: http://www.jewishencyclopedia.com/view.jsp?letter=S&artid=614. Original page at http://www.jewishencyclopedia.com/view_page.jsp?artid=614&letter=S&pid=0.

"History of Universalism." Christian Universalist Association. No pages. Online: http://www.christianuniversalist.org/articles/history.html.

Homer. *The Odyssey of Homer*. Trans. Samuel Butler, 1900. Online: http://www.sacred-texts.com/cla/homer/ody/index.htm.

Hontheim, Joseph. "Hell." *The Catholic Encyclopaedia*. Vol. 7. New York: Robert Appleton Company, 1913. No pages. Online: http://en.wikisource.org/wiki/Catholic_Encyclopedia_(1913)/Hell.

Howard-Brook, Wes and Anthony Gwyther. *Unveiling Empire: Reading Revelation Then and Now*. Maryknoll, NY: Orbis, 1999.

Isaak of Syria, *Daily Readings with Isaak of Syria*, edited by A. M. Allchin. Trans. Sebastian Brock. Springfield, IL: Templegate, 1989.

Irwin, Brian P. "Topheth." *EDB*, edited by David Noel Freedman, Allen C. Myers and Astrid B. Beck. Grand Rapids, MI: Eerdmans, 2000.

Jenkins, Philip. *The Lost History of Christianity: The Thousand-Year Golden Age of the Church in the Middle East, Africa, and Asia—and How It Died*. New York: HarperOne, 2008.

Jeremias, Joachim. *Jerusalem in the Time of Jesus*. Philadelphia, PA: Fortress, 1962.

Jerome, *Commentary on Matthew*. The Fathers of the Church. Translated by Thomas P. Scheck. Washington, D.C.: Catholic University of America Press, 2008.

Jersak, Brad and Michael Hardin, editors. *Stricken by God? Nonviolent Identification and the Victory of Christ*. Grand Rapids: Eerdmans, 2007.

Julian of Norwich, *Revelations of Divine Love (Short Text and Long Text)*. Trans. Elizabeth Spearing and A. C. Spearing. New York: Penguin, 1998.

John of the Cross. *Ascent of Mount Carmel*. Trans. E. Allison Peers. Online: http://www.ccel.org/ccel/teresa/way/formats/way1.0.pdf.

Bibliography

John Paul II. "General Audience: July 28, 1999." *John Paul II: Audiences.* No pages. Online: http://www.vatican.va/holy_father/john_paul_ii/audiences/1999/documents/hf_jp-ii_aud_28071999_en.html.

Josephus, Flavius. *Josephus's Discourse to the Greeks Concerning Hades.* Translated by William Whiston. Online: http://www.ccel.org/ccel/josephus/works/files/hades.htm.

————. *The Wars of the Jews; or the History of the Destruction of Jerusalem.* Translated by William Whiston. Online: http://www.ccel.org/j/josephus/works/JOSEPHUS.HTM.

Klaassen, Walter. *Armageddon and the Peaceable Kingdom.* Scottdale, PA, Windsor, ON: Herald, 1999.

Kennedy, Doralynn. "Commentary: The Rich Man and Lazarus." No pages. Online: http://searchwarp.com/swa223662.htm.

Keesmaat, Sylvia C. *Paul and His Story: (Re)interpreting the Exodus Tradition.* Sheffield, UK: Sheffield Academic Press, 1999.

Kirk-Duggan, Cheryl A. "Hell." *EDB,* edited by David Noel Freedman, Allen C. Myers and Astrid B. Beck. Grand Rapids, MI: Eerdmans, 2000.

Knowles, Michael. *Jeremiah in Matthew's Gospel: The Rejected-Prophet Motif in Matthaean Redaction.* Sheffield: JSOT, 1993.

Kolatch, Alfred J. *The Complete Dictionary of English and Hebrew First Names.* Middle Village, NY: Jonathan David, 1984.

Lane, Dermot. *Keeping Hope Alive: Stirrings in Christian Theology.* Eugene, OR: Wipf & Stock, 2005.

Lauter, Hermann-Josef. *Pastoralblatt.* Cited in Hans Urs von Balthasar, *Epilogue.* Translated by Edward T. Oakes. Fort Collins, CO: Ignatius, 1994.

Le Goff, Jacques. *The Birth of Purgatory.* Trans. Arthur Goldhammer. Chicago: University of Chicago Press, 1986.

Lewis, C. S. *The Great Divorce: A Dream.* San Francisco: HarperCollins, 2001.

Lightfoot, John. "The Valley of Hinnom." *A Commentary on the New Testament from the Talmud and Hebraica.* No pages. Online: http://philologos.org/__eb-jl/cent00.htm.

Lochet, Louis. *Die Hölle gehört zur Frohbotschaft eine Herausforderung.* Vienna and Munich: Herold, 1981.

————. *Jésus descendu aux enfers.* Paris: Cerf, 1979.

Longnecker, Bruce W. *2 Esdras.* Sheffield, UK: Sheffield Academic Press, 1995.

Lunde, J. "Heaven and Hell." *Dictionary of Jesus and the Gospels,* edited by Joel B. Green, Scot McKnight, and I. Howard Marshall. Downers Grove, IL: InterVarsity, 1992.

Luther, Martin. *The Bondage of the Will: A New Translation of De Servo Arbitrio (1525), Martin Luther's Reply to Erasmus of Rotterdam.* Translated by J. I. Packer and O. R. Johnston. Old Tappan, NJ: Revell, 1957.

MacDonald, George. *Life Essential: The Hope of the Gospel.* Wheaton, IL: Shaw, 1974.

————. *Lilith: A Romance.* Grand Rapids: Eerdmans, 1981.

MacDonald, Gregory. *Evangelical Universalism.* Eugene, OR: Cascade Books, 2006 & London: SPCK, 2008.

Masterman, E. W. G. "Hinnom, Valley of." *ISBE,* edited by James Orr. No Pages. Online: bible-history.com — ISBE.

Maurice, Frederick D. *Lectures on the Apocalypse; Book of Revelation of St. John the Divine.* London: MacMillan and Co., 1861. Online: http://www.preteristarchive.com/Books/pdf/1861_maurice_lectures-apocalypse.pdf.

Bibliography

McLaren, Brian. *The Last Word and the Word After That: A Tale of Faith, Doubt, and a New Kind of Christianity*. San Francisco, CA: Jossey-Bass, 2005.

Mendels, Doron. *The Rise and Fall of Jewish Nationalism: Jewish and Christian Ethnicity in Ancient Palestine*. Grand Rapids, MI: Eerdmans, 1992.

Merton, Thomas. *New Seeds of Contemplation*. New York: New Directions Pub. Co., 1961.

Metallinos, George. "Heaven and Hell: The Orthodox Understanding." *Orthodoxy in the Twenty-First Century*. December 27, 2008. No pages. Online: http://orthodoxy21 .blogspot.com/2008/12/heaven-and-hell-orthodox-understanding.html.

Mills, Watson E., and Roger Aubrey Bullard, editors. *Mercer Dictionary of the Bible*. Macon, GA: Mercer University Press, 1998.

Milton, John. *Paradise Lost*. New York: Viking, 1949.

Moberly, R. W. L. *The Old Testament of the Old Testament: Patriarchal Narratives and Mosaic Yahwism*. Overtures to Biblical Theology. Minneapolis, MN: Fortress, 1992.

Moltmann, Jurgen. *The Coming of God: Christian Eschatology*. Translated by Margaret Kohl. London: SCM, 1996.

———. *The Crucified God: The Cross as the Foundation and Criticism of Christian Theology*. Translated R. A. Wilson and J. Bowden. London: SCM, 1974).

———. "The Final Judgment: Sunrise of Christ's Liberating Justice." *Anglican Theological Review* 89 (2007) 565–76.

———. "The Presence of God's Future." *Anglican Theological Review* 89 (2007) 577–88.

———. *Theology of Hope*. London: SCM, 1967.

Montgomery, James A. "The Holy City and Gehenna." *JBL* 27/1 (1908) 34. Online: http:// www.archive.org/stream/holycitygehenna00montiala/holycitygehenna00montiala_ djvu.txt.

Morris, Henry M. *The Revelation Record: A Scientific and Devotional Commentary on the Prophetic Book of the End of Times*. Wheaton, IL: Tyndale, 1983.

Moule, C. F. D. *Punishment and Retribution: An Attempt to Delimit Their Scope in New Testament Thought*. New Testament Perspectives on Crime and Justice. Akron, PA. MCC U.S. Office of Criminal Justice, 1990.

Mulloy, John. "A Sharp Departure From Catholic Tradition." *The Wanderer* (March 19, 1987).

———. "Origen, Fr. von Balthasar, and Adrienne von Speyr." *The Wanderer* (February 5, 1987).

Murphy, Frederick. *Fallen is Babylon: The Revelation of John*. The New Testament in Context. Harrisburg, PA: Trinity, 1998.

The Mystery of Salvation: The Story of God's Gift: A Report by the Doctrine Commission of the General Synod of the Church of England. London: Church, 1995.

Nibley, Hugh W. "Baptism for the Dead in Ancient Times." *The Neil A. Maxwell Institute for Religious Scholarship*. No pages. Online: http://farms.byu.edu/publications/ transcripts/?id=67#r101.

Nickelsburg, George W. E. *1 Enoch 1: A Commentary on the Book of 1 Enoch, Chapters 1–36; 81–108*. Minneapolis, MN: Fortress Press, 2001.

Nickelsburg, George W. E., and James C. VanderKam. *1 Enoch: A New Translation*. Minneapolis, MN: Fortress, 2004.

Origen, "Homily 12 on Jeremiah." In *Origen*. Translated by Joseph W. Trigg. New York: Routledge, 1998.

Packer, James I. "Evangelicals and the Way of Salvation New Challenges to the Gospel: Universalism, and Justification by Faith." In *Evangelical Affirmations*, edited by K.

Bibliography

S. Kantzer and C. F. H. Henry, Grand Rapids: Zondervan, 1990. Online: http://www .ccel.us/EV.ch4.html.

————. "The Problem of Eternal Punishment." Leon Morris Lecture, 1990. Victoria, Australia: Evangelical Alliance Publishing, 1990; *Crux* 26 (1990) 18–25.

Peterson, Robert A. *Hell On Trial: The Case for Eternal Punishment.* Phillipsburg, NJ: P. & R., 1995.

Philo. *On Abraham.* The Works of Philo Judaeus the Contemporary of Josephus. Translated by Charles Duke Yonge. London, H. G. Bohn, 1854–1890. No pages. Online: http:// www.earlychristianwritings.com/yonge/book22.html.

Pinnock, Clark H. "The Destruction of the Finally Impenitent." *Criswell Theological Review:* 4.2 (1990), 243–259. Online: http://www.abc-coggc.org/jrad/volume2/ issue1/The%20Destruction%20of%20the%20Finally%20Impenitent.pdf.

Pink, Arthur. *Eternal Punishment.* Swengel, PA: Reiner. n.d.

Pitre, Brant. *Jesus, the Tribulation, and the End of the Exile: Restoration Eschatology and the Origin of the Atonement.* Tübingen: Mohr Siebeck; Grand Rapids, MI: Baker, 2005.

Plato, *Gorgias.* Trans. Benjamin Jowett. Online: http://www.sacred-texts.com/cla/plato/ gorgias.htm.

Pseudo-Dionysius the Areopagite: The Complete Works. The Classics of Western Spirituality: A Library of the Great Spiritual Masters. Translated by Colm Leibheid. Mahwah, NJ: Paulist, 1987.

Rahner, Karl. "Hell." *Encyclopaedia of Theology: the Concise Sacramentum Mundi,* edited by Karl Rahner. London & New York: Continuum, 1975.

Raphael, Simcha Paull. *Jewish Views of the Afterlife.* Lanham, MD: Jason Aronson, 1994. Cited in Sheldon Drobny, "The Concept of Cosmic Justice." *The Huffington Post,* 10 April 2009. Online: http://www.huffingtonpost.com/sheldon-drobny/the-concept-of-cosmic-jus_b_40957.html.

Ratzinger, Joseph. *Eschatology: Death and Eternal Life.* Dogmatic Theology. Vol. 9, edited by Johann Auer and Joseph Ratzinger. Washington, D.C.: Catholic University of America Press, 1988.

Reicke, Bo. "Gehenna." *The Oxford Companion to the Bible,* edited by Bruce M. Metzger and Michael D. Coogan. New York and Oxford: Oxford University Press, 1993.

Reiser, Marius. *Jesus and Judgment: The Eschatological Proclamation in Its Jewish Context.* Minneapolis, MN: Fortress, 1997.

Rice, Anne. *Called Out of Darkness: A Spiritual Confession.* New York: Knopf, 2008.

Rich, Tracey R. "Sages and Scholars." *Judaism 101.* No pages. Online: http://www.jewfaq .org/sages.htm.

Rissi, Mathias. *The Future of the World; an Exegetical Study of Revelation 19:11–22:15.* Studies in Biblical Theology. London: SCM, 1972.

Roberts, Alexander and James Donaldson, editors. *Ante-Nicene Fathers,* 25 vols. *Edinburgh:* T. & T. Clark, 1868–72. Online: http://en.wikisource.org/wiki/Ante-Nicene_Fathers.

Ross, Hugh. "The Physics of Sin." *Reasons to Believe.* No pages. Online: http://www.reasons .org/theology/christian-life/physics-sin.

Rowell, Geoffrey. *Hell and the Victorians: A Study of the Nineteenth Century Theological Controversies Concerning Eternal Punishment and the Future Life.* Oxford: Clarendon, 1974.

Rulandus, Martinus. *Lexicon of Alchemy.* Whitefish, MO: Kessinger Publishing, 1992. Online: http://books.google.ca/books?id=P9mpcTW4GpcC.

Bibliography

Salmond, Stewart D. F. "Hell." *HDB* 2:343–46. Online: http://www.ccel.org/ccel/hastings/dictv2/Page_343.html.

Schaff, Philip, editor. *Nicene and Post-Nicene Fathers of the Christian Church,* series 2, 14 vols. Edinburgh: T. & T. Clark, 1885. Online: http://www.ccel.org/fathers.html.

Scharen, Hans. "Gehenna in the Synoptics." *BSac* 155 (Jan–Mar 1998) 324-37. Online: http://faculty.gordon.edu/hu/bi/Ted_Hildebrandt/NTeSources/NTArticles/BSac-NT/Scharen-GenenaSyn-Pt1-BS.htm.

Schmidt, Carl. *Gesprache Jesu mit seinen Jungern nach der Auferstehung: Ein katholisch-apostolisches Sendschreiben des 2. Jarhhunderts.* Leipzig: Hinrich, 1908.

Schneider, J. "Basanos." *TDNT* (Abridged). Edited by Door Gerhard Kittel, Gerhard Friedrich, Geoffrey William Bromiley. Grand Rapids, MI: Eerdmans, 1985.

Segal, Alan. *Paul the Convert: The Apostolate and Apostasy of Saul the Pharisee.* New Haven: Yale University Press, 1990.

Simmons, Kurt. "The Bottomless Pit." No pages. Online: http://www.preteristcentral.com/pbpt-bottomless-pit.htm.

Singh, Sundar. *The Complete Works of Sundar Singh.* Madras, India: Christian Literature Society, 1986.

———. *Visions of Sadhu Sundar Singh of India.* Minneapolis: Osterhus, n.d.

Smith, David. "What Hope After Babel? Diversity and Community in Gen 11:1–9; Exod 1:1–14; Zeph 3:1–13 and Acts 2:1–13." *Horizons in Biblical Theology* 18 (1996) 169–91.

Smith II, Carl B. *No Longer Jews: The Search for Gnostic Origins.* Peabody, MA: Hendrickson, 2004.

Spencer, Richard A. "Hinnom, Valley of." *EDB*, edited by David Noel Freedman, Allen C. Myers, and Astrid B. Beck. Grand Rapids, MI: Eerdmans, 2000.

Spencer, Stephen J. *The Genesis Pursuit: The Lost History of Jesus Christ.* Longwood, FL: Xulon, 2006.

Stafford, Cardinal James Francis and Fr Gianfranco Girotti et al. *On the Occasion of the Pauline Year, the Eve of the Solemnity of Sts Peter and Paul, Pope Benedict XVI has Granted Special Indulgences to the Faithful* (10 May 2008). No pages. Online: http://www.annopaolino.org/Indulgenza%20ING.pdf.

Stanley, Jonathan D. "The Trouble with Judgment: Re-Christianizing the Final Judgment in Our Time." *I More than the Others: A Response to Evil and Suffering.* Annual Meeting of the Wesleyan Philosophical Society. Anderson University (March, 5 2009).

Stone, Michael Edward. *4 Ezra: A Commentary on the Book of Fourth Ezra.* Minneapolis, MN: Fortress, 1990.

Strabo. *The Geography of Strabo. Loeb Classical Library,* 8 vols. Trans. H. L. Jones. Harvard University Press, 1932. No pages. Online: http://penelope.uchicago.edu/Thayer/E/Roman/Texts/Strabo/.

Subhangi Devi Dasi. "Vedic Knowledge Online." No pages. Online: http://veda.harekrsna.cz/encyclopedia/dying.htm.

Swanson, Dennis M. "Expansion of Jerusalem in Jer 31:38–40: Now, Already, or Not Yet?" *TMSJ* 17 (2006) 25.

Terrien, Samuel. "The Metaphor of the Rock in Biblical Theology." *God in the Fray,* edited by Tod Linefelt and Timothy Beal. Minneapolis: Fortress, 1998.

Thayer, Thomas Baldwin. *Theology of Universalism.* Boston: Tompkins, 1865. Online: http://books.google.ca/books?id=ran9_zrfJNsC.

Tolle, Eckhart. *A New Earth: Awakening to Your Life's Purposes.* New York: Penguin, 2005.

Bibliography

Trumbower, Jeffrey A. *Rescue for the Dead: Posthumous Salvation for Non-Christians in Early Christianity. Oxford Studies in Historical Theology.* New York: Oxford University Press, 2001.

Turner, Alice K. *The History of Hell.* New York: Harcourt Brace, 1993.

Unger, Walter. "Focusing the Evangelical Vision." *Direction* 20 (1991) 3–17. Online: http://www.directionjournal.org/article/?692.

Virgil, *The Aeneid.* Trans. *John Dryden (1697). Online:* http://www.sacred-texts.com/cla/virgil/aen/index.htm.

Volf, Miroslav and William Katerberg, editors. *The Future of Hope: Christian Tradition amid Modernity and Postmodernity.* Grand Rapids: Eerdmans, 2004.

von Balthasar, Hans Urs. *Dare We Hope "That All Men Be Saved"? With A Short Discourse on Hell.* Translated by David Kipp and Lothar Krauth. San Francisco: Ignatius, 1988.

———. *Prayer.* Trans. Graham Harrison. San Francisco: Ignatius, 1986.

———. *Theo-drama: Theological Dramatic Theory. Vol. 5: The Last Act.* San Francisco: Ignatius, 1998.

von Speyr, Adrienne. *Apokalypse.* Einsiedeln: Johannesverlag, 1976.

Von Wyrick, Stephen. "Gehenna." *EDB,* edited by David Noel Freedman, Allen C. Myers, and Astrid B. Beck. Grand Rapids, MI: Eerdmans, 2000.

Vos, Geerhardus. "Lake of Fire." *ISBE,* edited by James Orr. No Pages. Online: bible-history.com — ISBE.

Walker, D. P. *The Decline of Hell: Seventeenth-Century Discussions of Eternal Torment.* London: Routledge & Kegan Paul, 1964.

Westerman, Claus and Ernst Jenni, editors. *Theological Lexicon of the Old Testament,* 3 Volumes. Peabody: Hendrickson, 1997.

Wilson, Benjamin. *The Emphatic Diaglott, I.B.S.A.,* 1942.

Wright, Nicholas Thomas. *The Climax of the Covenant: Christ and the Law in Pauline Theology.* Edinburgh: T. & T. Clark, 1991.

———. *Following Jesus: Biblical Reflections on Discipleship.* Grand Rapids: Eerdmans, 1994.

———. *Jesus and the Victory of God.* London: SPCK; Minneapolis: Fortress, 1996.

———. *The New Testament and the People of God.* London: SPCK; Minneapolis: Fortress, 1992.

———. *The Resurrection of the Son of God.* London: SPCK; Minneapolis: Fortress, 2003.

———. *Surprised by Hope: Rethinking Heaven, the Resurrection, and the Mission of the Church.* New York: HarperCollins, 2008.

———. "Your Questions to N. T. Wright." Beliefnet. No pages. Online: http://www.beliefnet.com/Faiths/Christianity/2000/07/Your-Questions-To-N-T-Wright.aspx.